THE HOLY SPIRIT
AND HIS WORK IN SOULS

Robert G. Griffin
6125 Hazel Ave. Apt 241
Orangevale, CA 95662
916-989-1889

The Holy Spirit and His Work in Souls

REV. EDWARD LEEN, C.S.Sp., M.A., D.D.

 Scepter

Nihil obstat	S. George Kieran-Hyland, s.t.d.
	Censor Deputatus
Imprimatur	Canon S. Banfi
	Vicar General, Southwark
	13 *April* 1937

Originally published by Sheed & Ward, New York, in 1939.
Reprinted with permission in 1998, 2008
by Scepter Publishers,
P.O. Box 211, New York, NY 10018
www.scepterpublishers.org

New edition © copyright 1998, 2008 by Scepter Publishers, Inc.

ISBN 978-1-59417-063-8
Printed in the United States of America

CONTENTS

FOREWORD

THE Holy Spirit is the divine artist whose *chef d'oeuvre* in creation is the sanctified human soul. To know an artist one must seek to acquire a knowledge both of his personality and of his works. This principle has directed the distribution of matter in the present work.

The first part, comprising eight chapters, deals with the person of the Holy Spirit. The remaining chapters focus on his operations in the human soul.

An analysis of the names which are ascribed to the Third Divine Person in the Liturgy and in theology discloses to us his distinctive personal characteristics. He proceeds from the Father and the Son by way of love. His name is *"Charitas."* A study of the various modes with which the love of God clothes itself in his dealings with his creatures gives us an insight into the distinctive character of the Third Person of the Blessed Trinity, as regards that which distinguishes his character from that of the Father and of the Son. The love of God, as shown forth in the creation and in the mystery of the Incarnation, is discussed in chapters one and three; the second chapter studies the Holy Spirit as the subsistent love of God.

The fourth chapter considers the purpose of the Holy Spirit in the great work of the Incarnation. He wedded the divinity of the Word to our humanity, in order that our humanity might in its turn be made participant in the divinity. Of the life that comes to us through this supernatural elevation, the Holy Spirit is the fountain. The fifth chapter is devoted to considerations on life in general and of that particular life which the soul shares with God.

The first of the gifts of the lover to the beloved is love itself. It is a prelude to all else that is given. The Holy Spirit, the love of God, is the Creator's first gift to his creature raised to the order of grace. Chapter six is a study of the Holy Spirit as gift of God most high.

Friendship is the third modality that the Creator's love assumes toward his creatures. It devolves on him who is styled in Scripture the "Spirit of the Lord Jesus" to cement the bonds of friendship between the creature and Creator. This is his *mission:* the sense of this theological term is explained in the seventh chapter. The mission of the Holy Spirit to the soul is not a passing one. He takes up his abode in a permanent manner in the souls of the just. This inhabitation, appropriated to the Third Person of the Blessed Trinity, is explained in the eighth chapter. It is shown to be an inchoate form of that perfect possession of God that is enjoyed by the blessed in heaven.

The existence of the Holy Spirit in the souls in which he takes up his residence is not an inactive existence. The Divine Spirit justifies the soul and does so by imparting to it a certain divine quality by means of the sanctifying grace which he pours forth in it. This is the theme of the ninth chapter.

Sharing in the nature of God, the Christian becomes a child of God. The adherent to Christ is born of water and of the Holy Spirit. The characteristics and privileges of the divine adoption are set forth in the tenth chapter. The child of God is destined to become a man of God. The concluding chapters deal with the principles of supernatural growth. These are the infused divine virtues, theological and moral, with the gifts of the Holy Spirit. The full development of the potentialities of grace issues in that sublime and blissful condition of soul outlined in the Beatitudes, with which the Savior prefaces his Sermon on the Mount. The concluding pages, then, discuss the fruits of the Spirit and of the Beatitudes.

The work has been prompted by a desire to popularize the wonders of Catholic theology and to give the ordinary reader a working knowledge of the divine life imparted by the Holy Spirit to the souls of the just. An insight into the operations of the Third Person of the Blessed Trinity is bound to promote an enlightened and active devotion to that divine person.

INTRODUCTION

An instinctive prompting of divine origin is moving souls to turn for a real existence to an intense interior life. They realize that hitherto their faith—the Christian faith—was not all to them that it could and should have been.

Many are beginning to understand that the faith is communicated to men by the Redeemer chiefly for this purpose: that they may be admitted to a participation of God's own divine life and helped to progress in that life. This explains the growing interest in the interior life—its laws, its manifestations and its means of progress—that has been such a characteristic of recent years. It is evidenced by the great wealth of literature dealing *ex professo* with the spiritual life that makes its appearance today. The great supply testifies to a wide demand and a very keen interest. It is characteristic of God that his answer to the challenge of the naturalism of the age should be a marked intensification of the supernatural life in those who remain faithful to him.

The soul is in us the fundamental principle of our life of nutrition, of movement, of sensation, of understanding and of willing. The soul is that through which, ultimately, we are able to nourish ourselves, have sensations, exercise thought and frame decisions.[1] Were there no such thing as the realm of divine grace, the life and the activities of our soul would be circumscribed within these limits. But when the soul is raised by grace to a supernatural condition—that is, to a condition superior to its natural one—then the field of its activities is immeasurably enlarged. It begins to have a new life proper to this new condition—a life with its own peculiar ideals, outlook, needs and aspirations. To this life, too, belongs its own hunger and thirst. Under the pressure of the imperious demands of this supernatural life, the soul must seek the wherewithal to satisfy this hunger and this thirst. Nothing found in the whole realm of nature, that is, nothing to be found throughout the whole length and breadth and depth of creation, can fulfill this function. Nothing created can appease the soul's hunger.

It is true that the supernatural life does not eclipse or destroy the natural life with its needs, its demands and its activities. The soul can therefore find exercise, as if it were not in a supernatural state at all, in the play of imagination and of thought and in the operations of the faculties of nutrition and sensation. And this life of sense and intellect can make it, at least for a time, insensible to the cravings of the appetites proper to the higher life. But this insensibility will not endure always. Sooner or later a distinct malaise is experienced—a sense of something being wrong. It is an

---

[1] It is thus defined by Aristotle: "The soul is that by which ultimately (that is, the remote principle by which) we live, we have sensations, we exercise local movement, and we think" (Aristotle, *On the Soul*, bk. II, chap. 2).

experience of emptiness, of want, of a need of something not to be found among all the objects which up to then were satisfying enough. This characteristic symptom points to the soul's being hungry: it is the soul's cry for its food. That food is nothing other than God himself. It is only God that can give supernatural life to the soul. It is only with God that life can be nourished, developed and brought to its maturity.

Our divine Savior, embracing in his universal vision all generations of men, felt his heart profoundly moved at the sadness and weariness that met his gaze on every side. Knowing his own power to relieve it and stirred by pity, he issued the loving invitation: "Come to me all you that labor and are heavy laden, and I will refresh you." [2] The heavy-hearted are not solely, or chiefly, those who are enduring actual misery and want, nor those only who are a prey to positive grief and sorrow, but also and perhaps, above all others, that great multitude who are crushed beneath the burden of life itself because of its weariness, emptiness, fruitlessness and futility. The dissatisfaction which consumes the hearts of men is found not only in those whose material necessities make them so clamorous. It exists, and even to a greater depth, in those who are freed from these harassing material cares. To those for whom, through present want of means and opportunity, earthly existence holds as yet unexplored possibilities, the resources of a worldly existence can offer the illusion of ultimate satisfaction. But what of those by whom all these possibilities have been exhausted? There never has been a period in which such a wealth of material comforts and advantages has been at the disposal of such a wide number as the present period. And yet not since Christianity began has dissatisfaction been so profound and universal.

The reason, perhaps, lies in this. Owing to the degree in which life has been accelerated due chiefly to the extreme rapidity which science has made possible in the means of communication, men can now, in a very short time, explore all the possibilities of new, hitherto untried, and therefore possibly pleasurable, experiences. When men move slowly there are always distant horizons rising one upon another to lure them on by pleasant anticipations. But when, because of the manner in which distances are swallowed up and space annihilated and years compressed into days, all the horizons in succession have been approached and there is no longer any distant vista to attract, what can result but a sense of blankness and disappointment? [3] When earth has still something to yield to men, men may, at least in some small measure, be content with earth. But when it has nothing more to give, and to many nowadays it has nothing more to give, men must turn elsewhere for an object, which, holding out hope, will stimulate effort.

The interior, supernatural life of the soul, as revealed to us in the lives of the saints of the Church of Christ, presents us with this very object. In that life of the soul there are inexhaustible possibilities and ever new

[2] Mt 11: 28.
[3] To take a simple instance: a journey which less than a century ago took months can now be accomplished in a few days or, perhaps, a few hours.

experiences; in that life man can be always pressing onward to new horizons. It is comprehensible then, that the thoughtful, the earnest, the unsuperficial are turning with a new interest to the study of the lives of the saints. This is not an interest of mere pious curiosity. It is inspired by the growing realization that the saints, and the saints alone, have found what all other men are vainly seeking—a real life. It is beginning to dawn on the intelligence of those who are sincerely searching for the truth and who, with unprejudiced minds, are seeking for a solution to the problem of existence that the real men and women are the saints and that it is only they who have known what life is.

A subtle but very definite change has taken place in modern times in the literature that deals with the lives of those heroic men and women on whom the Church bestows the honors of canonization. They are no longer regarded as interesting merely for the reason that they lead singular lives contrasting strangely with the lives of those with whom they are obliged to mingle; nor for the reason that occasionally they perform strange deeds surpassing the forces of nature; nor yet that they undertake and bring to a successful issue great and laborious enterprises; nor finally that they are, on the infallible authority of the Church, positively asserted to be in possession of the joys of the beatific vision. The interest in the saints is no longer the interest inspired by the wonder worker or the terrifying ascetic. It was natural that, in the ages of faith, when the saint differed from his fellowman only in this, that he made a more intense and rigid application of the ideals of living held in common with him by his neighbors, the writer/philosopher dwelt complacently on the marvelous and the uncommon in the history of his hero. But now between the saint and his *milieu*, even when that *milieu* is traditionally Christian, the cleavage is profound.

The saint differs from his fellows not merely in this, that he performs heroic penances, while theirs are of the mildest type; nor in this, that he works miracles, while their faith is not strong enough to move an anthill. It is not his doings and his sufferings and his achievements that set the saint apart from the modern Christian. It is his view of the meaning and purpose of the religion which he professes in common with others that marks him so singular even in an environment professedly Christian. It is in his system of thought, in his outlook on things, in his philosophy of life that the saint differs from his peers. In the days of faith it was in his actions, not in his thoughts, that the person of heroic sanctity differed from those about him. The ordinary run of mortals could then understand him even if they declined the effort of imitating him. But now, even in the world that calls itself Christian, the appreciations of true values in life, in conduct, in aims and ideals spring from principles that are un-Christian. The standards of value in human action are not only not Christian, they suffer by comparison with those taught and upheld by the philosophers of pagan antiquity.

Now is it possible to breathe contaminated air without having one's lungs affected by it? The present-day Christian is born into and grows up in a society almost wholly de-Christianized. His system of thought, that which in him determines his appreciations, his tastes and his judgments in all matters of moment for man as an individual or as a social being, is gradually corrupted by the prevailing errors. These errors float like malignant germs in every element in which ideas are conveyed to the mind—on television, in movies, in books, in plays, in art, in newspapers, in lectures and in every other means employed to propagate men's opinions. The individual Christians who, under the action of divine grace, find the strength and courage to revolt against the prevailing standards of value, instinctively turn to the saints for a satisfying scheme of existence.

It is the inner psychological life of the saint, not the external events of his career, that prove of interest for those who are weary of the unreality of the modern world. Those who take to spiritual literature at the present time are more desirous of knowing what the saint was, than what he did. His inner struggles with himself, his break away from the currents that flowed around him, the gradual triumph in him of grace over the resistance of nature, his occasional weaknesses, the courageous clinging to the principles of faith in those frequent eclipses of the supernatural when it is the world and its values that alone seem real, and the divinization of the soul appears to be but a hollow dream—it is all this that one looks to find revealed in the life story of the heroes of sanctity.

The writers of the day aim, in their works, at satisfying this legitimate desire. Men desire passionately to find some satisfying philosophy of life and are reduced to a mood alternating between disgust and despair by the shallow and unwholesome philosophies offered to them by the oracles of the hour. Earnest souls are beginning to regard the saints no longer merely as beings superlatively good and annoyingly singular, but as men and women who have received a deep initiation into the secret of living and who are, in consequence, apt to initiate others. It is felt that they alone know while all others are but groping in a state of more or less complete blindness. The saint is recognized to be the one who really succeeds in finding life and is, therefore, studied chiefly as an "essayist on living." As for the mentality of the saints themselves, a slight acquaintance with their story reveals that they considered their highest knowledge to be the knowledge of the art of communing spiritually with God, and that they regarded their own *real* existence to be the inner supernatural life of the soul, which grew and ripened through persevering contact with God.

At all ages of the Church there have appeared remarkable writings descriptive of the various stages and processes that mark the growth of the soul in the divine life infused into it by God. The output in the last century has been truly remarkable and betokens the awakening of the desire of initiation into this life on the part of great numbers of Christians. An interest in the process of sanctification naturally directs attention to that Person of the Blessed Trinity, to whom, by the law of appropriation, are attributed all the operations of sanctification in the Church itself and in individual members of it. With the widespread interest in the things of the spiritual life, there has grown up an eagerness to have a deeper and more accurate knowledge of the Holy Spirit. There are many indications that the years that are at hand will witness a great development of devotion to the Third Person of the Most Blessed Trinity. It is certain that an understanding of the role that the Holy Spirit plays in the supernatural formation of the soul would inspire the sincere Christian with a desire to address his prayers more frequently and more fervently to that person who, as it were, holds the keys to the treasures of divine grace. Souls whose aspirations rise higher than the mere avoidance of sin and who are eager to taste the happiness that is to be found in the union of the soul with God will find in personal devotion to the Holy Spirit a powerful aid in their efforts to grow in intimacy with God.

Every instructed Catholic knows that at baptism there is a wonderful and mysterious form of life infused into the soul of the regenerated child. There is no one who understands the teachings of our holy faith and does not know that our happiness in the next world and our perfection in this are both found in the development of this participation of the divine life given us gratuitously by God, our Father. The inauguration and the development of this supernatural life is our sanctification. And in Catholic theology all the work of sanctification is attributed—or appropriated, as is the technical term—to the Holy Spirit. It is only reasonable, then, that those who are anxious to grow in holiness should aspire to a deeper understanding—than is ordinarily possessed—of the personal characteristics and attributes of the Holy Spirit. It is hoped that the following pages, in spite of their imperfections, may contribute something to the satisfaction of this praiseworthy desire on the part of pious souls.

The First Mode of God's Love—
His Loving Kindness to His Creatures

WHEN theologians speak of divine goodness and divine love they generally use these words in a sense which they do not bear on the lips of the ordinary faithful. For the term "goodness," as applied to God, can have two significations, which, though an intimate connection reigns between them, differ somewhat one from the other. Several distinct shades of meaning can be attached, in theology, to the word "love," so that the notion expressed by it needs much careful qualification before it can be predicated of the Supreme Being. Since the pages to follow are devoted to a study of the Holy Spirit and of his operations in the soul, and since the Holy Spirit is the love of God personified, it is important that the terms, which recur again and again in discussing these subjects, be subjected to a close analysis in the very beginning. When vagueness of signification is allowed to attach itself to the terms employed in describing the relations that God, all gratuitously, allows to exist between his rational creatures and himself, there is risk that these relations may be hampered, complicated and placed on a false footing. It is all important for the soul to know how to approach God, how to address itself to him and how to bear itself becomingly in his presence. Mistakes will be made in all these respects if inaccurate notions of the spiritual commerce that should exist between creature and Creator are entertained through an incomplete, imperfect or incorrect apprehension of the terms that describe this intercourse. Even good souls may be unwittingly, at times, guilty of impertinence in their dealings with God, through lack of right understanding.

When Christians are, through some misfortune, faced with a future in which the prospects are all dark, they are wont to console themselves, and rightly, with the reflection that God is good. No statement could seem more simple. It would appear to carry its own explanation and require no further analysis. Yet this seemingly simple statement, "God is good," is one which calls for close examination if we are to grasp its real import.

The fundamental notion attaching to this word, "good," is seized when the term is considered as predicated of objects. A thing is said to be good when it adequately fulfills a purpose or supplies a need. A knife is good which cuts well. A horse is good when it performs satisfactorily the functions for which it is destined, i.e., when it runs swiftly if it is a racehorse or pulls a heavy load if it is a draught-horse. Food is good if it gives adequate nourishment. A plant is good when it is up to nature's standard. In human endeavors, that is good which satisfies a tendency in man. A good position for a man is one that he aims at and which when attained satisfies, at least to a certain extent, his ambition. Generally speaking, what any creature makes an object of pursuit is a "good" (real or apparent) for that creature. If it is something which the creature ought to seek and which, therefore, completes or perfects its being, it is a "real good," otherwise it is but an "apparent good."

Since what is "good" supplies or, at least, is thought to supply a need, it attracts or draws to the acquisition of itself. To acknowledge that a thing is good is to recognize in it a power to attract, a capacity to exercise an appeal. A thing may be good, that is, an object of choice, or choice-worthy, without being actually chosen or elected. But it cannot be elected unless it is seen to be attractive or appealing. Willingly to yield to the attraction—that is, to fix one's choice finally on what offers itself as "good" among others which can make a similar claim—is to love. To love a person is to decide that such a person is one's selection from among others who may be recognized to possess charm. There is, therefore, an intimate kinship between what is good and what is worthy of love. Attractiveness in persons is commonly taken to mean that graciousness of manners and manifestation of friendly interest which make those, toward whom these manners are exercised and in whom that interest is displayed, feel perfectly at their ease. But more accurately employed attractiveness means the aptitude to inspire affection. The lovable person is the one who, because of the excellent qualities or disposition that person possesses, is capable of calling forth the movement of love in others.

Love is a free surrender of the will to the attraction exercised on it by some good or goodness perceived to be present in persons or things. The active exercise of love, that which naturally follows on this satisfaction of the will in the object which draws it, is a movement of the whole being toward that person or that thing, with a view to union with it. It is "goodness"[1] which always attracts. It draws all creatures to itself. The philosophers tell us that all things tend toward the good. The good is simply that which supplies or is thought to be apt to supply a need of a being. It is always, when there is question of thinking creatures, regarded as something without which existence would be incomplete; as something the possession of which would contribute to a greater degree of happiness. To love is to be subjugated by the appeal that the excellence perceived in the beloved exercises on the will of the lover. It is a yielding or willing surrender to a charm that radiates from another being and then a movement to seek union with what enshrines that charm. The good draws like a magnet. The person that comes under the appeal of the good is restless, uneasy and unhappy until a union of some kind can be effected with the creature who possesses the excellent quality that attracts.

While the intelligence tends to draw its object to itself and unite it with itself (and that union, in fact, constitutes the act of knowing), the will on

---

[1] It will be already remarked that the word "goodness" is here used in a sense somewhat different from that which it bears in ordinary speech. When a person's goodness is spoken of, it is not, as a rule, his attractiveness that is meant. It is necessary to note that fundamentally, nevertheless, "goodness" is that in a person or thing which makes it attractive. It is not to be confounded with benignity—a term, however, closely akin to it.

the other hand does not draw but is drawn onward and outward to its object. It is in this sense that love is said to be ecstatic; that is, it moves the person that loves to regard his whole good as bound up in the being that he loves. If it is a person that is loved, the love that consists in being won by that person's charm naturally merges into the love of benevolence. Since the lover finds his good in the beloved, it is impossible that he should not ardently desire that what is his good should increase in goodness and should ever become more choice-worthy and attractive. In pursuing the well-being and the happiness of the beloved, that is, the good of the beloved, the lover is veritably seeking his own greater good.

When our divine Savior said to the ruler who had addressed him as "Good Master," that "there is none good but God alone,"[2] it is most probable that he used the word "good" in the sense that has just been developed. God is the universal magnet of all creatures. Every element of goodness that there is in things, everything therefore that has power to exercise an attraction, comes originally from God. If anything draws to itself, if anything stirs affection, if anything calls forth the movement of love, it is because it possesses a quality which is a participation of the infinite goodness of God. In creatures there is but a *measure* of appeal; God is *all* appeal—*all* attractiveness. He is winning in the extreme, not simply because there is in him some particular quality which is apt to call forth a deep affection, but because there is nothing in him which is not lovable. Creatures are only relatively good, that is, good in some measure or under some aspect. God is absolutely, that is, wholly, good. Every created being that is good has imperfection or limitation mingled with goodness. God alone is pure goodness, hence he is supremely choice-worthy. To love God is simply to allow one's will to fix its choice on God as being the good that is to be chosen in preference to anything else which competes for our affection. One may "feel" far more powerfully attracted toward other things, but if one resists the attraction and adheres to God—he loves God above all things.[3]

There is no goodness anywhere which has not its origin in him. And all that goodness accumulated together is incapable of equaling or exhausting his goodness. When inanimate things and irrational creatures under the impulse of nature tend by their native qualities and activities toward their perfection, that is, toward their good, they are really tending toward God. They are being drawn by the magnetic attraction of God; because all perfections in creation are, as it were, broken gleams of that infinite attractiveness which is identical with God.

But not all things which are good in themselves are proper objects of pursuit. When men, in their perversity, allow themselves to be won by the deceitful charm of that which flatters their sensuality or their pride, they can still be said in a certain sense to be tending toward God. Their

[2] Lk 18: 18–19.
[3] Love must not be confused with liking. It is possible to love what one does not like. Liking does not necessarily come under the control of the will. It is usually spontaneous and is an inclination of the sensibility to what pleases it.

misfortune lies in this, that in seeking after some good which is not meant for them by God, inasmuch as it does not perfect them as creatures or as rational beings, they put themselves at variance with God. They seek some good, it is true, and in that they are seeking some participation of the perfection of God. But the participation of God that they are pursuing is not the form of perfection for which they were created. Hence it is that in seeking it, they put themselves in opposition to God and so withdraw from him. At one and the same time they are apparently seeking God and in reality turning away from him. Thus they arrest their tendency toward God. The object which they seek (and not God himself) becomes the term or the final end of their desire. In this way they lose the power of tending toward their supreme and ultimate good. If, for instance, a man in his activity aims at what is just or prudent or brave or temperate, he is directing himself toward what perfects him as man, toward what constitutes his good as man. He is directing himself toward such a participation of the supreme good as was meant for him by that supreme good itself. The movement toward these objects carries him onward toward his ultimate perfection, his final and crowning good which is goodness itself. If, on the other hand, he yields to the attraction of an object which ministers to pride, sloth, cowardice or sensuality, he subjugates himself to what is powerless to carry him on toward God but has the very contrary effect of sweeping him away from God.

For man to be holy is nothing else than to love and to seek what is really and ultimately "good" for him as man. It consists in his will freely and fully surrendering itself to the attractiveness of God, who is supremely attractive and therefore merits to be sought above and beyond all else. Holiness lies in allowing oneself constantly to be drawn by this attractiveness considered as existing in God himself or in those things which, containing a good suitable to man as such, are apt to perfect his nature and bear him onward in his movement toward his ultimate good—God. Man is holy when by the infused virtue of charity, he loves God in himself, or when he loves God as found in the objects of the moral infused virtues of prudence, justice, fortitude and temperance. Man is holy when he finds God's goodness as existing in God himself or as found in objects worthy of man's choice, to be his good and meriting, therefore, to be sought after in every deliberate action. That God is good, then, means primarily that he, because of what he is, merits to be sought after in every movement of desire. It means that he is supremely attractive. That God is man's good means that he alone can fulfill man—that he alone can bring to their full evolution the quasi-infinite potentialities of man.

But that God is good can have another and somewhat different meaning from that which has been analyzed. He not only attracts us. He also bestows favors on us. God is not only good *for us*, he is also good *to us*. The latter kind of goodness is based on and springs from the former. That which in God is the source of the appeal exercised by him is what makes him supremely kind. His absolute goodness makes him eminently unselfish and therefore well disposed in the highest manner toward his creatures. When we speak of God as being good, it is of his attitude toward us, rather than of his power to attract us, that we are thinking.[4]

Good as applied to persons may mean that they possess certain powers and faculties which are well developed. Thus we speak of a good musician, a good advocate, a good teacher, etc. But when a man is spoken of as good, and there is no limiting qualification added, another and higher sense of the word "goodness" is introduced. The idea of goodness in this connection, like all simple notions, defies strict definition and will admit only of explanation or description. Though so difficult to define, everyone understands fairly well what goodness means. The person that is good is one that radiates a beneficent influence on all that come in contact with his personality. Goodness of disposition not only attracts and pleases like beauty, it also inspires trust and confidence. Those who are in distress or in need feel instinctively that there is strength, support and sympathy to be found in the good. These latter seem to hold treasures of life which, being more than sufficient for their own needs, can be dispensed with generosity to those whose natures are more hungry, starved or contracted. We turn spontaneously, under the stress of trial and suffering, to one on whose goodness we can count. Such a one is always helpful. The quality of goodness in him to whom we have recourse is the basis on which is founded our perfect trust that there we shall find an inexhaustible source of light and warmth and comfort.

Goodness is diffusive of itself. This not only signifies, as it ordinarily does for the philosopher, that whatever leads to what is good becomes, thereby, itself good;[5] it also signifies that goodness radiates an influence which tends to create an image of itself in all those who are apt to receive that image. There is no one but must have felt this subtle effect exercised by the personality of those endowed with that excellent quality of which there is question. The good by their very existence, by simply being good, tend to transform to their own likeness those who are not ill-disposed. One that is not deliberately perverse feels strength in their companionship, support in their sympathy and a moral uplifting in their mere presence. Just as the sun from its very nature cannot but diffuse light and heat, so the good, from the very fact that they are so, cannot but wish well to and strive to procure the advantage of those who are not unwilling to submit to their influence.

[4] The distinction between the two senses in which God is said to be good can be made clear by the use of terms which have the disadvantage of being somewhat technical. When God is said to be good in the sense that he is good for us, that is, our good, the term is used in its *ontological* sense. When God is said to be good in the sense that he is good to us, the term is used in what may be called its *moral* and more usual sense. In the previous paragraphs the word "good" was employed in its ontological signification. In the following paragraphs it will be employed according to its moral signification.

[5] Good is diffusive of itself. This expression is frequently cited and practically always not in its primary but in its derivative sense. Primarily its meaning is this: What is truly an end for men to seek is alone truly good. What leads to the end—because it leads to the end—becomes invested with the form of good. As conducing to the end, it participates in the nature of good which rightly belongs to the end alone.

19

If, in human intercourse, men of noble, kind and generous dispositions can so uplift others, how much more potent might be the effect of God on his creatures. This effect would be secured if the creatures would but allow themselves to come to God as to one whose sole object in his relations with them is to influence them for good. "If you then," he said, "who are evil, know how to give good gifts to your children, how much more will your Father who is in heaven give good things to those who ask him!"[6]

Men, of course, are free and can allow themselves or refuse to allow themselves to be changed for the better by their contact with God. Their reluctance to enter into that relation with their heavenly Father which should have as its ultimate effect the shaping of their spirit to his comes not always from perversity or a deliberate desire to keep apart from him. It is often attributable to a profound sense of unworthiness. Those who are conscious of being entangled in the meshes of sin, experience an instinctive shrinking from their Maker. They have the persuasion that One, who is infinitely pure and holy, can have nothing to do with beings worthless and defiled, such as they feel themselves to be. The sense of sinfulness very frequently, and that too, even in the case of souls who have received more than ordinary instruction, becomes a reason for not venturing on any but the most distant relations with God. Even the great St. Teresa fell into this error when, after she had received great favors from God, she lapsed into habits of infidelity to grace. Through a keen sense of unworthiness due to the imperfections into which she had allowed herself to drift, she shrank from close contact with God. She would, as it were, sink her individuality in her relations with him, by entering his presence only as one of a crowd. She gave up the practice of holding intimate intercourse with God in mental prayer. Her alienation from God was judged by her to be a justification for alienating herself still further. Bitterly did she deplore, in later years, this pernicious error.

It is true that far different are the relations between God and the just from those between God and sinners. But the Lord has multiplied his assurances to men that not even the inconstant and the weak and the ungrateful are excluded from the effects of his merciful regard and consideration. Nothing that men can do can paralyze the activity of the kindness of God in their regard or prevent its being extended toward them as long as they are in this life. Our badness cannot cause God's goodness to falter or to fail or even to waver. No matter how darkened the air may be by the fierce, dark storm clouds, the sun continues to pour out, steadily and unchangingly, its life-giving rays. Even so, God's goodness continues to pour its rays on his creatures, though the atmosphere in which they are enveloped is darkened by their stormy passions. It is the figure employed by Jesus Christ himself. "But I say to you, do good to them that hate you . . . that you may be the children of your Father who is in heaven, who maketh his sun to rise upon the good and bad, and raineth upon the just and the unjust."[7]

[6] Mt 7: 11; cf. Lk 11: 11.
[7] Mt 5: 44–45.

No coldness on the part of men can chill God's goodness to them. Nothing can cause God to change his attitude toward his creatures. It is true that in the pages of Scripture there are numerous texts which appear to state the contrary. They speak of God as being angry, as repenting of his previous kind actions, as withdrawing his favor, and as having many a revulsion of feeling in regard to those who had been the objects of his favors. But all these texts, rightly interpreted, simply express the disastrous consequences that, by the very nature of things, befall God's creatures when they break with him. They express not a change in God's dispositions toward men, but a change in the fortunes of men, following necessarily on their prevarications.

There are in general two classes of sinners. There are those who not only offend but cling to their offense, justify their action and even go so far as to have a decided aversion for God. Their sin is not one of weakness but of positive, determined and obstinate wickedness. There are others whose falls are real, grievous and even multiplied, but they recognize that they are sinners: they do not seek to justify their crimes. They sin but their sins are the outcome of weakness. They have not cast aside all fear of God: they are not determined to remain obdurate in their sinful state. God's kindness to sinners is manifested especially to those of this latter class. But yet even to the obstinate God is good and he pours his graces into their souls as long as there is a possibility of their turning to him.

It is a most consoling thought, incredible as it might often appear to those who are weighed down with the consciousness of sin, that God, the great, the holy and the good can, in a certain restricted sense of the term, love sinners, though he cannot entertain for them the love of friendship. St. Thomas Aquinas asks himself if it is possible for God to be thus disposed toward the erring, and he answers in the affirmative.[8] The reason he gives carries with it immediate conviction. His argument does not admit of reply. What is impossible for us, is possible for God. We cannot be drawn to another person unless our will is stirred by the attraction of some excellence existing in that person and endowing him with charm. We do not confer on the objects of our affection their charm and their appeal. Unless that charm existed in them, there would be no movement of us toward them, and they would not become objects of our love.

It is otherwise with God. He bestows on his creatures that which makes them lovable in his eyes. He finds no good in them that has not himself for its source. Whatever he gives must be good. How could he bestow anything that were otherwise?[9] To all his creatures without exception he has imparted much. They all share in some measure in the perfections, partakers of his own infinite perfection, which he has scattered with such profuse largesse through all creation. Hence it is that God has regard for all that has come from his hands. St. Denis, quoted by St. Thomas,[10] says that God, in the wealth of his loving kindness, goes out of himself and exercises

---

[8] St. Thomas Aquinas, *Summa Theologica* I, q. 20, a. 2, ad 4 [hereafter *S. Th.*].
[9] Lk 13: 11.
[10] *S. Th.* I, q. 20, a. 2, ad 1.

his providence in all things that exist (i.e., he works to provide for their good as if it were his own).

In the Book of Wisdom are to be read these words which, in the style of Scripture, express the very same thought as that dwelt upon by St. Thomas in the article of the *Summa Theologica* that has just been quoted. "For thou" (O Lord), says the sacred writer, "lovest all things that are, and hatest none of the things which thou hast made . . . and how could anything endure if thou wouldst not, or be preserved if not called by thee? But thou sparest all because they are thine, O Lord, who lovest souls." [11] It is a characteristic of love to wish well to, to be benevolent toward, another. All things in creation are indebted to the generosity of God. All things have been the recipients of the effect of his benevolence. If inanimate things, plants and animals can be the objects of ceaseless attention on the part of the Almighty, is it to be wondered at that rational creatures, even if they are sinners, should draw on themselves a far greater measure of the same kind regard? Even in their sins, while they are still capable of repentance, they are far more valuable in God's eyes than all the rest of creation taken together. A creature, endowed with reason and, therefore, with the power to know and to love God, has received from the hands of the Creator a gift that surpasses in value all the worth found in things incapable of thought. God's benevolence, that is to say, his goodwill, is proportioned to his gifts. He cares most for those to whom he gives most. He has more regard, then, for his rational creatures than for all the rest besides.

There is still another difference and one more profound between the goodwill extended by God to man and that extended to the other creatures inferior to man. These latter receive at once from their Maker all they are destined to receive from him. Their perfection, if we except living things, is attained, as it were, at one stride. In the case of irrational living things, it is true there is a beginning, a growth and a consummation. But the perfection capable of being attained by them is fixed, definite and limited. God is, as it were, satisfied in giving them merely that good which he has measured out for them. But with men (even when they prove ungrateful and resist his will—a thing which the inferior creatures never do), he acts otherwise. To rational beings he never tires of giving. [12]

He does not arrest the tide of his benevolence at the gifts of nature even when dealing with sinners. Over and above these gifts of nature he rains on them an incessant stream of actual graces which always have as their object

[11] Wis 11: 24–26.

[12] St. Thomas establishes the hierarchy of being on this basis—namely, the good destined for each grade of creatures and their mode of attaining it. At the summit of being is God in full possession of the infinite good without any effort. Next come the angels who attain the perfect good by one or by a small number of movements. In the third place come men, who attain the perfect good but by a multiplicity of movements. Next below men come plants and animals which attain an incomplete and imperfect good by one or more movements. Lastly come inanimate things which can reach out to no further being than that which they have in their beginning and so remain without movement (see *S. Th.* I, q. 77, a. 2).

the greater good of the recipient. He stimulates the will and enlightens the intelligence in order that the obstacles that lie between the soul and its supernatural good may be removed. He gives actual grace on actual grace to prepare the way for imparting far higher gifts than the gifts of nature. God's gifts are the measure of his regard. He aims at giving more in order that he may be able to love still more the object of his benevolence. God cannot, of course, extend his friendship, though he does extend his kindness and benevolence, to those who are estranged from him. But those who are at one time at enmity with him may, by repentance, afterward become his intimates. He foresees this possibility in the case of many, even in their prevarication, and, so, he deals with them with unwearying kindness. "But thou," says the sacred writer, "hast mercy upon all, because thou canst do all things, and overlookest the sins of men for the sake of repentance." [13] The holy king David had personal experience of the unchanging and unwavering loving kindness of God toward his erring creatures and could write, therefore, with deep feeling. "The Lord is gracious and merciful, patient and plenteous in mercy. The Lord is sweet to all, and his tender mercies are over all his works." [14] And again elsewhere he writes: "The Lord is compassionate and merciful, long suffering and plenteous in mercy. . . . He will not always be angry. . . . He hath not dealt with us according to our sins. . . . As a father hath compassion on his children, so hath the Lord compassion on them that fear him: For he knoweth our frame; he remembereth that we are dust." [15]

In a word, the Lord has a certain kind of love for sinners even as they are, and he aims at loving them in a loftier and more perfect manner if they consent to change to a nobler condition of soul by yielding to the solicitations of his grace.

There are profound reasons, based upon the very nature of things, that this should be so. In the first place we are all alike the work of God's hands. He has made us and we are his handiwork, stamped, even in our perversity, with his image. Every true artist loves his own creations more than he could be loved by them even were they endowed with life. The sculptor contemplates with pleasure the forms that spring from the marble at the touch of his genius. Poets love their own verses, and writers of prose are proverbially sensitive in regard to their own writings. As mothers love their children, even if they are to receive no love in return, so do artists love the fruits of their imagination and their creative skill. Perhaps this is implied in these words (than which perhaps there are no more touching in the whole of Scripture), whereby God speaking to the people by the mouth of his prophet said: "Can a woman forget her infant, so as not to have pity on the son of her womb? And if she should forget, yet I will not forget thee." [16]

There is still another reason to explain this kindly attitude of God toward us all indiscriminately. We stand to him not only in the relation of

[13] Wis 11: 23.
[14] Ps 145: 8, 9.
[15] Ps 102: 8–14.
[16] Is 49: 15.

the work of art to the artist, but also in that of the beneficiary to the benefactor. Now experience shows that it is a natural thing that a bond of affection should spring up between those who bestow kindnesses and those who receive them. The benefactor is drawn toward the person who is benefited, even when, as is so often the case, he is requited only with ingratitude. Those, who are conversant with persons who by natural inclination or by supernatural vocation devote themselves to works of mercy, cannot fail to notice and be struck by this phenomenon. Although this perseverance in doing good even to the ungrateful is oftentimes due to virtue hardly-won, it is not, even in those cases, unconnected with a deep instinct in human nature. Life is clung to and loved by all. Each one's life is very dear to himself.

We exist in living and doing. *"Vita est in motu,"* the philosophers tell us. The creator of a work finds his existence in a certain way actualized in the work he has made. Benefaction is an excellent form of activity. It is the exteriorization of an excellent inner quality, without which the act of kindness remains in a purely potential state—unexpressed, unactualized and, therefore, incomplete and imperfect. In the beneficiary then the benefactor sees what is good in himself given a living, concrete expression. He is drawn to the object of his kindness because that object, as it were, incarnates his own excellence. If it is natural to a man to love a good disposition of his own soul, it is only to be expected that he should find satisfaction in that disposition when given external expression in a benefit bestowed on another. As the picture sets forth in fairness of form and richness of coloring the glowing conceptions of the artistic faculty, so, in a somewhat similar way, the improved fortunes of those who have been charitably dealt with express in human conditions the benevolence which flowers in the souls of the good, the devoted and the self-forgetting. God is the Great Benefactor. Not only has he bestowed great and most precious gifts upon us, in the first instance; he has also, with great pain and labor to himself, restored them to us after we had lost them—the pain and labor being that of God made man.[17] If kindness draws the benefactor to the person who benefits, the drawing is far stronger when the bestowal of the benefit has involved much hardship and pain. "God so loved the world," St. John says, "as to give his only-begotten Son."[18] It has cost God the human life of his only-begotten Son to put the treasures of divine grace at our disposal. It is not then astonishing that he should have a deep interest in creatures for whom he has done so much.[19]

When, if we have not yet been converted to the Lord, we groan under the burden of sin, or when, having been at one time converted, we are

---

[17] "By whom he hath given us most great and precious promises" (2 Pet 1: 4).

[18] Jn 3: 16.

[19] This fact that a strong affection springs up in the hearts of benefactors in regard to those who are the recipients of their favors has been submitted to a very penetrating analysis by Aristotle in his *Nicomachean Ethics*, bk. IX, chap. 7 [hereafter *Nic. Ethics*]. He notes with his usual acumen that this affection is much deepened if the bestowal of the kindness costs the benefactor dearly.

crushed under the sense of our failure in the spiritual life, of our betrayal of God's trust and of our consequent unworthiness to appear in his presence, it is an instinct in us, in order to resist the temptation to utter discouragement and even despair, to take refuge in the thought of God's kindness. The considerations developed in the preceding pages show how justifiable it is to do this. The ideas that have been expressed, derived from Sacred Scripture, from theology and even from philosophy, should succeed in bringing home to us the almost incredible truth, namely, that God can have a certain love for us even when we are sinners. St. Paul touches on this consoling truth in his epistle to the Romans. He says: "God commendeth his charity toward us, because when as yet we were sinners according to the time, Christ died for us." [20] The more weak and the more sinful we find ourselves, the more we ought to dwell on the thought that God is our Creator and our Benefactor and that in spite of our waywardness we are still objects of his regard.

Seeing, then, that to us sinners this realization of God's goodness brings so much hope and consolation, it is surprising that we do not make it more commonly the subject of our thoughts and the object of our devotion. If this were done more frequently by those who find themselves entangled in sin or by those who have lapsed into a state of lukewarmness, the character of the spiritual life of both classes would undergo a speedy change. From the consideration of God's loving kindness would be derived not merely a firm expectation of forgiveness but in addition a strong incentive to virtue. There would come to the discouraged and the sluggish not only comfort, but inspiration as well. How often does it happen in the ordinary relations of life, that the affection of one who is devoted to us, if that affection resides in the heart of one who is pure and good, nerves us to resist the tendencies to evil and strengthens us to continue firm in the path of honor and rectitude!

If, in the commerce of life, we have been fortunate enough to come to know one whose nature is stamped with the character of goodness, we have recourse to such a one with perfect ease. In approaching him we have great confidence that he will place at our disposal all the resources which he can freely dispose of in our favor. Does it come sufficiently to the mind of the average Christian that what in men inspires these sentiments of trust and assurance exists in God in a preeminent manner? If it did, trustfulness in dealing with God would be pushed to far greater limits than is usually the case. Did we but realize God's infinite goodwill toward us, we would without fear or hesitancy or shrinking have recourse to him with an unlimited freedom and confidence. We would come to him with an assumption of the existence on his part of a generosity and promptitude to help, which would be proof against any measure of wretchedness and meanness on our part. Far from being displeased with such boldness, God would be greatly gratified. Unbounded confidence in his readiness to forgive his creatures and in the inexhaustibility of his mercy is one of the

---

[20] Rom 5: 8.

greatest compliments that can be paid him by his creatures; while on the other hand it is highly displeasing to him that we should narrow down his goodness to the limits of our own conceptions.[21] It is what we always tend unconsciously to do.

The words "God is good" are frequently on our lips. But as is the case with oft employed expressions, this statement has ceased to bear for us its full and literal significance. Our thoughts about God, if analyzed, would probably reveal that we regard him certainly as just and reasonable and perhaps considerate in his dealings with us; but scarcely anything more than that. It is saints that have the conviction that God is not only all that, but much more. They grasp that God is really and truly good even toward the wayward and the erring. This is because God is good not only with a goodness superior to that of men and angels, not only with a goodness which surpasses the power of men or angels to conceive, but with a goodness which is absolutely and positively infinite. There are the same limits to the goodness of God as to the Godhead itself—that is to say, no limits at all.

It is clear, from what has been said, that God verifies in himself all the significations that can attach to the predicate good. He is good because he is worthy of the uttermost love of his creatures, for he can fulfill every longing of their being. By tending toward him all seek their highest good and attain to their utmost perfection. God is good in the sense too that he is unwearied in his loving kindness to his creatures. That kindness is extended to all without exception. He loves them because in all things he pursues their good. But the love of God, in this sense, is not extended in equal measure to all persons. He is said to have a greater love for those on whom he bestows higher favors. In this sense he loves the just more than sinners, and, among the just, those who are more advanced in virtue than the less proficient. But if regard be had to the act of love itself, then it is true to say that it is with the same love God loves all his creatures. The act of his will cannot admit of greater or less intensity. In one simple unchanging act of the will, an act that admits of no development but is always equal to itself, God envelops creatures in his affection.[22] That love considered not in its effects but in itself will be the theme of the following chapter. As will be seen it is identified with the Holy Spirit himself.

[21] This displeasure of God at our measuring his dealings with creatures by our own standards is plainly hinted at in the response given by our Savior to the laborers called to his vineyard in the earlier hours. "Or is it not lawful for me to do what I will? Is thy eye evil because I am good?" (Mt 20: 15).

[22] S. Th. I, q. 20, a. 3.

2

The Holy Spirit—Divine Love Subsistent

GOD'S love for us is the source of all his benefits to us. It is in the Holy Spirit that he pours out this affection. An introduction to the knowledge of the Third Divine Person implies a study of love as it exists in God. It is from the contemplation of created things that we rise to a knowledge of God and his perfections—a knowledge which, though necessarily imperfect, is, as far as it goes, free from error. Whatever excellence is observable in nature must necessarily be found in God. Every quality there is in creatures, which does not in its very notion imply defect, can be assumed to belong to the Creator. These qualities or perfections, however, must exist in the Godhead in such a way as to be freed from all the limitations which affect them as existing in finite creatures. Not only must the perfections be stripped of the limitations which naturally attach to what is finite, they must as well, by an effort of intelligence, be endowed with the attribute of infinity. That any one of these perfections, therefore, which are scattered in such profusion throughout the universe, be predicated of God, it is necessary that it be purified of all that implies defect and limitation and be carried by thought to the supreme degree of excellence.

Love is one of those excellent things that are found in nature. It is "a good" in the sense in which everything that is real is, as such, good. It is "a good," moreover, in what might be called its dynamic aspect. For if love is called forth by and given to something that it becomes the lover to love, what is loved perfects the lover and carries him to a higher degree of perfection.[1] What a man loves gives him his place in the hierarchy of personality. He tends to become assimilated to the object of his choice, that is, of his preference. His determination of what is noble marks nobility of character. Love, in all that it implies of excellence and perfection (since it is numbered among created perfections), must exist in God in a preeminent manner. A study of the nature of love, as it is found in the human soul, will be an aid to us in our efforts to form a concept of divine love.

Having many points of resemblance, human and divine love differ, nevertheless, in many respects. In man, love, based as it is to a large extent on sensibility, is subject to vicissitudes. From being strong and ardent it can become feeble and cold. At times it flames up brightly. And again, because sensibility has been wounded or has ceased to be affected, it wavers, flickers and frequently dies out altogether. Even at its best it is not a man's whole self. In him there is a vast outpouring of energy, which has not as its purpose to procure the good of others. Even when a human being

---

[1] "Love of the good that is truly a good for the being that loves tends to perfect that being and bring it to a better condition. It is for this reason that man is in the highest measure perfected and elevated by the love of God" (*S. Th.* I, II, q. 28, a. 5 c).

becomes ardently attached to another, he does not consecrate all his thoughts to the object of his affection. A multitude of other objects can claim his attention at the same time and cause him to be distracted during long intervals from the dominant interest of his life. And it always remains possible that one affection should drive out another, no matter how strong that other may have been. Man's affections are fitful and changing. Because of that they are defective and unreliable. No one who is wise should place too much reliance on their stability. He is foolish "that trusteth in man and maketh flesh his arm."[2]

The majority of persons eagerly desire to be loved[3] and are prone to indulge the hope that the love once given will never be withheld. To this they aspire as to that which shall constitute one of the principal elements of their happiness. How frequent and cruel are the deceptions experienced in this matter! Love oftentimes betrays the person loved; as frequently or perhaps, more frequently, it betrays the lover himself. It is the penalty of human perversity that a man may bestow his affection on an object utterly unworthy of him, with consequent deterioration of himself. To love is in a certain sense to espouse the condition of the beloved, to make it one's own. In love there is always a species of abdication of one's self or relinquishing of self. This abdication is followed by a substitution. The lover's own individual and distinctive well-being ceases to be an object of pursuit. It is replaced as a term of desire and absorbing interest by the well-being of the beloved. What procures or enhances the good and happiness of the beloved beatifies the lover. The latter finds his happiness in what makes for the happiness of the object of his affection. This is to love truly.[4]

In all true love there is a species of worship, in virtue of which the lover implicitly acknowledges that the object of his worship is superior to himself; is more choice-worthy than himself; is a greater good to him than he would be to himself. There is a profound philosophic truth underlying the usage of the word "divinity," so common in erotic verse. To the person whose heart has been subjugated by the charm of the beloved, this latter becomes a sort of "divinity." Love therefore effects as it were a surrender of, or a submersion of, the being of the lover in the object of his affection. Between lover and loved there is effected a kind of identification. The lover becomes drawn to the condition of or clothed with the form of what he loves. If this object is base and beneath him, he is dragged downward by it. Not all love perfects. There is, alas! many an affection, the effect of which is to degrade. "The love of what is not in accord with the exigencies of the nature of the being that loves," says St. Thomas, "injures and lowers the lover."[5] A man's moral value can be

---

[2] Jer 17: 5.

[3] Aristotle, *Nic. Ethics*, bk. VIII, chap. 10.

[4] Aristotle writes with his habitual penetration and incisiveness as follows: "In loving their friend, men love what is good for themselves, since the good man, in becoming a friend, *becomes a good to him* whose friend he is. Accordingly, in this case, each at once loves what is good for himself and gives the other back an equivalent both in goodwill and in the kind of good" (*Nic. Ethics*, bk. VIII, chap. 7).

[5] *S. Th.* Ia, IIae, q. 28, a. 5.

accurately determined by a knowledge of the character of the persons or the quality of the things that win his affections. What a man loves reveals the man. Experience justifies the statement of Aristotle, quoted and approved of by St. Thomas, that the objects which a man deems choice-worthy and therefore to be sought after plainly manifest and accurately reflect the tendencies of the moral character.[6]

Love exists in God without any of the imperfections and limitations that attach to all human affections. All that it means of perfection is verified in him. The love of God is not wayward or fitful or changeable. It is not something that comes and goes in his being as thoughts, feelings and emotions come in us and then pass away. It is not a mere transient expression of his life. Subject to no vicissitudes, it partakes of the infinite perfection of the Godhead and is as eternal and immutable as is the divine nature itself. It knows neither waning nor eclipse.

The love of God has not to go outside the confines of the Divinity to find an object on which to fix itself: God's own infinite loveliness attracts him irresistibly. Even when God is drawn to his creatures it is still what is of himself in them that attracts him. Their aptitude to draw upon themselves the loving regard of their Creator is due to the participation of the infinite good with which he has endowed them—that infinite good being nothing other than himself, considered as infinitely attractive, as drawing all to itself by the power of its charm. God's love, being so pure, so perfect, so noble, can be aroused by nothing that is not God himself or that is not something of God himself bestowed on creatures. It is his own absolute charm that calls forth his love in every case, whereas the charm that wins the human heart exists prior to and independent of the love it provokes.[7]

The object, then, on which God's love is bestowed is never absent from his thoughts: it is ever before his mental gaze, provoking the outpourings of his tenderness and sustaining the vitality of his affections. And at the contemplation of this object, this fountain and source of all attractiveness that exists, this object of infinite loveliness and of limitless lovableness,[8] there arises in the Two Divine Persons, the Father and the Son, a mighty surge, as it were, of "spiritual emotion" (human language fails utterly in the description of these mysteries)—an infinite, a divine, a mighty heart-beat, a sigh of infinite satisfaction in the presence and in the absolute possession of what is supremely good and lovable. These ineffable wonders of love within the Godhead become more intelligible to us when we consider love as it is in those who are made to God's image and likeness.

---

[6] Aristotle, *Nic. Ethics*, bk. III, chap. 7, quoted in *S. Th.* Ia, IIae, q. 10, a. 3, and I, q. 83, a. 1, ad 5. *"Qualis unusquisque est talis finis videtur ei."*

[7] There is a profound difference between love in God and in creatures. The movement of love in creatures does not cause what is attractive in things, but, on the contrary, it is that attractiveness, real or imaginary, already existing which calls forth the affection. But the love of God creates that which is attractive in its objects and is therefore stirred only by what comes from God himself. God's love tends to make the beloved lovable and loving.

[8] God contemplates all created reality and, therefore, all created good in its archetypal form, which is the divine essence itself.

A person who is loved is said to abide, to be present, in the heart of the person who loves. That presence of the beloved in the lover is not, as it were, a static presence. It is dynamic. Love is in the will as a force, as a principle of movement. Being loved consists in existing in the will of the person who loves as a weight or force of attraction drawing that person strongly to oneself. An example will illustrate this. To sink an object which of its nature floats, one weights it with lead or stone. The heavy metal by its mass and momentum carries the object down to the depths of the water. So God existing in himself (as an object loved in the lover) bears God with irresistible force on toward the object that attracts him, namely, the divine essence perceived in all its infinite charm and appeal.[9] The full tide of God's love sets strongly toward and pours its waters on the shores of the divine loveliness. That loveliness is as a mighty magnet existing in all the energy of its magnetic attraction in the will common to the Father and the Son, and drawing them both with impetuous force toward itself. Figure has to be multiplied on figure, metaphor on metaphor in order to convey in weak, faltering, stammering, human language some idea of these ineffable mysteries. They are literally ineffable because they cannot be expressed.

The willing submission of God to this attractive force is God's holiness. Holiness is nothing else but a willed yielding and glad surrender to the appeal of the infinite good. Into this movement of love toward its object in the Godhead there is poured all the energy—all the reality—all the power of loving—all the divinity of God himself. The love of God is therefore a reality, possessing all the life, all the light, all the being of the great God. *It is, in consequence, truly God,* subsisting in the divine nature as God the Father and God the Son subsist in the divine nature. This love in God has all the perfections of the Father and Son. It shares their divinity. It is equal to them in all things because it possesses in common with them one and the same divine substance, holding it as they do in all its totality. The movement of love in God is, therefore, something divinely great. It is no mere transient emotion, stirring as it were the surface of his nature and then passing away. It is a substance—eternal, everlasting, unchanging, divine, subsistent. It is a divine person. It is subsistent love. It is love personified. It is the Holy Spirit.

At first sight there seems little connection between these terms, "Love of God" and "Holy Spirit." One may ask why the name "Holy Spirit" has been given distinctively to the Third Person of the Most Blessed Trinity. The reason of the name is found in the mode according to which the Holy Spirit proceeds from the Father and the Son. When God—in one comprehensive sweep of his infinite intelligence—embraces and comprehends all the infinite boundless reality that he is himself, there emerges in the divinity, in virtue of that infinite energy of the divine intelligence, a word or concept which is the exact, adequate, intelligible expression or statement of what God is. Through the fecundity of the divine intelligence,

[9] The famous saying of St. Augustine, *"Amor meus, pondus meum,"* conveys the meaning of these statements.

understood in the active sense, there is conceived a "divine expression," a "divine idea," which fully and perfectly signifies God. Our ideas truly but *inadequately* reveal what things are in their nature. The only-begotten "Idea of God," the Word of God, truly and *adequately* reveals what God is in his nature. This Divine Word, this intelligible expression of the Godhead, the Second Person of the Blessed Trinity, proceeding from and begotten of the Father, in virtue of the energy of the divine act of intellection of the Divine, is called by St. Paul (because of these very characteristics of his origin), "the brightness of the glory of God and the figure (that is, the exact and perfect image) of his substance." [10]

This term "Word," given to the Son of God because he proceeds from the Father by the way of intellectual operation, is intelligible to us, because there is a similitude of it in our own understanding of things. We apprehend or grasp or understand things in a mental word or concept or idea (as it is commonly called), which word or idea our intelligence produces out of its own vitality in the very act of intelligibly seizing the nature of a thing. Our mind grasps or understands the object in that idea. The idea is the mental image of the thing—its intelligible expression. It is the mind's statement to itself of what the thing is. Now, as in God comprehending himself, there emerges in the Divinity through the operation of the divine intelligence that divine reality which we call the "Word of God," so, too, in God loving himself there emerges within the bosom of the Godhead, through the operation of loving, a divine reality to which Scripture and Catholic theology give the name *Sanctus Spiritus*—in English, "Holy Spirit."

There is a good reason why this name, "Spirit," should be given to what proceeds from Father and Son through the operation of the divine will in loving. When the will is captivated by the appeal of an object, there follows a strong, loving impulse toward that which attracts. So, in God, when the infinite charm of the Divinity stands fully revealed in the Word, there arises a mighty onrush of impetuous movement toward that object of wondrous appeal. That movement arising from the depths of the Godhead, sweeping toward its object with impetuous force, is naturally likened to a rushing wind—a strong sigh of affection—a mighty breath proceeding from within under the pressure of love. *Spiritus* signifies breath or wind.

The connection of these terms with the name of the Third Person of the Blessed Trinity was present to our Lord's mind in the conversation with Nicodemus. "That which is born of the Spirit is spirit. The Spirit breatheth where he will, and thou knowest his voice, but thou knowest not whence he cometh and whither he goeth." [11] The same image reappears in the Acts of the Apostles, where the Holy Spirit's descent on the heralds of the Gospel is described in terms of flame and rushing wind. "And suddenly there came a sound from heaven, *as of a mighty wind coming* . . . and

[10] Heb 1: 3; cf. 2 Cor 4: 4: "The glory of Christ, *who is the image* of God"; Col 1: 15: "the Son . . . *who is the image* of the invisible God."
[11] Jn 3: 6–8.

there appeared to them parted tongues as it were of fire . . . and they were all filled with the Holy Spirit." [12] Fire and impetuous movement are the natural symbols of him whose procession from Father and Son is by the operation of love. St. Thomas says: "In God that which proceeds by way of love does not proceed as begotten but rather as a breath (*spiritus*), i.e., a breathing or sigh arising from love. By this term is meant a vital movement or impulse, inasmuch as one is said to be moved or impelled by love to do something." [13] So that infinite reality which arises or is called forth in the bosom of the Divinity when the Father and the Son are attracted by, and joyously submit to, the infinite drawing or appeal of the divine loveliness; that reality is the Holy Spirit—the infinitely pure breathing of love.

The term "holy" is appropriated to the Third Person of the Blessed Trinity because of the manner of his origin from the Father and the Son. Holiness is nothing else than a "willed" yielding to the appeal of the divine goodness. Creatures are holy in the exact measure in which they allow themselves to be subjugated by the attraction of that goodness which is in God. The Father and Son are carried toward it with an impetuous movement of infinite force. The reality, which originates in the Divinity in virtue of that divine satisfaction in the divine goodness, assumes to itself appropriately, as its very own, the attribute holy. Hence it is that Scripture and theology, aiming at characterizing in the personal name the mode in which the Third Divine Person proceeds from the First and the Second, have designated the Third Person "the Holy Spirit."

He is also called "Love," and this name belongs to him as the term "Word" is proper to the Son. All the divine life is comprised in the activity of the divine intellect and the activity of the divine will. There is a parallel between the two operations. As there proceeds from the intelligence, through the very fruitfulness of the divine intellection, [14] a divine person, the Word, so too there proceeds from the will, through the impetuosity of the divine loving, a divine person, who, for want of an exact term corresponding to the term "Word" as given to the Son, is called metaphorically—breath, a sigh of holiness, a flame, charity. All these terms are used to designate that reality which emerges in the will when the will has been captivated by the loveliness of an object. Or again to express the same thought in a slightly modified fashion: as within the Godhead through the operation of the intelligence there is originated a Word, so through the operation of the will there is originated a Living Love. The intellect, as it were, flowers in the Word; the will blossoms forth as a Love. [15]

[12] Acts 2: 2–4.
[13] *S. Th.* I, q. 27, a. 4.
[14] Intellection is to be understood actively. Its meaning would be accurately expressed by a present participle "intelliging"—if such a verb as "intellige" (corresponding to the Latin *intelligere*) existed in English.
[15] It is to be noticed that this term "Love in the Divinity" can have three distinct significations:
i. It can signify that, in the Father and Son, in virtue of which they both as one principle breathe forth the Spirit of Love. The theologians call this the "notional" sense of the term. [*Cont.*]

In this lies the wondrous attractiveness of the Third Person of the Blessed Trinity. He is *all* love. His personal characteristic is to *be* love. He is love and nothing but love. Everyone understands what is meant when a person is described as being "all heart." One who is so described is a person endowed with a loving and generous nature, and impelled by that nature to pour forth all its resources in the service and in the interest of others. By a metaphorical use of language, the Holy Spirit may be described as being "all heart." He is, as it were, the divine, the living, the uncreated heart of the great God. It is our solace and our ground of confidence to contemplate the Savior Jesus in that representation which sets visibly before us in his sacred heart the outstanding feature of his human character—his love. In it we find our hope, our consolation and our comfort.

Now, what the sacred heart is in the God Incarnate, *that* the Holy Spirit is in the God that dwells in light inaccessible—it is that unseen God contemplated as "Love personified"—in the literal sense of this phrase. Sinners and saints, the imperfect as well as the perfect, when they know that they have but too much reason to fear the blows of God's justice, instinctively take refuge in the thought of God's goodness and love. If the turning to this love of God considered abstractly (or in theological language, essentially) can bring trustfulness to the sinful, comfort to the weak and joy to the strong, how much more intense would these emotions be, if thoughts and affections were directed toward that one person who personifies—who, figuratively speaking, embodies in himself—the love of God. As the Holy Spirit is the link, the bond of union between Father and Son, so too it is in the Holy Spirit and through the Holy Spirit that the creature is united to the Creator. If by love we designate that in the will on which follows the impetuous movement by which the lover is carried with force toward the object of his affection, then truly may the Holy Spirit be said to be the love whereby God loves not only himself but us creatures as well. In the same way that God in the Word, which he begets, knows (that is, expresses to himself intellectually) both what he is himself and what we creatures are, so in the same way does he love himself and

---

ii. It can signify the operation of love itself. This is common to the Three Persons. Under this aspect, the term is taken in its "essential" sense.

iii. It can signify that reality which takes its origin in the will through the will's loving—just as if it were something wrought or effected or operated by the action of loving; theologians say—*id quod procedit in voluntate per modum operati,* i.e., that reality which originates in the will after the manner of something wrought or produced by the act of loving. Of course it is needless to state that in speaking of the Divine Persons no term can be used which would imply any one of them being caused or effected or produced. It is only words implying origin that can be applied to them. Hence theology does not say that the Holy Spirit is produced or effected by the divine energy of loving—but that he proceeds from Father and Son in virtue of that divine loving—as if he were the product of that act.

In this third sense of "Love"—as that reality which issues from the act of loving as though something effected or produced by it—the term is applied to the Holy Spirit personally. It is his personal name.

creatures in the Love which God, that is, the Father and the Son as one principle, breathes from the inmost depths of the divinity.[16] This truth of Catholic theology—that it is by the Holy Spirit that God the Father and God the Son love us—should, if it were clearly apprehended by Christians, exercise a powerful effect in promoting personal devotion to the Third Person of the Blessed Trinity. The interior life receives a great impetus when the soul realizes the characteristics of the Holy Spirit and understands that it may relate to him in the same distinctive way in which it has learned to relate to God the Father and God the Son.

[16] "Love considered notionally is nothing else than to breathe love; just as to speak means to pronounce a word, and to flower is to produce flowers. As then a tree is said to be in flower by its blossoms, so the Father is said to give mental expression by a Word, both to himself and to creatures. In the same way, too, the Father and the Son are said to love in the Holy Spirit both themselves and us" (*S. Th.* I, q. 37, a. 2).

3

God with Us—The Work of the Holy Spirit.
The Second Mode of God's Love

THOUGH the thought that God the Father and God the Son love us in the Holy Spirit, if dwelt on, is capable of exciting a tender devotion to the Third Person of the Blessed Trinity, and though there is much consolation to be found in this dogmatic truth, yet reflection on it is not unattended by a certain secret misgiving. Love is of various kinds. As considered in God it is one, being identical with the Holy Spirit; as extended to creatures, however, it can express itself in various ways. It is not difficult to understand that God's love for a saint and God's love for a sinner or even for a person who, though not actually in sin, is still far from heroic sanctity, must differ widely. The ordinary Christian is aware, perhaps too keenly aware, that he cannot expect from God the regard that is bestowed on the saint. Hence, while recognizing that God is not indifferent to him, he will ask himself uneasily, what is the real worth of that love on the part of God, of which he is assured he is the object.

It is easy enough to understand that God envelops us in the same regard which he bestows on all creatures, animate and inanimate alike, because he sees in them some vestiges of his own being and because he can use them as instruments of his glory. All things are the objects of God's thought and God's care. He assigns to each those possibilities which, being brought to fruition, realize the final end of all creation, which is the manifold showing forth of the Creator's artistry and perfection. We, with all other creatures, have our part in this universal benevolence of God. He gives us too that participation of the infinite good which is measured by our nature. But no human heart, in which the longings, common to all hearts, are not stifled, can be content with that purely impersonal affection of which all creation is the object. Obedient to its instincts it must aspire to a love less abstract and more personal, less metaphysical and more intimate, less one-sided and more reciprocal. Men delight in being loved more even than in being honored: for they desire love for its own sake, and honor for ulterior reasons.[1] Honor is valued only when it comes from those who are endowed with judgment, discernment and uprightness. Love has a value even when it is but the mute tribute of the lowly and the insignificant. That value is marvelously

---

[1] Aristotle, *Nic. Ethics,* bk. VIII, chap. 10. The philosopher acutely remarks that men have a craving to be honored by the good, because they find in that honor sure grounds for entertaining a good opinion of themselves. All are something great in their own eyes; by the honor received from the great and the discerning, this estimation of themselves is confirmed. But, on the other hand, being loved is sought for its own sake, as desirable in itself and independently of any ulterior considerations.

enhanced in the estimation of a person who finds himself loved by one eminent in qualities of mind and heart. What a happiness it would be for man if he could have an assurance that God extended to him, not merely mercy and kindness and condescension, not merely a considerate and watchful providence, but an affection such as is given by one human being to another! Any man, who is true to the instincts of his faith, would like to feel that he is loved by his Creator in spite of his short-comings.

"Friendship would seem to consist," says Aristotle, "more in loving than in being loved, a proof of which is furnished by the delight that mothers take in pouring out their love. Some mothers even give their children to be brought up by others and still, knowing them to be their own, they love them accordingly, and do not even look for a requital of their love." [2] That maternal affection of which the philosopher speaks not only does not look for a requital, it is even bestowed on those who by their evil conduct show themselves all unworthy of the love that is lavished on them.

We are all sinners and prove ourselves undeserving of the regard of our God: "If we say that we have no sin, we deceive ourselves, and the truth is not in us." [3] The consciousness of sin and of sinfulness weighs heavily upon every sincere soul. This consciousness is accompanied by the dread that the sinfulness, which is so keenly realized by the soul, renders impos-sible anything like tender and cordial relations between itself and its God. This fear seems to be only too well justified by many a text of Scripture which presents itself spontaneously to the memory. The inspired writer says in the Book of Proverbs: "The Lord is far from the wicked, and he will hear the prayers of the just." [4] And again we read in the Book of Sirach: "For the Highest hateth sinners and hath mercy on the penitent." [5]

The wayward and the wicked child, no matter how grievous may have been his misdeeds, can always count on an unwavering love in the heart of father and mother. Is it impossible for the creature that is sinful to experience nothing else but mercy and pardon on the part of his Creator? Must anything resembling that affection which the mother bears to her child wait on one's establishment in justice and holiness? If this were so, what fear and constraint in their relations with God would necessarily torment those for whom even ordinary sanctity is as yet a far off ideal! The sinner who longs to turn to the Lord would surely find great comfort and deep satisfaction in the thought that even in his wanderings he continued to be cherished by his God with an affection resembling that which the mother continues to bear toward her wayward child. And yet it would seem impossible that it could be so.

Between parent and child there exists a bond of nature which makes affection possible even when the child has forfeited his right to it by

[2] *Nic. Ethics*, bk. VIII, chap. 10.
[3] 1 Jn 1: 8.
[4] Prov 15: 29.
[5] Sir 12: 6.

wickedness or ingratitude or even rebellion. The father may be good while the child is evil, but the two remain one in their common nature and their common blood. But there would seem to be nothing in common between us, as sinners, and God. He is infinitely holy and we incline to all iniquity. His tastes are all heavenly, ours are of the earth, earthy. He is aloof from all our human concerns. He is unaffected by our human experiences. Throned in heaven he cannot share our interests, our trials, our emotions. Common experiences—for instance, sharing the same dangers, being involved in the same misfortunes—can draw together in friendly fashion men who before were indifferent to one another. The same hardships to face, the same trials to bear, the same interests to share—these things can establish close ties between men differing widely in moral worth. Misfortunes break down barriers: they place those who are affected by them on the same level. Nothing like this can happen, apparently, in the case of God and his creatures. Sanctification can obviously establish a bond between God and us. But where grace is absent, there seems no possibility of the existence of anything which could draw him to us in the bonds of mutual sympathy in the literal and etymological sense of the word.

Sinners as we are, yet we would aspire to a love of friendship as distinct from a mere benevolent regard. Such a love demands a certain community of nature, of life and of interest—an equality of some kind. People used to speak of trees as flinging their friendly shade over tired wayfarers to protect them from the heat of the summer sun, but they were perfectly well aware that this is the language of metaphor. Faithful as our dogs can be and appealing as can be the various kinds of domestic animals, we know well that we cannot be said, in any true sense, to love our dogs or horses. People use the term "love" loosely in speaking of their domestic pets, but nevertheless they would not maintain that the tie that binds friend to friend can exist between themselves and these creatures. For such a bond to exist there is required a mutual understanding and a power of mutual sympathy. "Friendship," says St. Thomas, "is based on some fellowship in life: since nothing is so proper to friendship as to live together. Now, irrational creatures can have no fellowship in human life, because this life is regulated by reason. Hence friendship with irrational creatures is impossible except metaphorically speaking."[6]

Now the Creator is more remote in his nature from us than we are from the animals. The distance that separates us from him is infinite; that which lies between us and them is finite. It would seem, then, that if the relation of loving friendship between us and irrational creatures is impossible, the impossibility is still more radical, still more profound, when there is question of the Creator and the creature. Philosophy in its highest flights never dreamed that the great God, the first cause of all things, could have any other relation to those things that depended on him except that of an overruling Providence. "One can lay down no accurate definition," says Aristotle, "as to how great must be that discrepancy between two men

[6] *S. Th.* IIa, IIae, q. 25, a. 3.

which makes friendship between them impossible. Though they may be widely separated from the point of view of personal advantages, friendship may still continue. But when the gap is very wide, as, for instance, between men and God, friendship is no longer possible."[7] In this conclusion the great philosopher was faithful to the deductions of human reason. No created intelligence could have dreamed that such a chasm would be bridged. No intellect not divine, even if this possibility were revealed to it, could have conceived the mode in which that infinite distance between God and man should be, as it were, annihilated.

St. Catherine of Siena speaks of Jesus Christ as the bridge that spans the space lying between Creator and creature. The figure is perfectly exact. For, by the Incarnation, God deigned to put himself on the same footing as man; by it he condescended to embrace the interests, partake of the conditions and share the vicissitudes of a human life on earth. The Second Person of the Most Blessed Trinity, by the humanity he assumed, brought it about that he, in spite of his own perfect holiness, could adapt himself more fittingly to the conditions of sinners. In the common humanity shared in by God and by man is found a bond of union between the two. By becoming man, the only-begotten Son of God can have for his fellow men that friendship which the upright can feel for their friends even when they have erred grievously. On earth friendship between two men is not necessarily severed when one of them suffers moral shipwreck. A friendship which could not survive such a catastrophe is neither deep nor true. The true friend is the one who knows us through and through, who is not blind to our shortcomings, and yet loves us.

St. Thomas, quoting Aristotle with approval, tells us that men are not to withhold the duties and offices of friendship from their friends who may have taken to evil ways. If it is laudable, by kindly and loving zeal, to aid a friend to recover his lost fortune, how much more laudable is it, by devoted affection, to aid him in recovering his virtue.[8] Jesus in taking flesh made himself the friend of men; for the very reason of his taking flesh was to confer on them the greatest benefit that friendship could bestow. He became incarnate to strike off from us the shackles of sin, to bestow on our souls the divine life of grace, and to throw open to us the treasures of heaven. And nobly and perseveringly did he, and does he, fulfill the duties of true friendship toward each one of us, as long as there remains a possibility of our taking the path of grace and virtue. Jesus as man can be the friend of sinners. What was implausible to God is possible for God made man. God, being infinitely perfect and holy, cannot love with the

---

[7] *Nic. Ethics*, bk. VIII, chap. 9.

[8] *S. Th.* IIa, IIae, q. 25, a. 6, ad 2; cf. *Nic. Ethics*, bk. IX, chap. 3. The great philosopher writes: "If one man admits another to his friendship, supposing him to be good, and that other turns out evil—is the first bound any longer to love him? Is it not impossible for him to do so, since there is nothing that commands affection, but only the good? . . . Should we then at once cast off the friendship? Surely not, except with those who are incurable in their wickedness. If they can still be reclaimed, we are bound to help them to recover their character even more than their property; inasmuch as to do so is more excellent and more properly a work of friendship."

love of friendship any but those who participate in his holiness and perfection. Sinners are necessarily debarred from his friendship, though, of course, they are not excluded from his kindness and mercy. There can be nothing in common, morally speaking, between God and the sinner as such. But there is much in common between the God-man and the sinner; there is the humanity common to them both. Hence, though God in his own nature cannot love but the holy and just, God made man can love even sinners.

God, existing in a human nature, is not fettered by the conditions which existence, according to the divine nature, in a certain sense, imposes on him. By the Incarnation God established that community of life and nature with us which makes it possible for him to have for us a love that otherwise would not be. Jesus in his lifetime was called the friend of sinners. He did not disclaim the title. Rather, he gloried in it and, in his most touching parables, amply justified it. Naturally speaking, his friendship with the just is of a higher and more perfect kind. Still, on his own admission, the feelings that he has in his heart for sinners are such as truly merit the name of friendship. Being in all respects like to us, save sin alone, he can enter into and sympathize with our aspirations and the secret trials and strivings of our souls.

All things that are possible to man are possible to him, except what is wrong. Men may entertain warm feelings of friendship toward each other even when one is virtuous and the other is not. In that, there is nothing that should not be; it is not sinful or imperfect. Friendship of a real kind (though, to be sure, this is not friendship in its most perfect form)[9] can be felt by the good for those who are not virtuous, as long as those latter have the possibility of virtue in them. So it is that our divine Lord, although himself so pure, so holy and so perfect, can have sympathy for us in our sinfulness and can have his heart drawn to us in spite of our wretchedness. He is capable of being swayed by every human appeal—again, of course, on condition that such an appeal contains nothing wrong in itself. If saints could love their parents and others who in various ways came into their lives, irrespective of their virtue or their lack of it, and that because of the ties of blood and humanity by which they were bound to parents and friends; and if, moreover, that is not urged against them as a fault, but rather applauded in them as a virtue, does not the same hold good with regard to the Saint of saints?

"Friendship," says Aristotle, "consists more in loving than in being loved, and it is those who love their friends that we single out for praise. Therefore, loving is thought to be the special virtue of friends."[10] If our

---

[9] Aristotle writes: "But the friendship of the good, who are alike in the character of their virtue, is perfect . . . for they are friends, not on any accidental grounds, but in virtue of their own inherent character, and their friendship continues as long as their goodness lasts, and virtue lasts well. . . . Such then are friends in an absolute sense . . . the others only in virtue of the resemblance they bear to them" (*Nic. Ethics,* bk. VIII, chaps. 4 and 6).

[10] *Nic. Ethics,* bk. VIII, chap. 10.

backslidings have not the power to kill the affection of the human hearts that are devoted to us, our sins cannot harden the heart of Jesus against us. There is no one so devoted to us as he: nor are we so dear to any one on earth as to him. He has spent himself utterly—even to the shedding of the last drop of his blood—in our interest. "And greater love," he himself said, "no man hath, than that a man lay down his life for his friends."[11] He asserts that his love for man was such that it constrained him to this extreme limit of sacrifice. On his own avowal, then, his affection for those whom by the Incarnation he had made his brethren could not be surpassed even by himself. His heart could hold no stronger feelings for us than it did. And it is to be remembered that this love of his for us was the love of a human heart extended to those who are so little deserving of such a wealth of affection.

It is to the Uncreated Love of God that we owe this divine invention by which God can be united with us sinners in the bonds of real friendship. To the Holy Spirit is appropriated every work of sanctification, and therefore, in a most special way, that work which is the source and fountain from which flows all our supernatural good. The Incarnation is stated explicitly in Sacred Scripture to be due to the operation of the Third Person of the Most Holy Trinity. The angel Gabriel said to Mary: "*The Holy Spirit* shall come upon thee, and the power of the Most High shall overshadow thee. And therefore the child which shall be born of thee shall be called holy, the Son of God."[12]

The Holy Spirit is the bond of union between the Father and the Son. He is, as it were, their living embrace. It is his characteristic to be the spirit of union. He fulfills the same role between God and God's rational creatures. In a previous chapter it was shown that it is in the Holy Spirit that God loves mankind with that species of affection which was named merciful kindness; this, as was said, is the only affection that can be extended by the Creator to men as long as these latter do not walk in the ways he has traced for them. The Holy Spirit, now, appears in a new exercise of his distinctive work of creating ties between the Creator and the creature—the work of drawing man to God.

Born as we are under the New Law it is hard for us to realize what difficulties would attend our efforts to deal familiarly with God, were we living outside that Law. It is very significant that while the pages of the Old Testament are eloquent as to the merciful and forgiving dispositions of God toward sinners, it is only in the pages of the New Testament that he is spoken of as the "friend of sinners."[13] It is impossible to exaggerate the importance of this change wrought in the relations between man and God by the Incarnation. It is incalculable to what degree this *chef d'oeuvre* of the Holy Spirit has smoothed away the difficulties that attend the efforts of frail, sinful man to enter into relations of intimacy with his Creator. There is an encouragement for souls in the thought that the God to whom they

[11] Jn 15: 13.
[12] Lk 1: 35.
[13] Mt 11: 19; see also Lk 15: 2.

are striving to return is human like themselves, with a human understanding and a human power of sympathy, whereas many such souls would be terrified and dismayed before the prospect of having to address themselves to a God "who inhabiteth light inaccessible."[14]

Such an encouragement is greatly needed by the soul that, discovering within itself a deep dissatisfaction with creatures combined with an immense yearning after God, labors nevertheless under a sense of utter powerlessness to come in contact with that being to which alone it is drawn. In this condition nothing but God can satisfy it. Everything else has begun to pall on it. It would have God, and nothing but him can stir its desires. Nothing on earth has any longer power to captivate it. God alone appeals to it, and yet with this great longing to draw near to God, there is a sense of inability to bring about the contact that is so desired. The soul realizes in the depths of its being that nothing can be united with God except what is Godlike and divine. It realizes only too well that its own sinfulness, its earthly instincts, its unheavenly tendencies make it unlike God and so present an insuperable obstacle to that oneness with him which conditions and makes possible the relation of a mutual friendship with the divine being. With extended hands and straining heart it reaches out over the immense void that is interposed between it and its God. It struggles desperately, almost despairingly, against the dual obstacle that its own finite nature and its sinful egoism raise between it and the all-holy and infinite Lord. The remoteness, the inaccessibility, the blinding sanctity of the Godhead that would appear to scorch and shrivel everything created that would draw nigh to it throws back the soul, baffled, disappointed and sorrowful within the finite limits of its own being. "I will rise and go about the city, in the streets and broad ways; I will seek him whom my soul loveth. I sought him and found him not."[15]

Only one who has had experience of it can form an image of the keenness of the pain that is felt by him for whom the whole earth has lost its savor, who is filled with consuming desire of God and yet sees no prospect of that torturing desire being satisfied. Such a person feels, as it were, suspended between heaven and earth and belonging to neither of the two. The soul has turned its back on the things of earth and yet finds many instincts in itself unresponsive to the appeal of the things of heaven. It feels oppressed by a complete helplessness to produce or have produced in itself that "likeness" to God which makes it possible for the soul to give itself to its Lord, and for the Lord to communicate himself to the soul. It knows full well that such a "likeness" is the condition of this mutual donation.

This desolate condition of the spirit is described in many places in Scripture, especially in the Psalms, but nowhere in more touching terms than in those that are found in the lamentations of the prophet Jeremiah. "Weeping she hath wept in the night, and her tears are on her cheeks. There is none to comfort her among all them that were dear to her."[16] And

[14] 1 Tim 6: 16.
[15] Song 3: 2.
[16] Lam 1: 2.

again he says: "Therefore do I weep, and my eyes run down with water, because the comforter, the relief of my soul, is far from me."[17] In its distress the poor finite creature will turn for comfort and consolation to the thought of the Incarnation. This mystery gives it a God, not remote, nor inaccessible, nor awe-inspiring. The Incarnation provides for the soul a being to whom it may easily turn; a being who, while being flawlessly perfect and therefore capable of being a stay of divine strength, yet shares in some measure the finiteness and limitations of the creatures that look to him for support in their weakness. Men can turn to the sacred humanity of Jesus with the assurance of being understood in their trials, infirmities, hopes and aspirations, with that understanding which comes through like experiences. "For we have not a high priest who cannot have compassion on our infirmities, but one tempted in all things like as we are, yet without sin."[18] "And whereas indeed he was the Son of God, he learned obedience by the things he suffered."[19]

The Church in her own gracious way, so human and so accommodated to our humanity, interprets and gives expression to the satisfaction that the limited, finite, human creature experiences in the thought of a God brought within the compass of its own experiences. The human heart grows warm and trustful in the presence of a God who moves in the sphere of human emotions, affections, feelings and experiences. In accents of exquisite naiveté, almost infantile in their simplicity, the Church gives apt expression to the feelings that the mystery of God made man stirs in the human heart. With a gladness that is tremulous and almost incoherent in its utterance she loves to exclaim as she bends over the manger: "For a child is born *to us*, a son is given *to us*."[20] What a wealth of relief, of pent-up emotion, of ecstasy is to be found in the words "to us." A son is given "to us"—to be close to us, to be one with us, to be finite like ourselves, to be sympathetic with the ways and moods of earthly existence—all this the words mean, and infinitely more. Those two words, "to us," are a concentrated expression of the tumult of glad emotion that arises in the soul of humanity when it has found a being to worship: who is at once infinite and finite; who is of a perfection which is transcendent and yet human; who is a prey to human weaknesses but free from human imperfections; whose native home is heaven yet whose name is *God with us;* who is one, in a word, who without losing that which belongs to the divine, is, nevertheless, eminently human. And it is the Holy Spirit who has fashioned that sacred humanity. It is the Holy Spirit who has given this child to us. It is the Holy Spirit who is the goodness of God as well as his love. Jesus is the gift made to us by the goodness of God. The act of giving is peculiarly appropriate to him who himself is the gift of God—*"Donum Dei"*—and in whom every gift of God comes to us.

[17] Lam 1: 16.
[18] Heb 4: 15.
[19] Heb 5: 8.
[20] Is 9: 6. Introit of the Third Mass on Christmas Day.

The soul, alive to the difficulties that beset its attempts to effect contact with God considered under the aspect of the divinity, will easily and readily turn to him considered under the aspect of his humanity. The love of our hearts can, since the days when the Word of God took flesh from one of his creatures, be given with a certain facility to him, the love of whom sanctifies. The child-saint Agnes, before her judges, exultingly proclaims this truth: "I love Christ," she said. "In loving him, I am chaste; in clinging to him, I am all pure; in being espoused to him, I bear the aureola of virginity."[21] It is not surprising, then, that our Savior himself said that, great as was St. John the Baptist and exalted above all the prophets, he was not as privileged as is the least one born under the New Law. "For I say to you, among those that are born of women, there is not a greater prophet than John the Baptist, but he that is the lesser in the kingdom of God is greater than he."[22]

It is as if God, debarred by the divinity from loving sinners with the love of friendship, overcame this "limitation," as it were, of the divinity, by forming to himself a humanity which is not subject to this "limitation."[23] God as God can extend to frail, sinful, erring human beings only mercy and kindness; God as man can pour out on them the affectionate and tender love of a human heart—a love, like that of a father or mother, which is chilled by neither waywardness, nor ingratitude, nor even insensibility. That love acquires a special tenderness when it is given to those who are struggling to abandon the ways of infidelity to God and to return to the paths of goodness and truth. Before God, as such, the poor soul that is conscious of its sinfulness must necessarily experience awe and fear and timidity. To God made man the same soul will come with trustfulness, with confidence, and with no misgivings as to the reception that awaits it. Shrinking is replaced by a confiding hopefulness. Where the majesty of the divinity would inspire terror, the humanness of the sacred humanity inspires confidence. "This is according to the eternal purpose [of God] which he had made in Christ Jesus our Lord, in whom we have boldness and access with confidence by our faith in him."[24] This attitude of boldness and confidence is encouraged in another text of St. Paul, saying: "For we have not a high priest who cannot have compassion on our infirmities. . . . Let us go therefore with confidence to the throne of grace, that we may obtain mercy and find grace in seasonable aid."[25] All men, whatever their condition of soul, can be drawn to the Son of Mary by the cords of Adam. There is charm, already, and much sweetness in the

---

[21] Response of the Third Lesson of the First Nocturn, Feast of St. Agnes, January 21; and Ceremonial of Profession of Religious Women.

[22] Mt 11: 11.

[23] It need scarcely be remarked that "limitation" is here a figure of speech; there is no limitation in the Divinity. But the word is apt to describe the ingenuity of God, as it were, in finding a way by which, being God, he can love sinners. To the Holy Spirit, to whom is appropriated the work of the Incarnation, we are indebted for this "invention" of divine goodness.

[24] Eph 3: 11–12.

[25] Heb 4: 15–16.

seeking him. What finding him is like only those can tell who have made the discovery.[26]

Sooner or later we turn from creatures in disappointment and disillusionment.

> Yea, faileth now even dream
> The dreamer, and the lute the lutanist;
> Even the linked fantasies, in whose blossomy twist
> I swung the earth a trinket at my wrist,
> Are yielding; cords of all too weak account
> For earth, with heavy griefs so overplussed.
>
> * * *
>
> And now my heart is as a broken fount,
> Wherein drippings stagnate, spilt down ever
> From the dank thoughts that shiver
> Upon the sighful branches of my mind.[27]

Life for those who search for happiness on paths other than those traced out by God is bound to end in disillusionment. It must be so. For when every experiment has been tried, the discovery will be made that life is all in loving and being loved. To live is ultimately to love and to be loved. As has already been pointed out, Aristotle acutely remarks that much as men desire to be honored, they ambition still more to be loved. The former ambition is more easily realized than the latter. It may, perhaps, be said that the latter is scarcely realizable at all—at least properly and perfectly. We may receive a certain measure of affection from human creatures, but perhaps only that. Why must this be so? The reason is that the love of a created being is not self-determined. It depends on an attractiveness to be discovered in the beloved. Human love, unlike God's love, does not create or impart that excellence which inspires love: it is called into being by something, the existence of which in the beloved is not due to the lover. Our love necessarily presupposes the existence of the good which causes it. Now, in truth, who of us merits to be loved? What good is there in us, of ourselves? This thought is beautifully expressed by Francis Thompson in the following two excerpts:

> And human love needs human meriting:
> *How hast thou merited—*
> Of all man's clotted clay the dingiest clot?
> *Alack, thou knowest not*
> How little worthy of any love thou art![28]

---

[26] From the words of the hymn *"Jesu Dulcis Memoria"*; the verse of which these words are a paraphrase runs thus:

> Jesu, spes poenitentibus!
> Quam pius es petentibus!
> Quam bonus Te quaerentibus
> Sed quid invenientibus!

[27] Francis Thompson, "The Hound of Heaven."
[28] Ibid.

None of us can be loved unless there exists in us that which is capable of calling forth love. And it is beyond the power of any man to make us worthy of love, because it cannot create that worth in us which makes us lovable. It has been said that it is beyond the power of any man; but there is an exception. There is one who can love us, because there is one who has it in his power to make us lovable.

> Strange, piteous, futile thing?
> Wherefore should any set thee love apart!
> *Seeing none but I makes much of naught.*

Jesus can take the "worthless" creature that he loves and give it the worth which makes it lovable. Through him comes the possibility of the full realization of man's highest ambition to be loved and to love. Jesus gives life in every sense. He has power to satisfy the fundamental aspiration of the human heart after the love that makes life. He, of himself, merits to be loved. He is worthy of all the love that human hearts can give him because even in his sacred humanity he is supremely attractive. Not only that, but he can impart to those who surrender to his attraction a participation of his charm. If then the soul is wise, if it desires to find an object of love which will uplift it, which will satisfy it, and which will yield to it what is denied by its own limitations—which will, in a word, complete and perfect and give it fullness of human life—it will turn to the loving contemplation of the human perfection of Jesus. This is the only way of escaping inevitable disillusionment.

It is the consciousness that we cannot find the resources of life in the limited conditions of our own being that drives us outside of ourselves in search of someone whose worth and virtue and goodness will complete our nature and supply its deficiencies. When we have, we think, found such a one, to that person is given all the affection of our heart. Again and again we are doomed to disappointment, again and again are we driven further afield in our vain search when we discover some striking want, some glaring defect, in the character we deemed flawless. Our idols are all found to have feet of clay. No such disillusionment can be ours when we seek in Jesus the complement of our existence, the fulfillment of our ideals. He is the perfect man and is capable of satisfying all the exigencies of the human heart. The human perfections of Jesus can supply every natural want that the soul finds in itself. In his friendship, therefore, is found a full human life. There is no risk where he is concerned of awaking one day to the discovery of some demand of our heart to which his human nature will fail to respond—there is no danger that any demand of our weakness and limitation will ever find him wanting. Those who, disillusioned with all else, are drawn to him find a source of inexhaustible life in the meditation on the varied human perfections which his daily intercourse with men revealed. No circumstance of human life, no accident, no sudden crisis ever found him at fault.

The most diverse and often seemingly opposed qualities are found to exist in him in a harmonious balance. He can be inflexibly strong while remaining inexpressibly tender. He can be exacting to the last degree and yet appreciative of the least element of good in those he deals with. He is of a holiness which sets him apart from man—"Which of you," he says, "shall convict me of sin?" [29]—and yet with the utmost ease he mingles with sinners of the worst type. He is uncompromisingly stern in his upbraidings and unfailingly tender in his pleadings. [30] He is of the most virile fearlessness and yet of a meekness that seems to yield before every storm. He unhesitatingly commits his followers to the most dire persecutions and yet consoles and comforts them with a solicitude that is like that of a mother in its tender devotedness and anxiety. And moreover, while all these perfections in him call forth our love and admiration, the sufferings and sorrows he endured permit our extending to him, as one more tried than ourselves, yet tried in ways like to ourselves, the whole sympathy of our hearts. All these endearing qualities are the expression of the Spirit of Jesus. The Holy Spirit is called in Scripture the Spirit of Jesus. The gracious character of the Savior is, at one and the same time, the creation and the earthly reflection of the character of the Third Person of the Blessed Trinity.

The benefits that come to sinful humanity by the Incarnation are not limited to all this. We are driven to Jesus as to the one creature among all creatures that can give satisfaction to all our cravings for human sympathy, understanding and love. But as soon as that contact with him is established, a new experience begins for us. The disappearance of the dissatisfaction with life, which we have felt, is followed by the emergence of different longings, greater ambitions, loftier aspirations. As we become friends with Jesus fresh horizons open up before us. The desires of our heart are enlarged and he is able to satisfy these new desires as he did those that prepared the way for them. The *Holy Spirit* has given us the sacred humanity of Jesus, by which, in spite of our sinfulness and the shrinking fear that comes of it, we can feel God as a friend to us. The work of the Holy Spirit does not end there. This but prepares the way for more intimate relations with the Divinity. It is his self-appointed task to establish those relations between God and men.

---

[29] Jn 8: 46.

[30] Contrast his fierce invectives on the Pharisees with his tears and tender reproaches to Jerusalem. "Jerusalem . . . how often would I have gathered thy children as the hen doth her brood under her wings, and thou wouldst not" (Lk 13: 34).

4

Jesus Was Born of the Flesh
That We Might Be Born of the Holy Spirit

IN the last chapter it was seen how the Word of God, in virtue of the created nature that he shares with men, can entertain toward all his brethren, just and unjust alike, feelings of a real, sincere and devoted affection. It goes without saying that he admitted those who were closer to himself, in tastes, aspirations and ideals, into more intimate relations with himself than were allowed to others less akin to him in mind and heart. He had his preferences. He loved some more than others. But, still, no man was excluded from his friendship. So much so that, as the Gospel testifies in many a page, it was not only the just that felt at home in his presence, but sinners too felt at their ease. The instinct of shrinking from God, that so often follows on a grievous transgression or infidelity, seems never to have been experienced by those who enjoyed the privilege of meeting Jesus in the intercourse of everyday life. There is positive testimony in the Gospel that the very opposite was the case. In St. Luke we read that "the publicans and sinners drew *near unto him* to hear him." [1] St. Matthew in another connection writes: "It came to pass as he was sitting at meat in the house, behold many publicans and sinners *came, and sat down with Jesus and his disciples.*" [2] These are but two out of the many texts of a similar import which manifest clearly that the Savior exercised a magnetic attraction over men who, at the time of coming in contact with him, were walking in the ways of sin. This is truly extraordinary.

That Jesus should exercise an ascendency over the just and the pure in mind and heart is only what might be expected. They could not but be attracted by his sanctity. But that sinners should not be awed and repelled by the same sanctity is very surprising. This could never be so unless the Son of Mary, in his attitude toward the weak and the erring, manifested something more than mere kindness and mere condescension. They could not feel such facility in approaching him unless they had the intimate realization that he truly loved them. Jesus has not changed his character or dispositions with the passage of time. It is, as St. Paul so eloquently expresses it, "Jesus Christ yesterday and today, and the same for ever." [3] And as he has not changed, so neither have men, at least in the vast majority. We are, alas! all of us, sinners and very closely akin in thought and affection to those sinful men who thronged the Savior's footsteps during his mortal life. That they were so free in their intercourse with Jesus, and that he did not discourage but rather openly approved

[1] Lk 15: 1.
[2] Mt 9: 10.
[3] Heb 13: 8.

such freedom, should be a great encouragement to the sinners of all times.

In the Incarnation the Holy Spirit verifies in an eminent manner his title of the Paraclete or the Comforter.[4] For what is calculated to bring more comfort to sin-laden hearts than the revelation that it has become possible that God, without abdicating any of the prerogatives of his divinity, should become and be called the friend of sinners? What can be more consoling than the revelation that God not only does not banish sinners from before his face, but actually seeks them out and shows a predilection for their company? It was by the operation of the Holy Spirit that the humanity of Jesus was formed. It is to the Holy Spirit also we owe those records in Scripture by which we are made certain that in very truth the attitude of God made man toward his erring creatures is one of friendship and love. For it is the Holy Spirit that inspired the sacred writers to commit to writing for our consolation and comfort those doings and sayings of the Savior which exemplify this attitude of God made man toward sinful humanity.

But consoling as it is for us that God has become our Emmanuel, that is, *God with us*; gratifying as it is for us that we can give our hearts without misgiving to one, who, though so perfect, is not aloof from us or disdainful of us, an incomparably greater privilege still is ours. *God stooped to our condition for the express purpose of raising us to his condition.* He shared our poverty with a view to communicating to us his riches. He clothed himself with our lowliness in order to invest us with his grandeur. He took from us our humanity with a view to bestowing on us his divinity. "A truly admirable exchange," says the Church, "in which the Creator of the human race, taking flesh, deigned to be born of the Virgin: and becoming man, by a virginal birth, bestowed on us his divinity."[5] "If God elects to enter into relations of exchange and barter with mankind, who can doubt that it is for our advantage? When he appears to borrow from us, it is with the intention of enriching his creditors. . . . He has gathered himself the bitter fruits of this ungrateful earth of ours, namely, weakness, misery and death. And what does he give in return for what he takes? He has brought us the veritable goods which belong to his heavenly kingdom which is his own possession and his patrimony. He has brought us innocence, peace, immortality, the distinction of the divine adoption, the assurance of a divine inheritance, *grace and the communication of the Holy Spirit.*"[6] But in order that man may profit in this wondrous barter, he must, on his side, dispose himself to further the purpose in view of which the Incarnation took place. The bargaining must not be all on one side. Everything is not done once that God has received what earth can communicate to him. When two persons settle on a transaction of exchange or barter, it is because each desires what the other can furnish.

[4] Paraclete means one who encourages, exhorts, cheers on, gives heart to and, therefore, comforts.

[5] Office of the Circumcision: Antiphon of Lauds and Vespers.

[6] Bossuet, Sermon for the Feast of the Annunciation.

The Son of God has shown, on his side, an eagerness, unparalleled by any creature, to receive from earth the portion or lot that belongs to fallen creatures—save sin alone. He has disdained nothing that belongs to our fallen nature—with the single exception of moral defect. He coveted all. He did not exercise selection among the miseries to which our nature is a prey when these miseries did not imply defect. He reached out—he bargained with man, as it were—for what man's fallen nature could give him. "He took all, even to the least things, all, even to the greatest infirmities. He wished to have hunger and thirst exactly as other men." [7] In the Incarnation he wished to make himself utterly like to men. Perfect in all his works, he would not be content with an imperfect resemblance. Wishing to resemble men, he would resemble them in all things possible. He would be man in the full sense of the term, otherwise his work, in this instance, would be imperfect. The Savior has shown in all this an avidity to get from humanity what humanity could give him. Humanity will not profit by this transaction unless it, on its side, has a like eagerness to receive from the Savior what he is willing to give in exchange for what he has received. It would be well if men exhibited as much keenness as God in this holy barter.

It is not unusual to observe that souls who seem desirous of sanctity and who employ the ordinary means of asceticism in order to acquire it are, at a certain period of their spiritual efforts, brought to a sort of a standstill. This phenomenon of arrest is fairly frequent in the lives of persons who give themselves to spirituality and is the subject, on their part, of many plaints and much searching of heart. When the soul, by sustained mortification, has shaken itself free from the trammels of sin and overcome all the external obstacles that oppose themselves to the approach to God, it would seem that sanctity should be within easy reach. [8] When, moreover, by sustained efforts of the imagination, one has learned to contemplate with admiration the human life of Christ on earth; when, by constant meditation, one has gazed into the soul of Jesus and established contact with the principles of moral perfection that have their source therein; when one has been able to glimpse the interior dispositions of mind and heart which have expressed themselves in an exterior life that compels the unwilling admiration even of the enemies of Christianity; when, in a wondering and rapturous realization of the common humanity that one shares with a being so perfect, one has poured forth one's soul in sympathy with the tragic opposition and dreadful sufferings that Jesus was to experience at the hands of those on whom he had lavished all the resources of his splendid nature; and when, finally, the soul, enamored of the moral beauty which it has learned to admire, strives to reproduce in its own acts the features of the ethical beauty of the human conduct of the Savior—then one would think that the utmost limit of man's spiritual endeavors and aspirations here below had been attained. Yet somehow, the soul has an

[7] Bossuet, Sermon on the Nativity of the Blessed Virgin Mary.
[8] Cf. Faber, *Growth in Holiness* (1925), pp. 319–323.

49

instinct that this is not so. Some deep want within it makes the soul suspect that there is still a world of spiritual experience that remains to be explored; and it is at a loss to know what to do in order to gain admittance to this world.

The soul's instinct is right. Man's perfection even here below is not attained in the admiration and practice of mere righteousness, even when the exemplar that one sets before oneself to imitate has all the radiant beauty of the moral perfection of Jesus Christ. God did not become man in order that we might pass from human imperfection to merely human perfection. The Second Person of the Most Holy Trinity became man to make us like to God and not simply like to a perfect man. In the admirable interchange of the Incarnation the soul's advantage is secured only when it strongly desires and looks to receive the divine in return for the human which it should be prepared to forego.

The love of the human perfections of our Lord, effective force as it is in the interior life, does not constitute the whole activity of that life. It is true that no soul can fully sound the almost infinite depths of created virtues that are in Jesus; yet, even if it did, it would be only to find that the limits reached open out on a world beyond—a world measureless and infinite—the world of the Divinity. The sacred humanity of Jesus, all perfect as it is, is not for us the *term*—it is the *way* that leads to this realm where man comes in contact with God himself. Hence it was that our Lord, speaking of himself as man, said: "I am the way."

In our prayerful relations with the Savior we should never lose sight of the fact that the humanity upon which we are fixing the gaze of our souls is a means to lead us on to the Divinity, which dwells in him corporally.[9] It can happen that our method of dealing with his life on earth may prove too human—that in the "exchange" spoken of we look for the merely human and not the divine.

This can present an obstacle to real progress and is the common cause of the arrest of which mention has been made above.[10] It is right to stress the importance of the use of the imagination in mental prayer. But souls imperfectly guided can easily fall into the mistake of dealing in a purely imaginative and intellectual way with the mysteries of the life of Jesus. If they have not a clear understanding of what union with God means, and if

[9] "For in him dwelleth all the fullness of the Godhead corporally" (Col 2: 9). This text means that the plenitude of the divine essence (not a mere participation of it as in other rational creatures who are in a state of justice) resides or dwells in the humanity of Christ and is united with that humanity substantially in the unity of One Person. The force of the adverb "corporally" is in this—that it signifies that the Divinity itself comes to us invested in the visible and tangible form of the Sacred Humanity (cf. Prat, *Théologie de St. Paul*, vol. 2, p. 184).

[10] It is not the place to develop here the reasons why humanity in its "bartering" with the Divinity proves so indifferent to its own advantage as not to seek to get from God what God is willing to give in this bargaining. These reasons will be found developed in any spiritual author. One of these is that souls think they are really seeking God when what they are really seeking is their own ethical perfection and immunization against moral disaster. It is frequently love of self, not love of God, that is the inspiration of spiritual endeavor.

they do not really desire that union, they will tend to overemphasize the human lineaments of the person of the Savior. This tendency is very pronounced among non-Catholic writers and ascetics. Catholics are not free from it, however. For, of the many souls practicing spirituality who persuade themselves that they are seeking union with God, not many are truly aspiring after that union, at least in any intimate form. Hence it is that in the case of many souls that give themselves to the practice of meditation, their study of the Gospel serves but to give scope to the play of fancy, to the satisfaction of the love of the ethically beautiful and to the speculative development of moral considerations. Persons of this type stand back, as it were, from the picture portrayed in the Gospel, to study it in a good light and from a favorable angle. They admire the beauty of the different virtues that go to complete that perfect work of the Divine Artist painted in human colors, namely, the moral character of Christ. They find intense satisfaction in the consideration of that beauty. But their attitude toward it remains, in great measure, aesthetic.

While having a vivid realization of the ideals, of the feelings, of the dispositions, of all the perfection in thought and act, of Jesus, these souls remain without perception of the vital relation that should exist between his inner life and their own. Their attitude toward the Incarnate God easily becomes one of mere barren admiration without any formative or transforming effect on their own life. They, as a consequence, remain strangely uninfluenced by that on which they meditate. They are to a great extent insensible and unresponsive to the Divinity which aims at working on, and transforming them to, the image of God through the Sacred Humanity. The tendency of such souls to consider too exclusively the human in the man-God makes them fail to realize that the moral perfection of Jesus is not meant to be for them a mere object of contemplation—and, therefore, something outside of themselves—but rather an instrument which, in the hands of the Divinity, is to penetrate into their interior, forming and fashioning thought and tastes and affections to the living likeness of the thought and tastes and affections of the humanity of Christ. And all this interior conformation to the spirit of Jesus is meant to go on in the soul at the expense of what is found there of the soul's own spirit.

This molding of the soul to the mind of Christ is not the final end of the spiritual endeavor. It only prepares the way for something higher. It is an adaptation for union with the Divinity dwelling substantially in the sacred humanity. In God's plan that sacred humanity is the Way that leads to the Divine. Cast in it and receiving its form the soul of man is ready to receive the impress of God. The human charm of Christ is meant to *attract*, not to *arrest*, the gaze of the soul. Its function is to draw us to the Divinity, which reveals itself to us through the human features of the Savior in a manner calculated to win our confidence and affection.

To effect this approach to the Divinity which resides in our divine Lord, it is necessary for us to submit our whole being to the spirit of his life. Our own attempts at living a life of goodness must be deliberately modeled on his perfect conduct. No mere objective and artistic study of the life of the Son of Mary, as something outside of and apart from ourselves, will effect much change in our souls. It will certainly fail to give us a real comprehension of the Incarnate God and of the nature of the work of the Redemption. Our idea of him will, to use a word borrowed from Cardinal Newman, remain "notional" and as such will be without vitalizing effect on us, as far as the supernatural life is concerned. If the Incarnation is to fulfill its purpose in our own individual selves, we must make the life of Jesus ours. His human life is not merely to be admired by us, nor even imitated; it must be lived by us—lived in its spirit.

To live our life in the spirit of Jesus means that the attitude of soul, the ideals and principles that characterized, governed and directed the conduct of Jesus, must be made to govern and direct our conduct. "Let that mind be in you, which was also in Christ Jesus." [11] To live thus is to put on Christ. Our Lord had a created human nature which was indebted to God for all it was and had. At all times he recognized this truth. He lived in docile subjection to God. "I always do the things that please him," [12] he said. It is in this fundamental attitude of soul that we are to be *one* with him. The necessity of this perfect conformity of our outlook and our bearing to the outlook and bearing of Jesus is inculcated by God himself on two occasions in a miraculous locution from heaven. The first occasion was immediately after the baptism of Jesus, when God made his voice heard from heaven, saying: "This is my beloved Son, with whom I am well pleased." [13]

The second occasion was at the Transfiguration, in which the same words were used with the significant addition: "Hear ye him." [14] It was as if God said to man: "The human life of Jesus Christ is eminently pleasing to me; yours shall be pleasing in the measure in which it is animated by the spirit of his." There is more demanded of us than a mere walking in the light of his example. It is by means of a fusion or identification of a mystical kind between Jesus and ourselves that we prepare for the inflow of the divine into our souls. It is thus that Jesus, from being the *Way*, becomes also the *Truth*, which is equivalent to being the *Life*. [15]

No one, it would naturally be thought, could be better circumstanced than were the apostles to acquire an intimate knowledge of Jesus and to be fashioned in his likeness. And yet the story transmitted to us by the Evangelists bears clear testimony to the fact that they remained to an

[11] Phil 2: 5.
[12] Jn 8: 29.
[13] Mt 3: 17.
[14] Mt 17: 5.
[15] Jn 14: 6. We should not imagine that because our Lord tells us he is the Way that a time comes in spiritual progress when we shall cease to meditate on the events of his life. We should never cease to meditate on the Sacred Humanity, but our meditations will take on, ultimately, a somewhat changed character. The hidden Divinity will begin to manifest itself more unmistakably through the human features that first attracted our gaze. "He standeth behind our wall . . . looking through the lattice" (Song 2:9). Christ is the way we must always walk in, but at the same time he leads to God hidden in him.

extraordinary degree unaffected by his example and teaching. They were influenced, of course, in a certain way, but not in that way in which the Savior himself aimed at influencing them. They scarcely understood at all what he wished to *effect in them*, though they had some little comprehension of what he meant to *do through them*.

After three years' close contact their knowledge remained very superficial. They did not know him for what he was. Neither did they know what was his real action and his real purpose. The sense of the Master's words: "My Father worketh until now and I *work*," [16] was completely veiled to them. Hence Jesus had to say to them sadly on the last day of his earthly pilgrimage: "So long a time have I been with you, and have you not known me?" [17] It had, as yet, hardly dawned on them that the whole object of their three years' intercourse was that God should establish contact and union with their souls. They persistently assigned another and far different purpose to the following of Jesus. The clearness of bodily vision they enjoyed obscured for them the spiritual. Looking upon him as an individual among individuals, singularly perfect, it is true, they regarded his life as uniquely his and incommunicable, as would be the life of any other leader among men. They could admire it, but it was his. It did not occur to them that his life should and could be theirs. They saw no relation between him and themselves except such as is established by social and daily intercourse, based upon a deep admiration and love and warmed by an enthusiastic loyalty and partisanship. To their minds the bond between him and them was of no other nature than that which exists between a great leader and his devoted followers. "They had no real knowledge of the divine mediation and of the divine priesthood of Jesus and of all the communications of grace that were vested in him, and of all the power over all creatures that results therefrom, until after the Ascension, when the Holy Spirit at Pentecost enlightened them." [18] Previous to that they had recognized him as a savior but they had no accurate idea of what salvation meant.

It was after Pentecost when the apostles grasped that the life of Jesus was not a life limited and defined and circumscribed by the concrete historical incidents of which they had been the privileged eyewitnesses. Enlightened by the Holy Spirit they understood that the life they had witnessed was, in a true sense, universal and was meant to be shared in and participated in by a multitude of human beings forming one with Christ by living his life. At Pentecost the apostles understood, at length, that in the economy of the Redemption the lives of Christ and of his members were not to be as two distinct circles having merely external contact, but rather as two circles tending to become concentric. The Paraclete showed that the way of salvation (or sanctification—for it is one and the same thing) for man was that he should, in a mystical way, merge his life in that of Christ. Man secures the advantages procured for him by the Incarnation, through

[16] Jn 5: 17.
[17] Jn 14: 9.
[18] Ven. Libermann, *Commentary on St. John* 1:51.

53

effecting a mystical identity between his own individual human acts and those of Christ on earth.

This identity is primarily wrought by grace and the sacraments. But it becomes effective when the union produced by the sacraments is made operative. The sacraments are but the beginning of the union with Christ. The development of this union consists in man's performing the daily actions of his life in the spirit of Christ, in espousing the ideals of Christ and in sharing the thoughts and affections of Christ. Man, united with Christ by the sacraments, effects this identity with Christ by sharing his loves and his hatreds. Man is one with Christ when he thinks as Christ thought, loves as Christ loved, and hates as Christ hated—when, in a word, he sets before his intellect and will those objects on which were set the intellect and will of Christ. It is in this way only that the "oneness" between Christ and his *adherents* is vital with a divinely vitalizing effect. All this the apostles saw when the Holy Spirit had descended on them. Up to that time their way of seeing Jesus and dealing with him was too natural and too human to permit their rising to the spiritual and supernatural view of things. To remedy this defect it was needful that the Sacred Humanity should be withdrawn from their bodily sight and contact.

The apostles could not understand Christ until he left them. "But I tell you the truth: it is to your advantage that I go," [19] said our Lord to them. To our way of looking at things nothing could seem less advantageous. What gain could compensate for the loss of the privilege of living in close human companionship with Jesus? The Master foresaw an immense advantage for his followers in his leaving them, and he assigns the reason, saying, "For if I go not, the Paraclete will not come to you." [20] Their too human and natural love for him had to yield place to a love which, in its mode, was to be infinitely higher than human. The earthly had to fade away in order that the heavenly might not any longer be obscured.

How many there are who in their spiritual life deal with the Savior in the same external imaginative way in which the apostles related to him! They are content to be of his company, to admire his qualities and to pity his distresses. They would willingly be in his train, but do not desire to walk in his footsteps. "And yet if Christ made himself part of humanity, it is as head of a body. If he has lived our life, it was, doubtless, in view of sanctifying it, but it was also in view of teaching us to direct it, as he does, toward his heavenly Father." [21] The ultimate aim, then, that the Son of God had, in coming on earth, was not to attract our gaze by a beauty purely human, but to direct our gaze to a beauty that is divine. He became man not merely to love us humanly and to have that love reciprocated in the same way, but to give us the power to live and to love divinely. God loved us in the Creation in the way that has been already explained in a previous chapter. God loves us in the Incarnation with a love which is distinguished from the love manifested in Creation by an extreme tender-

[19] Jn 16: 7.
[20] Ibid.
[21] Jules Lebreton, *La Vie Chrétienne.*

ness of affection. That tender affection shown to us by God made man devoted itself to the task of preparing and forming us so that we could be loved by God in a manner which transcends the two forms of affection that have been touched upon. God stooped to share our nature in order that we might be able to participate in his divine nature, and so become for him an object on which he could bestow a love like to that with which he loves himself. This loving design of God in our regard is expressed each morning at Mass in the prayers recited at the mingling of the water with the wine. The priest says: "O God, grant that we may be made partakers of his divinity, who has deigned to share our humanity, Jesus Christ, thy Son, our Lord."

In these words the main purpose of the Incarnation is touched upon. They are an echo of those St. John uses when speaking of the effects of the coming of the Divine Word among men. "But," he says, "as many as received him, he gave them power to be made the children of God." [22] So charged with meaning are these few words, so incredible in their import, that the average person feels a certain shrinking from their obvious signification. The responsibility that they impose on us is overwhelming, because the grandeur to which they bid us aspire strikes us with dizziness and with something almost akin to dismay. *"Noblesse oblige"*—and the obligations attached to a nobility which St. John tells us may be ours are extremely exacting. Human cowardice and sloth and the human inclination to what is ignoble will instinctively take refuge in the notion that the words used by St. John are but a metaphor. Fallen nature's instinctive aversion for real dignity—the dignity that is of God—will impel it to consider salvation under any other aspect rather than that suggested by the words of the evangelist. It is true, of course, that the Redemption may be considered from several points of view and described accordingly in different ways. It may be viewed as a liberation from the captivity under Satan, or as a striking off of the shackles of sin, or as a cancelling of the condemnation weighing upon the children of Adam, or as the lifting of a curse, or as the expiation of sins, or as the acquittal of the debt due to the justice of God because of man's prevarications, or as a rescue from eternal damnation, or as a renewal of a right of entry into Paradise. The Redemption is all this, and our tendency to regard things materially and selfishly will cause us to envisage it by preference under the aspect that promises to make no other demand on us than that of laying hold of an advantage won for us.

Now, salvation means something far greater for us than the mere liberation from sin and its consequences here and hereafter. It means more even than the admission to a life free from miseries and containing all happiness. Salvation consists rather in establishing us in that condition by virtue of which the eternal life of God becomes ours, according to the normal right of succession to an inheritance. The Incarnation has won for us the possibility of becoming adoptive children of God, "and if children,

[22] Jn 1: 12.

heirs also; heirs of God and joint heirs with Christ"—according to the words of St. Paul.[23]

The sanctifying grace which we receive through union with our Redeemer makes us children of God, as St. John states in the text already cited. One has a totally inadequate conception of the effect of sanctifying or habitual grace, as it is called, if it is regarded as producing a condition of soul characterized by merely negative properties—such as freedom from sin and from the punishment due to sin. The infusion of habitual grace into our souls is the genesis of a life, the vital activities of which far transcend the energies of the highest form of moral life. Grace does not merely purify the heart; it does not merely aid it to withdraw its affections from what is unworthy of man; nor does it merely create in the human heart a love for the moral good. It does far more than this. The grace that comes to us from Jesus Christ bestows on the soul a life which surpasses and leaves far behind all that can find its origin in the limited resources of the whole realm of nature. *By grace we are empowered to love not only the man in the man-God, but even the God in him, and that, too, with the love of friendship.*

This would seem impossible, seeing that the reciprocal affection, which perfect friendship implies, postulates a community of nature and therefore a life in common, with common tastes, common tendencies, common ideals and aspirations. Does it not appear absurd to pretend that there can be between the human and the divine a mutual understanding and a common objective? To love God, as such, and to be loved by him in turn with a reciprocal and like affection—to effect this union of love there is needed a bond between God and man which shall be woven of divine elements. Jesus can love humanly, but God himself as God cannot love except divinely and cannot love with a love of friendship anything that is not divine. If we are to reciprocate this affection on the part of God we must be able to love with a love greater than any created heart is capable of. We must be able to love with an affection which is divine in its principle.

Who can free the soul from its created limitations, lift it above itself and establish terms of real intimacy between the created and the uncreated Spirit? *It is the Third Person of the Blessed Trinity that by means of sanctifying grace accomplishes this marvel* "because the charity of God is poured forth in our hearts by the Holy Spirit, who is given to us."[24] We have seen that the Holy Spirit, in the work of the Incarnation, brought God down to man. He crowns this wonder by one more dazzling still. He raises man up to God. He sets the foot of mortal man in a world infinitely remote from the one to which he would naturally be confined by the possibilities of his own nature left to its own resources. He places man in a sphere where he can approach God and where God, without waiving the rights of divinity, can draw near to him. The Holy Spirit pours a life

[23] Rom 8: 17; cf. 1 Pet 3: 7, where the apostle enjoins on husbands to give honor to their wives "as to the co-heirs of the grace of life."

[24] Rom 5: 5.

and a vitality into the human soul which enables it to exercise its faculties on the same object on which converge the intellect and the will of God—this object being the Divinity itself—the infinite truth and the infinite good. In a word, the Holy Spirit, by communicating himself to the soul in the inpouring of divine charity, makes that soul "deiform," or like unto God. By the imparting of grace, of which he, Subsistent Grace, is the source, he divinizes the soul. He bestows on it the condition of God, in a finite measure, and thus permits the creature and the Creator to embrace in an affection which is in its mode divine and truly bears the name of friendship.

God becoming man became a friend of man. Man being made "deiform" by the Holy Spirit becomes a friend of God. The Holy Spirit having "humanized" God to effect a community of nature between Creator and creature on the human plane now divinizes man to effect that community of nature on the divine plane. He has made it possible that God should love us with the love of friendship not only humanly but divinely—and this is the third mode of God's love for man. By this, God loves us, not only with the human created love of the heart of Jesus, but with the Divine Uncreated Love in which God is enamored of the Divine Loveliness itself.[25]

"How can such things be?" one is tempted to exclaim. So asked Nicodemus of old, as the shades of night gathered over Jerusalem at the close of one of the early days of the ministry of Jesus. The question sprang to the lips of the Jewish doctor as our Lord slightly lifted for the gaze of his wondering soul the veil that hid this mystery from human view, allowing him to catch a glimpse of this dazzling destiny of man. "Unless one is *born again* of water and of the Holy Spirit, he cannot enter into the kingdom of God," said our Lord.[26] The power of thought and of love that we have acquired by our first birth—the birth according to the flesh—cannot even in its highest development carry us beyond the limits of the created universe. Through these powers even if submitted to an independent evolution God could not be known in himself. Our ideas of him would be limited to what we could derive from the study of created perfections. We could see him only in his created works, not in himself. We could *know something about him* but we could *not know him.* To penetrate further, to make our way into a world where we breathe the "native air of God," where we can meet him, in a certain measure, on equal terms, there is needed a new birth, a new generation, in virtue of which we receive a higher nature, equipped with divine powers and faculties—that is, faculties that participate in the divine energy. God can love, with the love with which he loves himself, only what is divine and Godlike; hence that we are the objects of his loving complacency, we must to some extent be "divinized." That we should love God in himself, it is required that we participate in the divine energy of loving the divine. It is Jesus Christ who

<hr>

[25] All this subject will be fully developed later on. Only what is needed to maintain the sequence and orderly development of the ideas is stated here.

[26] Jn 3: 5.

has merited this "supernature" for us—*it is the Holy Spirit, the giver of all good gifts, who forms it in us.* We are born spiritually of the Holy Spirit, "By whom [that is, Jesus] he hath given us great and precious promises, that by these you may be made partakers of the divine nature." [27]

[27] 2 Pet 1: 1–4.

5

The Holy Spirit—the Fount of Life

CONFORMING the spirit of our life to the spirit of the life of Christ should not be the final end of spiritual endeavor. Its object is to dispose the soul for vital and intimate union with the divinity that dwells in Christ. It is the Holy Spirit, by the graces he imparts, who enables the soul to mold its actions to the form of the human doings of Jesus and to dispose itself for the divine union. Having thus formed us, in the mode of our actions, to the form of Christ, the Holy Spirit communicates to us the very life of God. This inpouring of the divine life is what the Apostle desires for his followers, saying: "The grace of our Lord Jesus Christ and the charity of God and the fellowship of the Holy Spirit be with you all." [1] The logical gradation in the text is worthy of note. The following pages will be devoted to examining what is meant by the divine life and to explaining why the title "Fount of Life" is attributed to the Holy Spirit.

Ultimate notions are proverbially difficult to define, though all men know fairly well what they stand for. These notions are expressed in terms which are in common and daily use. It is easy for a person to fall into the illusion that he is in full possession of the meaning of words because he habitually uses them, but a call to set out the sense of the terms employed to name elemental things immediately reveals the difficulty that such an explanation presents. There is about these fundamental realities a deceitful simplicity which lures the average man into the belief that he will find no difficulty in defining them. The effort to do so quickly dissipates the illusion and often ends in perplexity and even irritation. The truth is that the simpler the notion, the greater keenness and penetration of mind it demands if a clear and satisfying analysis of it is to be given. Ultimate things scarcely admit of definition. At most they admit but of description and illustration by means of concrete instances in which the notion of these simple realities is verified. The idea of "the good" analyzed in a preceding chapter is a case in point. Beauty, unity and movement are further instances. Life is another. It shows itself extremely elusive the moment the attempt is made to lay hold of this notion and exhibit its meaning captive in phrases of clarity and precision.

"Life" is a term designating a reality of universal experience. Even the youngest manifest a certain understanding of what that reality is. A child two or three years of age will be careful to treat in a different manner objects animate and inanimate. It knows full well that it cannot deal with live objects as freely as it deals with those which are not alive. It distinguishes with facility between a toy mechanical dog and the live animal. But

[1] 2 Cor 13: 14.

even when that child has reached adult years and becomes, perhaps, a philosopher, it will find its intelligence severely tasked to set forth with precision, fullness and accuracy all that is involved in the simple statement, "it is alive."

In the hymn *"Veni Creator Spiritus,"* the Holy Spirit receives among other titles that of *"Fons Vivus,"* or "Fount of Life." An analysis of the nature of life is necessarily demanded if there is to be had a clear understanding of the implications of this phrase. To ponder the question, what is life? is to find that it is an easier thing to ask the question than to answer it satisfactorily. One finds that things of the most diverse kinds are said to be "living things." The most obvious instance of life is presented in the human beings with whom we associate. The phenomena of birth and death obtrude themselves constantly on our notice. For each individual we assign the period that elapses between coming into the world and the leaving of it as the span of life. When death intervenes it is understood that life is extinct—it has ceased. It is true that those who have the faith, and even those who have it not but are imbued with the principles of a sound philosophy, hold that, in the case of human beings, the cessation of life brought about by what is called death is somewhat relative. Such persons hold that the vital principle in men continues to exist and to live, in the real sense of life, even after the body has become inanimate. But no such survival is asserted in the case of animals. They too live, but death is for them the final term of an existence, which, for the majority, at least, of animals, is brief.

Passing from the realm of animals to the realm of plants, one finds that the world of living things has not yet been left behind. Although it is not so usual for ordinary people to associate the notion of life with trees and flowers and all the other things that spring from the fecundity of the earth, they are not unaware that the plants that they tend so carefully and the vegetables that they cultivate so assiduously for household needs are, in a very true and real sense, alive. Though they do not so readily speak of a vital principle when there is question of plants as they do when it is a question of men and animals, they know that there is an essential difference between, for instance, wood as it is used in the construction of houses and as it exists in its native forest. People, as a rule, shrink from using the terms "animal soul" and "plant soul"—owing to the restricted significance that the word "soul" has for them—yet they will, without hesitation, admit the legitimacy of the usage of the term once it is declared to be synonymous with "inner vital principle" or, simply, "the principle of life."

Leaving the plant world one finds that one has not yet quite quitted the realms in which the term "living" finds its application. One hears of "living waters." The phrase is used to denote running streams, gushing fountains, wells of fresh water and the like. The appellation is never given to stagnant pools—in fact, living waters are so named as opposed to these pools. The familiar name of the Dead Sea will instantly occur to the mind. It is so called because it is regarded as lifeless, if contrasted with moving or living waters. But in spite of the usage of the term "living" in this last connection, there is no one who is unaware that its sense is entirely different from that which it bears as applied to plants, animals or men. Even a child will not consider a running stream to be alive in the same way as it considers a running dog or horse to be alive.

It is curious that although the use of the term "living" in the case of springs and streams is clearly metaphorical, it is this usage that guides us to an apprehension of what is common in all these different forms of life that have been passed in review. It is the apparently spontaneous movement of the water—starting, apparently, of its own impulse from the earth and constantly renewing itself if it is a well, or pursuing a course of its own accord to the sea if it is a stream—that causes the source or stream to be described as "living waters." For a living thing is commonly understood to be that which has the power of moving itself and has that power of its own nature. A thing that moves itself but has the principle of its motion outside itself is not said to be alive. Neither a locomotive nor an automobile is said to be living. Though both in a certain sense are said to be self-moving (whence the term "automobile"), the cause of their movement is not in or from themselves. The most perfectly constructed motor car will never move unless its pistons are subjected to the pressure of exploded gas.

If a thing then is to be considered a *living* thing it must not owe the origin of its vital movement to anything outside itself. The principle of such movement must be *immanent:* that is, in and a part of itself. The most characteristic expression of life is self-movement—that is, movement of which the thing that is described as living is the originating cause. So much so that when there is a complete cessation of this self-movement, death is said to have intervened—life is said to have become extinct. In this connection, of course, movement has a very wide sense and does not mean merely transference from place to place—that is, mere locomotion. Breathing, seeing, imagining, thinking, willing—all these are comprehended under the notion of movement.

The movements in living things which spring from the life principle are directed to life's purposes. They are exercised by the living thing with a view to its attaining its fullest measure of life. It is true, therefore, to say that this movement springs from life and is directed toward life. A study of plants reveals this clearly. All the manifold activities discernible in the nutritive, augmentative and reproductive processes in the plant aim at evolving its life to the utmost. When the growing thing has attained its full stature and has exercised its fecundity in reproducing its kind, the cycle of its life is closed. There is no further progress possible for it. The development of the plant, which up to that point was easy to mark and which was evidently the objective aimed at by all the vital processes going on within it, ceases at the moment that full size has been attained and the seed which is to perpetuate its existence has been elaborated. It may continue to live after that, but the process of decay has already set in.

The activities that characterize animal life, while embracing all that are found in the vegetable kingdom, are much more complex and varied. The animal enjoys consciousness, whereas the plant does not. The horse or the dog can *enjoy* life, because it has a consciousness of living. The passions of gladness, affection, rivalry, fear, excitement, anger, hate—all these can be experienced by the creatures that constitute the animal kingdom. Their movements are not so restricted or so fixed as are those of the plants. All that falls under the senses can call their activities into play. They are sensitive to sights and sounds and scents, and they can modify their attitude to things, according to whether these sights and sounds and other qualities that affect the senses are pleasing or the reverse. They are sensitive to kindness and to ill-treatment. They can be attracted by the former and repelled by the latter. They have a keen instinct for seeking out what is advantageous to the particular species to which they belong and avoiding what is hurtful. The whole range of emotional experience is open to irrational creatures, but their life is circumscribed by that experience. It admits of no further development.

All the activities of animal life are directed toward the experience of pleasure and pain and the perpetuation of the species. When a racehorse, for instance, has reached its greatest muscular development, has put forth its utmost speed, has felt all the emotions of struggle in a race, has enjoyed the keen satisfaction that comes from the exercise of its powers, has tasted the delights of rapid motion and has reproduced its kind— its life is completed, though its existence may not yet be terminated. If there is added to the enumeration just made the experience of the satisfaction of hunger and thirst, one has assigned the complete end toward which the movements of the animal have been directed. The fullest experience of animal life is something that is definite, fixed and attainable by the normal brute in each species placed in normal conditions. Having reached that well-defined limit, the animal has fulfilled the purpose of its creation: all the movements which it has called forth from itself have attained their objective and realized their purpose.

Man, in his turn, is subject to the law which governs all living and growing things. Incomplete, like them, at the start, he is meant by the Author of nature to reach the fullness of life, proper to him as man, and that by the exercise of vital activity springing from the vital powers with which he is endowed. But he differs in two important respects from the plant and the animal. Firstly, he is not directed toward the goal of a full human life by a law imposing itself on him with necessity from without or from within. The normal plant or the normal animal set in normal conditions must reach the perfection of plant or animal life. The normal man placed in normal conditions *ought* to reach the fullness of human life but *does not necessarily do so.* It is in his power[2] to attain to or to miss the goal. That is his glory. "God made man from the beginning and left him in the hand of his own counsel."[3] Man can discern for himself the path along which lies his development into a full human life; he can choose to pursue

[2] "In his power" must be understood with all the limitations and qualifications set down in theology. Here there is simply question of man's power of freely cooperating or not cooperating with the means given him to attain the perfection of manhood.

[3] Eccles 15: 14.

or not to pursue that path. A normal animal cannot miss being an animal (given normal conditions) and enjoying the fullness of animal life: a man can miss being a man and having the experience of a full human life.

There is another aspect in which the life of man differs from that of the creatures of the animal and plant kingdoms. As has been noted, their measure of life (in the strict sense of the word "measure") is limited, fixed and determined. It is not so with man, at least not on this side of the grave. His life reaches out toward infinity. It would never be possible for him in this world to attain a point of perfection in human existence, beyond which progress would be impossible. At a certain stage of its vital activity, it ceases to be possible for plant or animal to be any more perfect in its kind. All higher experience of plant or animal life is closed to it. But man can go on indefinitely developing in manhood, that is, in the perfection of human life.[4]

The reason is that the objects to which tend the faculties that make man to be man and distinguish him from all other living things are not limited or finite. The powers which differentiate man from the animal and from the plant are his intellect and his will. Anything or everything that is true is an object on which his intellect may exercise itself. Anything or everything that has any element of good in it can stir the will to its appropriate activity. It is by the usage of his reason and his will that he is to bring to himself the perfection of life which is distinctively human. A man is not a perfect man when the processes of nutrition have evolved his bodily frame to its fullest stature and strength. Neither is he a perfect man when his senses and his imagination and his emotional faculties have developed all the energy and put forth all the activity of which they are capable. The development of bodily perfections will give him the perfection of plant life; the full evolution and exercise of his sense faculties will procure him the fullness of animal life—his own proper life as man lies beyond and above both these perfections. Now just as an animal is perfect in its kind when its sense life has been brought to its highest perfection, so, in a parallel way, is it with man: he too is perfect when his rational life, that is, his life of intellect and will, has been brought to its appropriate perfection.[5]

---

[4] We know from our faith that progress ceases with death. If man is found "just" at that moment, he merits the beatific vision during all eternity, and his degree of vision remains unchanged forever, admitting of no increase. The measure of his vision of God is proportioned to the degree of divine charity which he had reached at the point of departure from this world. But if man were left indefinitely in this world, since his perfection lies in the love of God, and since there is no limit to be assigned to that love, he would go on indefinitely increasing in perfection.

If, on the other hand, men were created not with a supernatural destiny, but with a natural destiny there is no solid reason to oppose the view that his final goal would be an unending and indefinite approximation to an ever-receding final goal in rational existence. The reason is that it is only the actual infinite that is God himself, seen in himself, that can exhaust all the possibilities of the human intellect and the human will. Our souls are a capacity for the infinite, and that capacity can be crowned only by the infinite.

[5] Cf. Aristotle, *Nic. Ethics*, bk. I, chap. 6. "What then precisely will this characteristic function of man (as man) be? Mere vegetative life it evidently cannot be, that being

For man does not start with the perfection of manhood, that is, in the enjoyment and possession of a perfect human life. That perfection is a goal toward which he is to strive and which he is to reach by the growth and development which is specifically human and which, as has been pointed out, is not mere bodily or sense development. The initial incompleteness of man generates a desire to have what is wanting supplied. The reason and the will enter into play with the dawn of conscious deliberate existence: all their activities are called forth by the desire of a full life, which is aimed at through these activities. In this moral existence, which is the existence proper to man as such, the intellect is pressed into the service of the will. Man can be forged to perfection only by actions which become him as man and by the attainment of objects the acquisition of which supplies the needs of his rational life. He makes progress toward a complete human life by acts and objects of acts suited to his nature as a reasonable being. It is the function of the intellect to discern from among possible courses of action and possible objects of choice those that are truly good for man. It is by the will that man executes these actions and reaches out after these objects and so perfects himself. His good as man is one that is compassed by action.[6] This end of action is frustrated when the intellect occupies itself with what is false and the will seeks what is not truly good for man—what does not become him as a rational creature. Error, unreality and the choice of what misbecomes a man corrupt human life. The objects which a person pursues and which he lays hold of may indeed procure, to a certain extent, his well-being in the order of plant or animal existence; but they may fail to perfect him as man.

Life, as has been said, manifests itself in movement. This movement, in the case of plants and animals, is unerringly directed toward its proper term—the creature's perfection. It is governed by a purpose to attain, and that purpose is attained. No movement is aimless or objectless. A living thing sets itself in motion always in view of reaching a definite end—a term, a point of repose where the movement ceases. So it is with man. All man's agitation, all his strivings, all his conations are governed by a purpose and directed toward an objective. He too sets himself in activity with a view to arriving at a term where all further striving ceases and where that native incompleteness of which he is so innately conscious will be supplied. The purpose of his self-originated movement is to arrive at a state of repose—at a full life, where he shall find himself free from the

---

common even to plants, whereas what is sought is a function special to man. We may, therefore, eliminate from our consideration the life of mere nourishment and growth. Next in development is a kind of conscious, sensitive life; but evidently this also is a life shared in common with other organizations—the horse and the ox. The remaining alternative is that the special function of man is a life developed by the action of that part of our nature which contains reason. Of this part of our nature, one element is, as it were, obedient to reason: the other element contains reason and consciously exercises it. . . . We must assume the true life of man to be one manifested in conscious activity, since thus only does life seem to be predicated in its more absolute and perfect sense."

[6] Aristotle, *Nic. Ethics*, bk. I, chap. 5.

limitations and drawbacks and wants which, making themselves acutely felt, are an incessant stimulus to action and effort.

God himself is intensely active, because he is intensely alive. But his activity is an infinite repose, because he is in the full possession and the active enjoyment of all that can be the term of endeavor, namely, *life*. God has not only fullness of life, he is life itself—absolute, infinite—knowing neither limitation nor want. His repose is not a repose of inactivity but the repose of a fully satisfied and satisfying activity, free from pain and effort and striving toward something further to be attained by that activity. Our vital efforts, the energies we put forth even when misguided, are a straining after a repose of this kind. We move but to be at rest.[7] Were we granted the satisfaction of all human aspirations, were we to reach the full perfection of human life, all restlessness would disappear and we should enter into repose.

What kind of effort or what form of rational activity is it that guides us securely and unerringly toward the much-desired term? What are those objects we must aim at, the attainment of which by our efforts will bring us a complete existence and a full life such as is proper to man? They are those that come within the scope of the virtues of the intellect and the will. St. Paul gives a brief and typical (though incomplete) list of them in his epistle to the Philippians. In this epistle he exhorts the Christians to act in such a way that the effect of their activity will be an advancement in the perfection of the life proper to them as reasonable beings. "For the rest, brethren, whatsoever things are *true*, whatsoever *modest*, whatsoever *just*, whatsoever *holy*, whatsoever *lovely*, whatsoever *of good fame*, if there be any *virtue*, if any *praise of discipline*, think on these things."[8] The instruction of the Apostle paraphrased would run thus: If the things you make the object of thought and pursuit are such as come within the range of the virtues I here enumerate, you will be able to give satisfaction to that desire of an ever fuller and more perfect life which incessantly agitates you.

The life of man is rational and spiritual. The end of life's activities for him will be that life of reason in its most perfect expression. Acts only that spring from reason or that are under the control of reason carry him onward toward his consummation. His sense activities as unregulated by reason are merely animal. If they are to become human they must be brought under the sway and the control of reason. Only those acts that are good for man, as man, contribute to the perfection of man. Acts are good or bad according to whether the objects to which they are directed are good or bad. What is bad for man—and that is, what is unreasonable

---

[7] An image of this law of all activity is found in the different departments of human endeavor. For instance, a man works hard at a business for years with a view to retiring from it in the end in order to enjoy, on the strength of an acquired affluence, the repose he promises himself as a reward of his efforts.

[8] Phil 4: 8. It is to be noted that these virtues, as Christian virtues, produce a perfection that is far higher than mere rational perfection. But here they are considered only under their rational aspect—that is, as being in conformity to reason. Under that aspect they go to constitute a merely human or rational perfection.

and therefore unnatural for him—contracts, limits, diminishes and impoverishes the life that is specifically his. Objects of pursuit unworthy of a reasonable being militate against his perfection. On the other hand, all that which, in action, wins the approval of right reason tends to promote, develop and expand his life as man. It ministers to his perfection.

Now, life takes its character from the activity in which it is exercised. And that activity is determined, in its turn, as to its moral value by the objects toward which it is directed. As a consequence, the things which we desire manifest the moral level of our existence. St. Thomas says that the activity in which a man takes a special delight, to which he is inclined and which he makes his principal aim, may be called, by a figure of speech, his life.[9] And Aristotle says, much in the same sense, that every pleasure implies a corresponding character in the man who feels it, so that a man, unless he is just, cannot feel the pleasure that the just man feels.[10] A person necessarily devotes his energies to that which tends to satisfy him. His life can be best described in terms of the pursuits to which he gives himself. When a man gives his activity of mind and will to what is trivial and indifferent, he is said to be leading an empty life. One who is all absorbed in what goes to promote his physical well-being leads a healthy, animal existence. A man lives an intellectual life when he consecrates his energies to the cultivation of his mental faculties. He who forms high ideals, but does not use his will to realize them, lives the life of the dreamer. A life characterized by inactivity and sloth is a useless and barren life, while one empty of objective is an aimless life. A life which has high objects of thought and is spent in pursuit of them is the noble and good and, therefore, the true life of man. To think high things, to form worthy ideals and to labor to realize them in action—that is human life in the true sense of the term. To have noble objects of thought and to pursue them unflinchingly is to realize our potentialities and to develop our manhood. The value of life, therefore, is in exact proportion to the nobility of what constitutes the object of thought and the term of endeavor.

When our inquiry is transferred to the life of God, the same principle holds true: namely, that the worth of a life is measured by the value of the objects of thought and affection to which it is consecrated. The life of God is infinitely perfect. Like that of his rational creatures, it expresses itself in the activities of thought and of will. Its perfection is measured by the grandeur of the object on which the divine intelligence is exercised and by the force with which the divine will adheres to the good laid bare in the act of divine intellection. God's life is, in its perfection, infinitely superior to that which belongs by nature to his creatures. The angels rank highest in the order of creation. Yet the life of the greatest among these, even if indefinitely perfected, would fall infinitely short of what the life of God is. The life of God is superior not only in perfection but in its kind to that of any being created or capable of being created. It is ineffable. It is incapable

[9] *S. Th.* I, q. 18, a. 2, ad 2; and IIa, IIae, q. 179, a. 1.
[10] *Nic. Ethics,* bk. X, chap. 2.

of definition. The reason is that the object on which God's intelligence is exercised could never become an object for a created intellect, no matter to what degree of natural perfection such an intellect might be raised. And in its turn the creature's love, not having set before it the infinite loveliness of what is revealed to the divine intelligence, could never approximate to the nature of God's love.

The object of God's thought is supremely noble and supremely beautiful. It is the Divinity itself in all its reality. The whole energy of his mind is given to the adequate comprehension of this supremely perfect intelligible object. God has before his mind, as the term of his contemplation, "All Reality," all that is verified in the term "Being"—pure, perfect Being, without any admixture of "what is not." "What is" is his name. Whatever has any taint of nothingness is excluded from his definition. God said to Moses: "I am who am. . . . Thus shalt thou say to the children of Israel: He who is hath sent me to you." [11] The object of God's contemplation, that which gives full exercise to his intelligence, constitutes in itself all perfection, all reality in such a manner that outside of it and beside it there is nothing. For whatever reality there is besides God is real only to the extent that it participates in some measure in the reality which is God. No creature can have what is not already in a supereminent manner in God. And this sum total of all perfection, which lies before God as the object of his intellectual contemplation, is infinitely desirable, infinitely attractive, infinitely appealing. For God there is nothing in it to militate against its attractiveness. It does not show itself as involving hardship or pain in the attainment. There is nothing to tarnish its splendor, nothing to dim its luster. There is nothing in it to conflict with or diminish its character as "good." It is pure, white, dazzling, unalloyed reality. It is *what is* and all *that is*. Its attractiveness is not, as in created things, a mere aspect, accompanied by much that does not attract. It is lovable through and through—it is very substantial loveliness, subsistent attractiveness—an object, when clearly seen (as it is by God), essentially compelling and calling forth love. And to this most worthy object of thought and desire, God is drawn with infinite force. He embraces with his whole being the infinite good which he contemplates. That is God's life—spent in the most noble exercise of thought and of love.

In contrasting the life of man as such with the life of plants and of animals, it was pointed out that the highest evolution of human life in the order of nature was the perfection of rational life. Man as a reasonable being is perfect when he thinks those thoughts and loves those objects which become him as man—and does so consistently and unfailingly. This is perfect human life, but it falls infinitely short of the life of God. Man cannot of himself transcend the finite limits of his own life; he cannot taste a higher life than that which is circumscribed by the full range of his mind and will exercised on objects proportioned to them. His life of thought and love will be limited to the compass of the natural power of the spirit that is

[11] Ex 3: 14.

in him. *If he is to rise beyond these limitations and to enjoy a life similar to that of God, man must necessarily know what God knows and love what God loves. To rise to God's life he must participate in the nobility of God's thoughts and God's affections.*

How can this be done? No one can know, the Apostle says, the hidden things of God, except the Spirit of God. "So the things also that are of God no man knoweth, but the Spirit of God." [12] Just as the realm of what is divine is open to exploration by the Spirit of God, so the realm of what is human circumscribes the activity of the mind of men. "For what person knoweth the things of a man but the spirit of the man that is in him?" [13] If then our vision is limited to what is human, the same limitation must lie upon our affections and our aspirations. We can love only what we know, though our love is not necessarily proportioned to our knowledge. To love nobly and in a way that would be patterned on the manner of loving of God, we should necessarily be able to explore in some measure the inner beauty of the Divinity. No mere knowledge about God, no mere knowledge of him derived from the study of created things can bring us this vision and so set us within reach of the happiness that is God's because of the superabounding vitality of his existence. To be able to quit the narrow limits of a merely rational existence, it is necessary that our powers of knowing and loving participate in some measure in the energy of the powers of knowing and of loving that belongs to God. This participation is given by sanctifying grace.

It would be impossible for us to reach God's life and God's happiness were we left with nothing more than a human spirit in us. It is not impossible if we have a divine spirit in us. "For the Spirit searcheth all things, yea, the deep things of God." [14] If the Divine Spirit is given to us, resides in our inmost being, and becomes, in a true sense, ours, then the whole realm of the Divinity is flung open to our gaze. The Holy Spirit is in us by grace. In him we see God. "Now we have received not the spirit of this world, but the Spirit that is of God; that we may know the things that are given us by God." [15] To enable us to enter into his own life, God gives us his own Spirit—the Holy Spirit—to be in us the source of the vision of the divine, and of the love of the divine. With the Holy Spirit in our souls we are enabled to transcend the limits of our finite nature, to scale the heights of heaven and to fix with undazzled eyes the flashing intelligibility of the Divinity. This vision is blinding for every created eye, but not for the eye of God. It is not blinding for our gaze when we possess the Holy Spirit, for then our faculty of seeing is strengthened by a participation of the penetrating intuition of God's own intelligence. The same Divine Spirit in us enables us to move with love toward what he reveals to us. We have, in a word, through the Holy Spirit, the same object of thought and the same object of affection as God himself has—that is, we

[12] I Cor 2: 11.
[13] Ibid.
[14] I Cor 2: 10.
[15] I Cor 2: 12.

have God's own life. The Holy Spirit is the source of this life in us: he is "*Fons Vivus.*"

The Holy Spirit enables us to rise to the energy and nobility of God's life. He becomes in us the principle of the tastes, tendencies and aspirations of a soul's life which has taken on the features of God's own existence and partakes of its elevated character. Our life becomes divine in the measure in which the Third Person is the source and the inspiration of the deliberate acts of the soul—to the extent, that is, that the intellect admits his illuminations and the will obeys his instinctive promptings.

The life of an intelligent being is to know and to love—and love is ultimate. It is so in the life of the Blessed Trinity. The Holy Spirit, who proceeds from Father and Son, by the way of love, closes the divine processions. When our souls put on the divine form they necessarily reproduce the character of the divine life. In them will be reproduced an image of the divine processions. The intellect elevated by grace will exercise its activity in the endeavor to gain an ever more penetrating vision of God, as far as he can be known by faith. When the exercise of faith is stimulated by the keen desire to acquire a more intimate knowledge of One to whom the soul already feels itself drawn, then love, of ever greater intensity, is developed in the will. In this activity inspired by grace we know in order to love.

If the highest life consists in knowing and loving what is best, life resolves itself for us, here on earth, into the love of the Supreme Good. The energy and power of life on earth is measured by the energy of the love of God. Men put forth all their vital activity in order to secure life—more life, and nothing but life. Their thirst for life can be gratified only in one way, and that is by the development in their souls of a great knowledge and intense love of God. "Now this is eternal life; that they may *know* thee, the only true God, and Jesus Christ, whom thou hast sent." [16] If then men's strivings have not as their consequence a growth in knowledge and love of God, they are fruitless and vain. Their gropings after "life" are thwarted. They may move from point to point on the earth's surface with ever greater speed, but their movement brings them to no position of rest or satiety. The more quickly they girdle the globe, the more rapidly they return to the place whence they set out. Such movement brings men nowhere. The activity that brings men to the experience of having got somewhere, of having moved to some purpose, of having aimed at a goal which marks a progress in life, is the movement of the soul toward God in knowledge and love. The Holy Spirit is, in the soul, the force which originates and maintains and intensifies that movement.

The ordinary Christian will ask himself if it is possible that his soul could be the theater of such marvels. Those who believe yearn, as is natural, to have some realization of them in their consciousness. It is hard for us to bring home to ourselves the reality of the supernatural world within us, because we can be conscious only of the natural activities of

[16] Jn 17: 3.

intellect and will. The supernatural cannot, ordinarily speaking, enter into natural consciousness. Grace is a supernatural thing. Its operations are a mystery, and the world of grace is a mysterious world—impenetrable to the spirit of man as such. The spirit of man can know but the things that pertain to human nature, and grace is not of these. But the divine mysteries of grace are clear to the Spirit of God, and that Spirit, being within the soul, imparts to it somewhat of his own vision of things in a mysterious way that is beyond the reach of sense and reason. That a thing so vital and intimate to us should be so shrouded in the mists of darkness and mystery ought not be a surprise for us. In the world of nature, the proper sphere of the investigations of the human mind, how many mysteries there are! "If I have spoken to you of earthly things," said our Lord, "and you believe not, how will you believe if I shall speak to you of heavenly things?" [17] Our faith teaches us that things are so, and that should be sufficient for us. A tender and humble devotion to the Holy Spirit, the source of all this wonderful inner life, will effect in our souls a firm conviction of its reality, a deep appreciation of its value and an ardent desire for its growth and increase.

[17] Jn 3: 12.

6

The Holy Spirit—Gift of God Most High

THE exchanging of gifts is a custom which, from the very beginning of things, has existed among men drawn together by the bonds of social intercourse. Its universality shows that it springs from an instinct that strikes its roots deep in our nature. Like all elemental practices it has a deep significance and a wide usefulness. Were it to disappear as a feature of human relations, its going would mark the departure of something which acts as a preservative of what is sound and good in human nature as God made it. The Creator meant all men to be closely knit together by stronger than earthly bonds. For he planned a greater solidarity between them than that which springs from common interests, uniting persons of the same state, or than that which has its origin in a common kinship, drawing together those who share the same blood. The Creator, as we know by our faith, predestined the whole of mankind to form one mystical body, united together by the bond of divine charity—a tie stronger and more potent in itself than any that could be found in the natural order of things.

Whatever tends to create division, whatever tends to isolate, to segregate, to individualize, goes counter to God's original design. The more, then, that a theory of life or a course of action issues, of its nature, in the breaking up of the body of mankind into isolated units, the more subversive it is of God's chosen order. Whereas, on the other hand, whatever operates to unite, to draw together and to make as one is marked with a divine approval; for it contributes, in some measure, greater or less according to its importance, toward securing God's ideal of human life. Manifestly, whatever fosters individualism is evil and works against nature.

Greed and covetousness, the desire to have more than our due share of the things of earth, develop the evil traits of that selfishness which is the radical defect in fallen human nature. He who yields to selfishness and greed sets himself apart from his neighbor, enters into rivalry with those whose interests compete with his own, hardens into an unfeeling individualism and thus becomes a disruptive element in the social life of mankind. This evil tendency is in all men since the fall. Sin severed man from God. It destroyed the links which held together in a wonderful harmony the different faculties in the individual man; and it sundered the ties which unified the individuals that compose the human race. Sin has in it an appalling force of disintegration. When the chain by which a number of beads are linked together to form an ornament is snapped, the beads fall asunder in disorder and confusion. So sin snapped the chain which held together in a harmonious and beautiful unity at one and the same time the members of the race and the diverse powers of these members. The fruit of sin is disunion and individualism.

Now, generosity in giving is an excellent antidote against the virus that has been introduced into our "spiritual system" by original sin. To give means always to deprive oneself. It has in it the element of self-sacrifice. It militates against the hateful greed that is ever aiming at acquiring for self at the expense of others. Giving has a unifying effect, for it establishes a bond between the giver and the recipient. It has a purifying and elevating effect, for it stirs up in the benefactor and the beneficiary dispositions which refine human nature. It helps the person who receives by supplying some material need of his and by calling forth in him feelings of gratitude. Gratitude has a wholesome and chastening effect on the human soul. Giving a gift profits the giver even more than the receiver, for it keeps alive, fosters and develops in the soul those elements of good which run danger of being corrupted by selfishness. It would not, perhaps, be hazardous to think that all these considerations find their justification in that statement of our Savior not recorded in the Gospels but preserved for us by the great Apostle: "It is more blessed to give than to receive." [1]

The exchanging of gifts is, then, an excellent custom; but, like all things that become of common and frequent usage among men, it has in process of time lost much of its original significance and its native character. In the beginning it was something very real and had a certain sacredness attached to it; now it has become, in many cases, a matter of convention. What was meant to be, and should ever have remained exclusively, the external expression of a deep and sincere feeling of the human heart, too often, at present, degenerates into a mere formality. Men, in giving, are frequently moved by a spirit of calculation or constrained by the usages of a society grown artificial. They give with a view to a return in kind, or they give because it is expected of them. Their action lacks the spontaneity that is needed in order that the object bestowed may be a *gift* and not a mere *present.*

There is a profound distinction between these two notions. As indicative of spiritual values they are very unequal. The worth of the *present* can be measured in terms of money: it is greater or less according to the price which the object bestowed fetches in the market. The gift may have a value in exchange, but its worth is to a great extent independent of such a value. In the *gift* are to be found elements which defy the calculations of the marketplace. For a gift is something that is invested with human emotion and feeling. Not everything that is given by man to man merits the name. That an object bestowed be really and truly a gift, the bestowal must be prompted and inspired by an affection for the person who receives the gift. The object, moreover, must be given in a pure spirit of disinterestedness and without any looking for a personal advantage to accrue to the giver from his action. The only advantage to be sought is that of the beneficiary.

[1] Acts 20: 35.

What is given must be surrendered completely to the recipient to have and to use as may seem good to him. The giving must aim at procuring in some measure the good, the well-being and the contentment of the person on whom the object is bestowed.

What is implied in the term "gift" will be more fully grasped by contrasting it with other things which resemble it. When a man gives to his servant what the latter has contracted to receive for his labor, what is handed over is called a *wage*. When a person, seeking to procure something he needs for his own personal advantage, gives a sum of money for it, it is a mere transaction of *sale* and *purchase*. When a man is menaced with danger or death and renounces a portion of his property in favor of those who hold his life or liberty in their hands, he is said to pay a *ransom*. When a kind and generous master shows his appreciation of loyal and devoted service by handing over to his hired man more than is the latter's legal due, the excess over the stipulated sum is not a wage but a sign that the servant's fidelity merits special recognition. But even when all these elements of self-interest and personal advantage are absent on the part of the donor, as when a group of men combine together to confer something on a man to honor his virtue or his talents, an instinctive sense of the fitness of things makes us describe this token of appreciation as a *presentation* rather than a gift. What men receive from those who organize contests in the physical or mental arena is called a *reward* or a *prize*. Even when the exchange of things is between acquaintances, the artificiality and unreality of modern life has brought it about that no better term than "presents" can be applied to the objects which change hands. For men give to one another at fixed times, at certain seasons, on the occasion of particular social happenings, simply because it is "the proper thing" to do so. The act does not come purely from the heart. It is *form*, not *feeling*, that inspires it.

There may be absent the desire of receiving the equivalent in turn, but there is present the expectation that in similar circumstances one will be treated as one has treated others. In these cases men, in giving, are moved rather by a desire to rid themselves of an obligation that convention forces on them than urged on by a sentiment that can find its rest and satisfaction only in procuring the good of another. But when, in giving, the love of friendship exists between the giver and the receiver, then the donation[2] is invested with a character which exalts it far above these numerous forms of bestowal that have been just enumerated. That which is given to another through the promptings of friendship is purely gratuitous. The friend who gives looks for no return in kind. Such a return may indeed be made, but his act of generosity is not inspired by the hope of it. It is the good of the recipient that is before all else intended. "The sole cause of a gratuitous gift," says St. Thomas, "is love; for if we give gratuitously to a person, it is only because we seek his good."[3] It is because the object which is handed over is thought capable of procuring this good that it is selected in

---

[2] Note that "donation" is taken here in the active, not passive, sense; it is equivalent to "donating."

[3] *S. Th.* I, q. 38, a. 2.

preference to some other object. Love inclines the lover to find his happiness in securing the happiness of the beloved. The natural ardor with which one seeks one's own bliss is devoted to procuring the bliss of the object of one's affection. Love has the effect of "depersonalizing," as it were, the individual whom it sways and transferring all his energies in the pursuit of good to securing what will contribute to the happiness of the person who is loved. These energies for procuring good work for, and in, the interest of the beloved as if it were the lover's own good that was being sought. It is in this sense that love is said to cause "ecstasy," that is, the going out of oneself, the relinquishing of oneself—the abdication, as it were, of oneself. True affection is utterly unselfish. It can find satisfaction only in what brings something of happiness and joy into the life of the person who is the object of the affection. Human beings never weary of giving to the person they love. All that is looked for in the giving is that what is alienated or handed over should be acceptable to the being that is loved and bring him pleasure or advantage.

The assurance that the thing bestowed—the gift—supplies some want or satisfies some need on the part of the recipient brings immense satisfaction. The satisfaction deepens into happiness when the pleasure showing in the eyes of the beloved one on the receipt of the gift reveals that the object has been well chosen. There is great joy felt in the fact that love has been proved to be sincere by its keenness in discerning what could contribute to the good or the well-being of the person who is the object of that love. Mere acquaintanceship can never impart that keen-sightedness as to another's needs and requirements that belongs to a sincere and deep affection.

All these considerations serve to bring into clear light the elements that go to constitute the essence of a gift. The giving must proceed from love.[4] Its object must be the advantage of the recipient and not of the donor. No return may be looked for—at least, the intention of anything like compensation must be excluded from the act of beneficence. Of course, where reciprocity of affection exists such a return will be made. The actual repayment in gratitude, in increase of love, or even in an object equivalent in value to what has been received does not destroy the nature of a gift and make it to be a giving of some other kind. But the desire of such repayment or an interested expectation of it, exercising an influence on the act of giving, would rob it of the value that belongs to it as a love-inspired act. To admit a motive other than that of procuring the happiness of the one to whom the thing is given is to bring the whole transaction down to the level of convention or selfish calculation. Furthermore, what is handed over must be regarded as becoming the absolute property of the recipient. The latter must be able to use what he has received in the way that best serves his interests and must, in doing this, be assured that he is responding exactly to the wishes of the donor. That a thing be a gift it is furthermore required that it be something which it is in the moral power of the giver to

[4] S. Th. I, sent., d. 18, a. 2.

transfer. It must be his property, and he must have the right to do with it according to his will. If a man were to bestow on another what is not part of his own belongings, this act would not be termed a donation in the proper sense of the term. A man cannot make a gift of what is not his own property but belongs to another.[5] The motive in giving a gift must always be that another who is dear to the giver may have in his possession, to enjoy and to use and to profit by, what had previously been in the power of the donor to use at his discretion.

The love of friendship, which uniquely considers the advantage of the friend, is the essential thing in all these elements that go to constitute a gift. That being so, the value of the gift is not measured by its intrinsic or mercantile worth. An object fetching but a small price in exchange, if given with love, outweighs, in the estimation of the recipient, something far more precious bestowed with indifference or through custom. To use a saying that has lost neither its force nor its truth through frequent usage, it is not so much the intrinsic value of the gift of the lover that is valued as the love with which it is given. What we ourselves experience when things are given to us by those whom we cherish and who, on their side, hold us dear, clearly shows this. What we receive may have, indeed, relatively great monetary value, but it does not become on that account a cherished object for us, unless its great price is an indication of the sacrifice the donor was willing to make in order to give us pleasure. Even if the gift happens to be something which supplies a long felt want in our life, its value for us lies not in its aptitude to fill this gap in our possessions. It is not its utility in itself but that utility, as discovered by an affection that was keen-sighted where our needs were concerned, that causes us to treasure what has been given. As we look upon it we delightedly picture to ourselves the prolonged thought, the anxious investigation, the loving inquiry, the affectionate search which were all pressed into service in order that it should be well with us because of what has been given to us.

All this is verified in the relations of God to his creatures. God is the great giver. "Every best gift," says St. James, "and every perfect gift is from above, coming down from the Father of lights."[6] What men aim at in bestowing gifts, in the true sense of that word, is what God aims at, too, in his kindnesses to us. *In giving, his purpose is to secure our happiness by what he bestows on us.* The difference between the gifts of God to us and those that come to us from creatures lies in this, that God can realize the purpose intended in all giving, whereas his creatures cannot. We, when we love, ardently desire to procure the happiness of those who are dear to us. But our power falls very far short of our desires. Let us tax our possessions, exterior and interior, to the utmost, what we have to bestow is but little. The best that we are able to give can bring little more than a transient satisfaction to those whom we desire to gratify and content permanently. Even when we give not merely all that we have, but also all that we are, not

[5] For example, a public official transmitting state aid to the poor cannot said to be giving them *a gift*.

[6] Jas I: 17.

merely our goods, but ourselves, in the sense in which a man can give himself,[7] we still fail to secure the lasting happiness of the being we love. The measure of happiness is the measure of life. It is by what is spiritual in us that we live. We cannot impart life—that is, real life—to another by the bestowal of material objects, not even by the lavishing of affection. Nothing can give us an increase in perfection of life except what can enter into and impart itself to the spiritual element in us. Enlargement or increase of life lies in the enlargement or the increase of the vitality of the soul. Nothing created can cross the threshold of the spirit. Nothing created can, in its own nature, enter into, unite itself with and so give expansion to the human soul. This power belongs to God alone.

What is impossible to man is possible to God. The gift of the creature can enrich us only materially: that of God can enrich us spiritually. The creature can give itself to us only in a figurative and metaphorical sense: God can give himself to us in a literal and real sense. What the creature bestows can gratify us: what God bestows has the power to vivify us. The creature, by its gift, can bring us pleasure: God, by his gift, can bring us happiness. He who, in creating us, gave us our being has alone the power to add to and increase the measure of the being he has given. If then God could become our possession, he would be the gift supreme. A thing may be excellent in itself, but if there is something in its own nature or in the circumstances in which it exists which precludes the possibility of its being given to us, it can never be a gift as far as we are concerned. To be a gift a thing must not only be good in itself; it must also have an aptitude to be bestowed, an aptitude to pass over into the possession of one who did not previously hold it as his own. It must be "give-able." Can God himself be the object of a donation? Can God be as something given and handed over to the possession of another? The question would seem almost like an irreverence. How can the infinite become the "property" of the finite, the Creator be possessed by the creature?

Unaided human reason could reveal to us many of the attributes of God—his simplicity, his eternity, his immutability, his infinite power, his universal presence, his infinite goodness, his boundless wisdom—but it could never discern among his attributes the "aptitude to be given," that is, the possibility of his being a "gift" for his creatures. It is to the keenness of the vision of faith alone that this marvel reveals itself. That infused virtue, by which our intelligence is given a force of penetration infinitely beyond the range of its natural capacity, teaches us that not only can God be imparted to us, but that the benevolent purpose he had in bringing intellectual and reasonable creatures into existence was to give them himself to the full measure in which they can participate in him.[8]

[7] A man can give not only what is in his possession but also himself to another in friendship (*S. Th.* I, sent., d. 15, a. 3, ad 1).

[8] The primary purpose in creation was that the infinite perfection of God should be shown forth in other beings who should be reflections of his existence and of his beauty. Among these beings were to be some who should be images of the self-conscious life of God—of his life of knowing and loving. These would thus not only reflect the beauty of

We are created to serve God. That is true, but we are created not merely for that. We are created to use our wills to unite ourselves to God, by bringing these wills into conformity with his. Yet even this is not the ultimate end of our creation. This is but a means to something else. To serve God might appear an all-sufficient end for us; to keep our wills in conformity with that of God might appear to be the highest destiny that it is possible for us to achieve. Neither the one nor the other is the ultimate end of the existence given us by God. We serve God and we keep ourselves submissive to him by so doing (for union with God is impossible if our will is at variance with his) only in order that God may, through that union, be able to give himself to us—to give us a participation in the treasure of his own being—to "impregnate" our spirit with his life and so bring us to that fullness of existence after which we are ever thirsting. We are bidden to serve God and to keep our wills in harmony with his uniquely because that is the condition to be realized on the part of the creature in order that the Creator may be given—may become for the creature a gift actually received.

Yes, God is a gift that is in God's own power to bestow. In God are found in a manner that is most perfect all the elements that enter into the very notion of a gift. God is not only good: he is by his essence the supreme good itself and therefore capable of satisfying every want. "Thou art my God and I have no good apart from thee."[9] The sovereign good has in itself as such a tendency to communicate itself to others.[10] God gives himself in pure liberality. God cannot receive any compensation from his creatures and, therefore, does not act in view of any advantage to accrue to himself from his action, but in a spirit of pure and disinterested liberality.[11] It is in the power of God to communicate himself that he is capable of becoming a gift—that is, something given. He can enrich, benefit and beatify the creatures on whom he is bestowed. He is communicated with supreme liberality and without any hope or possibility of there being a return in kind. He is, therefore, the gift most perfect in every aspect.

To temper somewhat for us the dazzling splendor of this mystery of our faith, to make it appear to us not so incredible as we should instinctively

---

God but would be able to recognize that they do so. The greatness and happiness of intelligent beings consist in the fidelity with which they reflect the perfections of God in themselves. Hence it is that the glory of God and the happiness of the faithful creature are materially, though not formally, identical.

[9] Ps 15: 2.

[10] See St. Thomas Aquinas, commentary on the *De Divinis Nominibus* of Dionysius. The Areopagite compares the sun to almighty God. The heavenly luminary, he says, irradiates all things with its light, and it has not to persuade itself to do so. It floods things with light because it is what it is—because, in a manner of speaking, it cannot help doing so. So God, in an analogical way, diffuses his goodness on all capable of receiving it, or willing to receive it—and that because he is what he is, sovereignly good.

[11] *S. Th.* I, sent. 1, d. 18, q. 1, a. 3. It is clear that the giving which aims at the utility of the giver can never be attributed to God. Wherefore he, in a singular and unique manner, is said to be liberal. He is uniquely liberal because all but he aim, in giving, at some temporal or spiritual advantage. Therefore there is no gift which is perfectly disinterested except that of God. And love is the motive of all liberal giving.

judge it to be, and to initiate us gradually into the full realization of its wonders is one of the objects of the institution of the Blessed Eucharist. In face of the fact of the Incarnate God giving himself to us under the Sacred Species (the consecrated Host), we cannot be overpowered by the mystery of the Blessed Trinity itself, in the reality of its own divine life, communicating itself to the human soul. The former communion is a preparation for, and a sacramental sign of, the latter.[12] "If anyone loves me" (and so unites himself with me in the sacrament of love), says our divine Lord, "my Father will love him, and we (that is, the Father and the Holy Spirit and the Son as God) will come to him and will make our abode with him."[13] And in the same chapter we read, "I will ask the Father, and he shall give you another Paraclete—the Spirit of truth, whom the world cannot receive, because it seeth him not, nor knoweth him; but you shall know him; because he shall abide with you, and shall be in you."[14] These texts show conclusively that when we are in such dispositions that our will is conformed to that of Jesus, then God, Father, Son and Holy Spirit, communicates himself to us. In the communion of the Blessed Eucharist, the presence of the Incarnate God endures only as long as the Sacred Species remains unassimilated to our substance—at most a comparatively short space of time. But in the communion in which God gives himself to the soul, *the presence of God is not transient. God is given as a gift and therefore to be our permanent possession.*

God remains in the possession of the soul as long as the soul wills to hold him as its own. No matter how excellent our spiritual state is, the real presence in us, after the reception of the Blessed Eucharist, ceases after the lapse of a portion of time that can be counted in minutes. On the other hand, the real presence of the Blessed Trinity abides in our soul as long as we remain in those dispositions which made a sanctifying reception of the Blessed Sacrament possible. That possession of God would endure for all eternity were we never thereafter to put ourselves at variance with his will. The fundamental disposition of the soul of Jesus was one of submission to and conformity with the divine will. "In the head of the book it is written of me that I should do thy will, O God."[15] We are one with our Savior as man when there is in us this submission to the will of our heavenly Father, as that will is expressed to us in the laws that regulate our lives as men and as members of the Church. It is only by rebellion against these laws that we break with Jesus and so lose the infinite gift that has been given us—God himself. In his human life our Lord showed us how to serve God and remain united with him, union being a consequence of service. Disservice

---

[12] The Holy Communion might in a wide sense be called a means to the indwelling of the Blessed Trinity in the human soul. It is true that at the moment of baptism the Three Divine Persons take up their abode in the soul of the infant. But baptism involves in a certain way a desire of the Eucharist, since of its nature it tends toward it. In baptism there is a *votum improprie dictum* of the Blessed Sacrament (cf. Billot, *De Sacr. in gen.*, vol. I, 5th ed., p. 328).

[13] Jn 14: 23.

[14] Jn 14: 16–17.

[15] Heb 10: 7.

spells disunion. We have only to shape our human life after the pattern traced by our Lord, to live that according to principles by which he governed his actions, to cultivate the attitude toward God and man which he exhibited and to develop the dispositions of soul which characterized him, in order to fulfill the conditions which make it possible that God, instead of being for us merely "giveable," becomes "given."

To imitate Jesus Christ is to walk in the path of life which he has traced out for us. To walk the path he has traced is to serve God. Service of God means conformity of will to God's will. That conformity of will conditions God's bestowing himself on us as a gift. God is infinite in all things. He is infinite in kindness and generosity. That infinite generosity moves him to bestow upon others all that lies within the limits of his resources; and his resources have no limits. Infinitely generous and having at his command infinite riches, he bestows infinitely. He gives all that is in his power to give and, therefore, gives himself.

And it is not as if God must be importuned in order that this donation may be made to his creatures. He is ever ready to be given and is actually donated in the very instant in which the condition of receptivity exists on our part. His purpose in creating angels and men was that of making them happy with his own happiness. They have only to accept that happiness by admitting God into their souls.

Before the fall, man was in the perfect condition of receptivity, and God imparted himself to the human soul in a measure that increased with every conscious deliberate act. Sin made the communication of God impossible. The ingress into the soul was barred to the Creator by the deliberate action of the creature's will. The wickedness of sin wrought a dreadful change in man. Sin not only emptied the soul of the Divinity but left in it, as well, an aversion from the divine. But sin did not change God. He always remained communicable, always remained *a gift*, ready and apt to be given to his rational creatures. In order that from being communicable he should be actually communicated nothing was needed but that the aptitude to receive him should reappear once more in man. The Word became flesh to restore this receptivity in fallen humanity and actually revived it in those who consented to enroll themselves in his following: "But to all who received him, who believed in his name, he gave power to become children of God." [16] God's dealings with us do not consist in binding and fettering our wills by numberless restrictions and laws.

Once the Redemption has been accomplished and the original rupture between God and his rational creatures has been healed, God's every action in their regard is directed solely and exclusively to overcoming the reluctance to accept him as a gift—a reluctance that still clings to man's nature even after original sin has been forgiven. But the moment that the rational creature comes to look upon God as his supreme good and rejects as false and as merely apparent goods all things that do not lead to him, at that moment as surely as the sun streams into an apartment when the

[16] Jn 1: 12

79

blinds are drawn aside, God streams into the soul.[17] All that is needed in order that man should receive, possess and hold as his own the Creator and sovereign Lord of all things is that he should desire God above all else, and all other things in subordination to that supreme love of God. God, as has been said, cannot look to a return for his giving. If he could be said to look for any return, it would be to see the infinite happiness which he himself enjoys reflected in the souls of men and in the angelic spirits.

One thing only God demands of us; and in giving it we enrich ourselves, not him. His free, liberal and gratuitous communication to us of the riches of his own life, that is, of himself, requires that we should freely respond to his advances and should give to him the adhesion of our wills, the love and loyalty of our hearts. His great glory lies in this, that we, being free, surrender this freedom to him and yield ourselves to the spell of his divine charms. The moment that God discerns this harmony of will between the creature and himself, he instantly lavishes on that creature the gifts that he has destined for it. He gives because he loves.

Love, as has been stated many times already, is the chief constituent element in a gift—so much so that, when the giving is without affection to prompt and inspire it, what is given is but a present. The first, therefore, of gifts, the source of all others, and that in virtue of which these others are given, is love itself. St. Thomas writes: "Is it not because we love a person that we gratuitously confer a benefit on him? The first thing that we give him is the love by which we wish that what is good should be his. Consequently love is the first gift, since from it flow all other gifts." [18] Hence it is that when our will yields submission to God, the first thing that he bestows on us, as a prelude to all else, is his love. His providence and his care are extended to all the works of his hands without exception, but his love is given to those who choose him in preference to all creatures.

Of all things that life here below yields to us, there is nothing that has such power to give us a surpassing contentment and gratification as the affection of the pure, the noble and the good. The love that comes to us from such a source is a treasure of great price. When we become the object of it, not only is the affection itself treasured exceedingly by us, but, as well, everything that witnesses to it. We look eagerly for the signs, indications and tokens of the affection borne to us, and we set high value upon the most insignificant of these tokens. A word, a look, a gesture, the most trivial thing in itself, if it is used to manifest outwardly the warmth of the affection which may be felt for us, is eagerly welcomed and has power to stir us to the very depths of our being. This is because of the significance with which these apparently trivial things are charged. Creatures speak of giving their affection to us. The expression is exact enough but, in ultimate analysis, is only a figure of speech.

Creatures can have affection for us but can bestow on us, put us in possession of, nothing more than outward signs and tokens of the feelings

[17] See St. John of the Cross, *Ascent of Mount Carmel* II.
[18] *S. Th.* I, q. 38, a. 2.

they entertain toward us. Created love can reach its object only by representation. Love itself must remain imprisoned in the human heart. It is part of the creature's being and not detachable from it. But if the love which is felt for us could take substantial form and come to us not merely in representative signs, but in its own reality, as a living entity, how inexpressibly dear to us would this living love be! How far it would outweigh in value every token of itself which until then it would have used to manifest itself to us! If we could receive love itself, as distinct from the mere manifestations of it, the gift would, as it were, intoxicate us with happiness. If a few written words can be jealously preserved by us as a treasured possession, it is scarcely possible to realize what the joy of life would be could we keep with us, and hold as our own to keep and to cherish, the very love which a human heart bears to us.

In the loving relations of the Creator and the creature this apparently unrealizable dream becomes a reality. With God all things are possible. It is not in signs and tokens but in its own inmost reality that his love is given. For love in God is not an affective movement of his will that comes and goes, rises and then disappears. The strongest affections in us creatures are not realities that can exist independently of the soul in which they take their rise. They are not ourselves, any more than the shape, color or form of a thing is the thing itself. As the color can come and go on the human countenance and leave that countenance what it was, so can the affections come and go in the soul and leave it what it was—at least in its substance. These dispositions of soul are but a reality belonging to a greater reality. They have but an unsubstantial existence and are utterly dependent on the abiding reality in which they rise and disappear. But the movement of love in God is not like that. It is no transient, passing, accidental modification of his being. The love of God is a living, substantial reality. As the vital energy of the shrub finds its fairest and ultimate expression in the flower, so may the Holy Spirit be considered the full flower of the love of God. He is, as it were, the efflorescence of the divine energy of loving in the Godhead. He is the full and perfect expression of that energy of love. He blossoms forth from the vital energy of loving in God as the flower from the vital energy of the shrub.

When, therefore, God deigns to bestow his love on us, he is not limited to mere signs or pledges of it. What he can give, in giving his love, is a living, substantial reality. *For God to give us his love is to give us the Holy Spirit.* Only of God is it literally true to say that he gives us his love. In giving us the Holy Spirit, it is the very love of the Godhead that he transfers to us, to become our treasure and our possession. This is the justification of the title which the Church assigns to the Holy Spirit in the hymn *"Veni Creator"*—*"Altissimi Donum Dei,"* Gift of God Most High. Bewildering as this is to our mortal conceptions of things, we must accept it in all its absolute literalness. It is no metaphor. Just as something that is given us by one who loves us is meant to become our absolute property and to procure our well-being by its possession and its use, so the Holy Spirit is given to us by God the Father and the Son as a gift to hold, to keep and to cherish, to embrace and to possess in our souls as our very own. The Holy Spirit, the gift of God to us, becomes ours, when given.

There are two names which, by reason of the nature of his procession from the Father and the Son, are the appropriate and personal names of the Third Person of the Blessed Trinity. He is named "Love" and "Gift"; and of these two names, that of Gift characterizes him more perfectly than that of Love. For love of itself signifies, as has been explained above, something in and of a substance. It expresses a modification of a being—a movement of the will. In the language of philosophy it is a term which designates something "accidental." In philosophy an "accident" is something which can come and go in a substance and leave that substance unchanged in itself. It means something that demands of its very nature to exist in something else and to belong to that something else.

Now, a gift does signify a thing, a substance—as well as a certain relation between a giver and a recipient. The Holy Spirit, the Spirit of love, is something eminent in the order of substance. For he is a person, and a person who is divine. Personality marks independence in existence. A person does not belong to or inhere in another. The Holy Spirit being a divine person, a term that implies of itself the notion of substance is more appropriate to him than one that does not do so. Hence the word "Gift" names him more perfectly than the word "Love," though both titles are his. And since a gift means something that passes from the benefactor to the beneficiary because of the love of the former for the latter, it can be appropriately applied to the Holy Spirit, who proceeds from the love of the Father and the Son and is bestowed on us because of the love of God for us. Leo XIII writes in his great encyclical on the Holy Spirit: "We have said that the Holy Spirit gives himself. 'The charity of God is poured forth in our hearts by the Holy Spirit who is given to us.'[19] For he not only brings to us his divine gifts, but he is the author of them and is himself the Supreme Gift, who, proceeding from the Father and the Son, is justly believed to be and is called 'Gift of God Most High.' "

[19] Rom 5: 5.

7

The Mission of the Holy Spirit—
the Third Mode of God's Love

OUR divine Lord, on the eve of his death, spoke to his apostles of many things which must have been to them extremely mysterious at that time. During the three years in which they had lived in his society, had absorbed his teaching, and had striven to mold themselves to his spirit, he had come to be all in all to them. Their words to him, when they in a vague way apprehended that the dramatic crisis of his life was drawing near, give clear evidence of this. Their horizons both spiritual and material were bounded by him. The thought of looking beyond or outside him did not arise in their minds. It was unthinkable for them that their life should have any other need than the need of him. If they were to give expression to their attitude toward Jesus they could appropriate for themselves the words of the Psalmist: "I have said unto the Lord, 'Thou art my Lord; I have no good beyond thee.'"[1]

A certain statement of the Savior himself, in which may be detected a note of pathos, would certainly seem to have encouraged that attitude. The accent of Jesus, vibrant with deep emotion and ardent love as he mentioned the name of his Father, stirred in Philip the apostle an eager desire to gaze on the face of One who called forth such a wealth of affection in the heart of the Master. He said to Jesus: "Lord, show us the Father, and it is enough for us."[2] The reply of the Savior was: "So long a time have I been with you, and have you not known me, Philip? He that seeth me, seeth the Father also. How sayest thou, 'show us the Father'? Do you not believe that I am in the Father and the Father in me?"[3] There is a reproach conveyed in these words. Philip is taxed for having, after so many months, so ill profited of the doctrinal instruction conveyed to him by the Divine Master as not to know that Jesus and the Father are one. The doctrine had been expressly stated on a previous occasion in the hearing even of the scribes and Pharisees. It had been then set forth in such unmistakable terms that the life of the Savior was imperiled as a consequence. When Jesus said: "I and the Father are one,"[4] the Jews, we are told, took up stones to cast at him. The words addressed to Philip not only convey a reproach: they seem also to express pain on the part of the Savior. He was grieved that his apostle, privileged to gaze upon the Master, should not find in that vision all that his heart could long for.

[1] Ps 16: 2.
[2] Jn 14: 8.
[3] Jn 14: 9–10.
[4] Jn 10: 30.

And yet, when the sad moment of departure was drawing near, the Lord does not try to console his followers by mere assurances of remembrance in the kingdom to which he is hastening. That is not the main burden of his discourse. He tells them that he will be replaced by another. "And I will pray the Father, and he will give you *another Counselor* to be with you forever. The Spirit of truth, whom the world cannot receive, because it neither sees him nor knows him; you know him, for he dwells with you, and will be in you."[5] These are not the words of one who finds in assurances of everlasting fidelity the only consolation to give to his followers, grieving at the impending separation. There is, rather, a deliberate effacement of self and a substitution of another in his place with them. He returns to the same theme later on, when he could read in their inmost souls their belief that no one could take his place and that no Paraclete that he could send would compensate them for his loss. He said to them: "If I do not go, the Counselor will not come to you; but if I go, I will send him to you."[6] And again: "When he, the Spirit of truth, is come, he will teach you all truth."[7] These words of the Savior are addressed not exclusively to the apostles, but to all those who through their teaching would be won to belief in him. He said: "And not for them only do I pray, but for them also who through their word shall believe in me."[8]

The whole tenor of our Lord's discourse shows that he was thinking in terms of the entire body of Christianity. It is clear, too, that he envisaged the "mission" or the sending of the Holy Spirit by his Father and by himself, after his return to the bosom of the Father, as the *grand event* to which his whole life was directed. For him, clearly, it was the crowning circumstance on which converged all those acts culminating in the Passion, which he wrought for the salvation of mankind. This mission, this dispatching from heaven to the souls of men of an ambassador wholly divine in nature and in person, was evidently looked forward to by the Savior as the full fruit of his whole earthly mission and his life work.

The invisible coming of the Holy Spirit—so frequently accompanied in the early years of the Church by external manifestations of its effects—was vividly realized by the first Christians as the invariable accompaniment of justification. This truth of faith, namely, that the Holy Spirit is sent to the justified soul, was a powerful incentive to them to lead a life not only of exterior rectitude but of great inward purity. The Apostle's words, warning them not to sadden the Divine Envoy who abided in the midst of the inward spiritual kingdom, had for them a persuasiveness that they have not for Christians of more recent times. When he said to his contemporaries: "Grieve not the Holy Spirit,"[9] his words stirred emotions in them which are not aroused by the same words addressed to the faithful of our own day; for in the minds of these latter, the sweet and wondrous and most consol-

[5] Jn 14: 16–17.
[6] Jn 16: 7.
[7] Jn 16: 13.
[8] Jn 17: 20.
[9] Eph 4: 30.

ing doctrine of the special and abiding presence of the Holy Spirit in the soul enjoying the grace of God has become greatly obscured. If they hear this truth of faith referred to, they are little moved by it, for they do not grasp its import in any but the vaguest manner. Yet it is a doctrine that is of fundamental importance (in the literal and exact sense of the term "fundamental") both in the ordinary Christian life that limits its aspirations to the observance of the precepts and in the more developed form that is dissatisfied with anything short of procuring the good pleasure of God in all things. It is a doctrine that is intimately bound up with an adequate understanding of what constitutes the "supernatural" in religion—so intimately that it is scarcely possible to have an adequate idea of the supernatural without having a clear understanding of the invisible mission of the Holy Spirit to the soul and all that flows from this mission by way of consequence. There is no adequate apprehension of what supernatural religion means without a good grasp of the effects of sanctifying grace— called by the theologians *gratia gratum faciens*, that is, the gift of God which makes the rational creature pleasing and acceptable to God.

St. Thomas tells us that "a Divine Person is capable of *being sent* insofar as he exists in someone in a new way; and of *being given* insofar as he is had (that is, held or possessed) by someone; and it is sanctifying grace that accounts for both these effects."[10] The sending or "mission" of the Holy Spirit is intrinsically connected with the conferring of sanctifying grace in the work of justification. The mission of a divine person is a wholly supernatural event. It has no counterpart or parallel in any of the relations which exist between the world of nature and God. The term "supernatural" is of constant use on the lips of Catholics, and yet it may well be doubted if the number to which it conveys a precise and definite meaning is very considerable. The causes of this are partly historical. A stressing of one aspect of faith, even when that stressing is necessary, weakens the attention that may be called for by another aspect.

In the great revolt of the sixteenth century, the denial on the part of Protestants of the necessity and even of the possibility of good works drove the Catholic theologians to emphasize the freedom of man and the moral aspect of religion. The acrid discussions among the Catholic theologians themselves on the thorny questions relating to actual grace helped to rivet attention still closer to the theology of human acts and their efficacy for salvation. The necessary insistence on the truth that man, by the aid of grace, can perform works meritorious of eternal life and that faith divorced from good works did not avail toward salvation came gradually to generate, in the average mind, the idea that morality was the principal element of supernatural religion instead of being, as it is, merely a condition of it. This notion could not, of course, take definite shape and win positive assent in the mind of the believer. But that it is there in a vague way is easily proved if an analysis be instituted of the notion of the "supernatural" that floats in the ordinary Christian mind. It will be

[10] *S. Th.* I, q. 43, a. 3 c.

85

discovered that the term conveys for such a one an idea belonging rather to the moral than to the physical order.[11] It will be found to imply something good in the order of *human conduct* rather than of something of good arising from *divine contact*. It is understood as something affecting conduct rather than being, *action* rather than *form of existence*. The exposition of that section of theology which discusses the Holy Spirit, the Author and Source, by appropriation, of all the operations in the world of grace, sheds full light on what is essential in religion and gives a clear understanding of Catholicity as a system supernatural in its means and in its end and not a mere form of higher morality.

The way in which the truths of our faith are presented to us in our early years is, perhaps, to some extent, if indirectly, responsible for the superficial and very inadequate notion that is commonly held of the consoling doctrine of the abiding presence of God in the soul. We are taught in the first days of our Christian instruction that God is everywhere. This truth does not, as a rule, offer any difficulty to the child's mind. For it is closely associated with the idea of the divine omnipotence. It is true that the notion of God being able to do all things is a far easier one to grasp than the notion of God being present everywhere. The child is in continual contact with persons whom it sees achieve, with ease, things it could not itself attempt. Power and knowledge seem to it to belong to its father and mother. From this experience it readily and easily ascends to the notion of a being who can do all things and who knows all things. And with the direct clear logic of childhood, the little one reasons implicitly that, since with God nothing is impossible, it cannot be impossible for him to be everywhere. The matter rests there for the child. It feels no impulse to institute an inquiry into the nature of that omnipresence. It is content with the knowledge that it is so; it feels no curiosity to know how it is so. When in later years the child becomes an adult and learns that God is in the soul in grace, this information is connected with what was learned in the early lessons in catechism and is taken to be nothing but a particular application of the attribute of omnipresence.

It is rather unfortunate that through this mental association the doctrine of the presence of the Holy Spirit in the souls of the just is brought into relation with another notion of our early years which was anything but a comforting one. For with the information that God was everywhere was conveyed another truth, logically to be deduced from the fact of the omnipresence, namely, that all things, even our most secret thoughts, are naked and open to his eyes. The idea that one is continually under the observation of an all-seeing eye, cold, penetrating, dispassionate, critical

---

[11] The word "physical" as used here needs a little explanation. It is to be understood in its philosophic sense. In this connection it means a reality which exists independently of the mind—one which is not a mental construct. It is opposed to something purely logical, a being of reason. It is what in ordinary language is meant by the term "real." It signifies what is a constituent element of an extra-mental reality. The reason for entering into this explanation will be made clear when sanctifying grace is discussed in a subsequent chapter.

and condemnatory, brings a chill to many a childish heart. No doubt the little one has been taught that God is his father, but in many cases the truth of God's constant watchfulness leaves a deeper impression than the truth of his fatherhood. It is a misfortune that the first idea of God should be that of a sleepless, watchful and rather fault-finding observer. How this must falsify relations with God from the outset! And very often the early impression receives no correction afterward when the presence of the Holy Spirit in the soul is dealt with in connection with the question of habitual or sanctifying grace.

Every Christian knows from what he has learned concerning the "oneness" in nature in the Blessed Trinity, that where the Holy Spirit is, the other Two Persons must be also. The soul, again because of first impressions, feels more uneasy than comforted by that presence. If the interior attitude of the person brought up on this Jansenistic[12] idea of a watchful and critical God were analyzed, it would be revealed as being somewhat of the following nature. He knows that when he is in the state of grace the Holy Spirit is present in his soul. Coupled with that knowledge is the belief that God is keenly on the alert to discover that fatal lapse in thought or in action which would justify him in taking his departure from the soul once more. This may seem a harsh and rude picture of the ideas called forth by the doctrine of God's presence in the soul of the just, but it is to be feared that it is fairly exact in the case of a goodly number of Christians. There can be no doubt that the notion of the indwelling of the Holy Spirit in the souls of the justified encountering such a mentality is calculated to be more terrifying than consoling. What a change could be wrought if it were brought home to all children from the beginning that God is, indeed, watchful, but watchful rather for the purpose of doing us good than of finding us at fault. What a different idea would be had of God if the child were taught, from the beginning, that God's vigilance was a vigilance of love and not of disapproval—the vigilance of the loving father and not that of the suspicious warden![13]

That presence of the Holy Spirit in the soul of the just, which is a consequence of his mission to them, is not, it may be stated from the outset, a mere form of the omnipresence of God, though it presupposes that omnipresence. It is something very different in its nature and in its effects. To understand clearly in what the difference lies, it will be necessary, first, to enter into some explanation of the mode by which God is present in all things in general.

It must not be supposed that once things have been created they continue to exist of themselves by their own native resources without any need of further aid from God. This is not so. Things not only must be

---

[12] Though Jansenism may be dead as a professed doctrine, it survives in many modalities of religious thought and practice.

[13] It need scarcely be pointed out that there are many who, from their tenderest years, are taught to dwell on the fatherly solicitude of God. But too frequently it is the idea of God as the just and inflexible judge that is stressed in the instruction of the young.

created by God, they require as well to be maintained in being by his sustaining power. That continued conservation is a kind of prolonged creation. Creatures do not receive their existence, as it were, all at once. It is doled out to them moment by moment. It is, to use another metaphor, distilled to them drop by drop. If God ceased for a moment to impart those partial existences to a thing, that thing would instantly cease to be. It would lapse back into nothingness. All things remain perpetually suspended on God, depending utterly on him for each particle of existence they enjoy. Everything, then, that exists is held up in existence by God.

Now this holding up is not as when we hold up things in our hand through our external contact with them. God does not hold things superficially and sustain them in that way. He holds things in existence by being in their very inmost depths, giving them not only their nature and their natural existence but, in addition, every movement of energy that they put forth. He not only gives things *being*, he gives them *action* as well. He is more intimate with each form of reality than it is with itself. He is in the depths of the rose making it exist as that particular kind of rose. He is in the colors of the rose leaves, imparting to them the living brilliancy of their hues. He is in the depths of man's soul; he is in every interior and exterior act; he is in man's thoughts, reasonings and decisions. What is more, man has to draw on God for the very energy he puts forth in the very act of sin. God's power is ever actively engaged in this work of conservation with regard to every form of reality. He is in the heart of those realities that abide identical with themselves under a multiplicity of changes and are called "substances." He is intimate with those that come and go and have but a transient and fugitive existence in things which are called, in philosophical language, "accidents," because they exist in substances without affecting any essential change in these substances. Were God's act of conservation to be relaxed for a single instant in the case of any form of reality whatever—spiritual, material, mental, moral, sensitive, inorganic, accident, substance—that form of reality would simply cease to be. God's power is put forth in every pulse of organic or inorganic being, in repose and in movement, in every slightest change.

Now every agent must be, through his action, present to that on which he acts. By his action the worker is in contact with the materials of his art. Since every being and every aspect of being is the effect of God's creative or conservative action, God's power and exercise of that power is present to and in everything to the very depths of its reality—even to that extreme where it touches on the confines of nothingness. Where anything, therefore, is, there God must be. Where he is not, nothing can be. If anything were to escape the pervading presence of God, it would do so to its cost; it would mean for it a plunge into annihilation. That is the reason, not only why God is everywhere, but why he *must* be everywhere—everywhere meaning where anything is. He is there in virtue of the exercise of his "conserving" power. Now, in the Divinity the power of operation is identified with the essence. Where, therefore, the divine power is, there the divine essence must be, because the two are identical. This is the explanation of what the theologians mean when they state that God is everywhere by his power, his presence and his essence.

God, therefore, envelops all reality, since he himself is the source of all that is real and positive in the heavens, on the earth and under the earth. Now this universal presence, though of the same nature in all things, is not in all respects the same. It exists in a limitless variety of degrees. Though fully present to all, God can be present in things to a greater or less extent. He is more intimately present where his operation is more potent and attains to higher effects in the order of being. He is more deeply present in those effects which reflect more perfectly his perfections. The greater[14] the output of divine energy, the closer the presence: one is in direct proportion to the other. He is more present to the plant than to the earth from which it draws its nourishment, because the plant is living and the earth is not. Living is a higher form of being than the mere existence enjoyed by inorganic things. He is more present to the animal than to the plant on which it browses—for sentient life is higher in the scale of being than non-sentient or vegetative life. This presence goes on deepening the higher we ascend in the scale of life, attaining its utmost intimacy in the most spiritual operations of the human intellect and will—that is, if consideration is limited to the natural order and to the material universe. Minerals, plants and animals cannot have any awareness of this intimate presence of God in them. Man, on the other hand, can submit this presence to the analysis of his mind and, arriving at some understanding of it, can conceive a natural regard for the source of this creative and conserving power to which he owes his existence.

God may be said to be present in the effects of his creative and conserving power in yet another sense. He is present, as has been stated, in these effects as producing them: he is present in them, too, inasmuch as each of them is a participation more or less remote of the divine perfections. God is in what he creates much in the same way as the mind and genius of man find concrete expression in and are reflected in the works of his hands. It is said that "the style is the man." The more perfect the work, the more of the artist that is found in it. His whole artistic power, that which is best in him, considered as an artist, finds its highest expression in his masterpiece. In a similar way God, as being the divine artist from whose hands all things come, is found in creatures not by a division of his substance but inasmuch as each is an image or vestige of his being, by way of participation. Those creatures which share more fully the divine perfection are, by that fact, closer to God, more intimately bound up with him. He, on his side, is nearer to them than to others. God, then, exists more perfectly in those creatures which benefit in larger measure of his bounty, and these in their turn are more closely united with him the richer the gifts of nature which they receive from his hands.

[14] "The greater output" is to be understood with regard to the term of the energy, that is, the effect in nature, not with regard to the principle. There is no greater or less in the divine operation itself, except as considered "terminative," as the theologians express it.

Now, "beyond and above the common and universal manner in which God is in all things by essence, power and presence, as a cause is in the effects which participate in the virtues of that cause, there is another and special way which is particular to rational beings. In some of these God is present as an object known and loved is in the being that knows and loves the object, i.e., as a thing known in the knower and a thing loved in the lover. And because a creature endowed with intelligence can, in the exercise of its activities of knowing and loving, gain[15] God himself in the reality of his own nature and personality, it follows that instead of saying that God is in such beings, we say rather that he dwells in them as in his temple. No other effect of God's activity except sanctifying (i.e., habitual) grace can be the cause of this new and special presence of a divine being in the created spirit. It is only in and through sanctifying grace, then, that a divine person is sent and proceeds from another in a procession that has as its term an effect that belongs to time."[16] These words of St. Thomas usher the reader into the very heart and center of the whole supernatural system and bring him close to that veil which, to the searching gaze of faith, permits the passage of some dim rays of that inner glory of which St. Paul speaks, saying: "Eye hath not seen nor ear heard, neither hath it entered into the heart of man, what things God hath prepared for them that love him."[17]

In the words quoted from St. Thomas there is question of a kind of presence of God in the soul of the just which finds no parallel whatsoever in nature. It must be a wonderful sensation for the pilot when, beating his way upward through the atmosphere vitiated by earth's exhalations and then through the heavy clouds hanging like a canopy over that atmosphere, he emerges suddenly into a world flooded with untainted splendor, a world of pure sunshine, a world where the radiant beams that stream directly from the great source of all material light suffer no dimness. This experience bears an analogy to that which thrills the mind of the theologian when, having mounted through all the different degrees of God's presence in nature, he emerges into the contemplation of this radiant presence of the Holy Spirit in the soul through divine habitual grace. In the lower regions the light that streams from the Divinity falls on the soul in broken and refracted rays. Here the everlasting fount of light and glory pours out its beams on the soul through the intervening veil of faith. That veil does not refract, distort or divert those beams; it merely arrests the

---

[15] "Gain" in the sense in which by effort one succeeds in reaching a term aimed at (e.g., "The fugitive gained the frontier"). The Latin phrase is *attingit ad Deum*. The translation, "attains to God," does not convey the sense of the expression. One has to think of the soul striving to cause its acts of knowledge and love to traverse an immense space and finally come to fix themselves on a distant object. That object at an infinite distance is God himself. Without grace the acts of will and intellect must necessarily fall short and terminate at created reflections of God, that is, the things of the material universe. By grace they can go onward, traverse the infinite distance and come to rest in the adorable person of God himself.

[16] *S. Th.* I, q. 43, a. 3 c.

[17] I Cor 2: 9.

radiance which otherwise would scorch and shrivel the soul as yet inapt to bear their full splendor.

What has been already said in speaking of the ordinary, natural presence of God in things will help to give some understanding of this marvelous effect of divine grace. This effect has a dual aspect. It will make for clearness to consider these two aspects successively. This divine presence that comes from grace may be considered on the side of the Creator and on the side of the creature. Let it be first considered on the side of the Creator.

It has been stated that the force and virtue of God's action on a thing measures the intimacy of his presence in that thing. By infusing grace into the soul, God is producing an effect of a kind infinitely superior to anything he causes in the order of nature. St. Thomas assures us that the grace of a single individual surpasses in worth the natural good of the whole material universe.[18] In the same way he says that, comparing operations from the point of view of their results, the operation that consists in bestowing grace on a soul is far superior to that which is exercised in the creation of the world. There is in fact no comparison to be instituted between the power put forth in God's action when he, for instance, is sanctifying the soul of the child in baptism and that which he exercises when he is moving and strengthening the intellect of a mighty philosopher to probe the secrets of nature and to penetrate to the ultimate reasons of things. God is always present where his action is. He is present in both these operations just mentioned, but his presence in one is infinitely closer than his presence in the other. God is more deeply, vitally and intimately present to the soul when he is imparting to it the least degree of sanctifying grace than he would be were he moving it to the highest activity of intellect possible to the created spirit in the life of its natural mode of operation. Even in the relations of men with one another or with things, the degree of presence is not measured by mere spatial conditions but by interest and affection. We are more present to those in whom we are interested than to those who may be much closer to us in space. The artist is more present to the work which engages all his powers than to that which can be executed with less effort and absorption of mind.

Now, in conferring grace on a creature God calls upon the resources not only of his omnipotence, but also of his goodness. The magnitude of the effect aimed at in the sanctification of a soul demands (speaking figuratively) an "intentness" on the part of God not required in the creation of the universe. St. Augustine assures us that it is a more stupendous work to justify a sinner than to call a world into being. If then we consider the grandeur of the operation, the closeness of the tie that it involves between the creature and the Creator, and the nature of the effect it produces (namely, the imparting to the soul of a participation of the divine nature), there is given, apparently, an exhaustive explanation of all that is

[18] *S. Th.* I, II, q. 113, a. 9, ad 2.

involved in that singular presence of God in the soul that is a consequence of divine sanctifying grace.

Yet this is not so. There remains much more to be said. The considerations just developed do not give a sufficient justification for the terms used by St. Thomas (and all Catholic theologians) in studying this theological question. In the passage already cited, from the *Summa Theologica,* are to be read these words: "A Divine Person is capable of being sent *insofar as he exists in someone in a new way;* and of being given insofar as he is had (that is, held or possessed) by someone; and it is sanctifying grace that accounts for both these effects. . . . *Hence it is by reason of sanctifying grace that a Divine Person is sent,* or temporally proceeds. . . . *Hence the Holy Spirit is given and sent."* [19] These words present the great mystery in a new light. There is question of a presence that wears features other than those that can be discerned in a presence the nature of which is determined by an intense application of energy and the production of an eminent effect. There is a special contact with the soul which, though necessarily common to the Blessed Trinity, is by appropriation attributed to the Holy Spirit as belonging to him in a singular and personal manner. It is a contact which is not expressed by a word primarily signifying *action on* the soul as one would naturally expect from the considerations developed in the previous paragraphs.

Theology speaks of this contact as established by a "sending" or "mission" of one of the Divine Persons, and that Person, the Holy Spirit. The usage of this strange term, in connection with a Divine Person and the habitual restriction of its usage to the Third Person of the Most Holy Trinity, should lead one to suspect that an analysis of its implications would reveal aspects in the presence of God by grace in the soul that so far have not presented themselves. How can God be "sent" to any place since God is necessarily everywhere by power, essence and operation? Why is it that, although the Son is also spoken of as being "sent," it is, as a rule, the Holy Spirit that is mentioned in this connection? The answer to these two questions brings us into the very heart of the central mystery of our faith. The term "mission," as illuminated by its own inner meaning and its full implications, sheds a flood of light upon the whole economy of the relations of God with fallen humanity.

This economy, surveyed from the vantage point of God's extraordinary goodness, falls into three grand "moments" or divisions.[20] The history of the human race from the instant it emerged from the gates of Paradise might be represented in three great bands of different hue, each colored by the particular love that God shows to fallen man at each

---

[19] *S. Th.* I, q. 43, a. 3 c.

[20] In tracing the relations of God to fallen man, it may be necessary to remark that it is not temporal sequence that is taken into account. The condition of man is shown in the *real sequence*—the sequence of the divine decrees. It is the real sequence of cause and effect. Though from the temporal point of view men were friends of God before Jesus came, from the causal point of view such friendship became possible only by his passion and death. Man was severed from God until the death of Christ.

of these three stages.[21] Scarcely had the fall taken place when it became clear that the break with God was not irrevocable and that one day the bonds of friendship, sundered by man's sin, should be knit together once again. Man became a sinner but was not abandoned to his fate. God did not close his heart to his creature's misery, though that misery was brought about by the creature's own rebellion and ingratitude. During all the long ages that followed, the Lord continued to give to man all that his divine uncreated heart could extend to him. Love of friendship was impossible because of man's unredeemed state—but the love of beneficent kindness was not fettered by the same restrictions. The Creator poured out his merciful kindness on his sinful erring creatures, heedless of the repeated rebuffs that his love had to experience. With a divine realization of the corruption of the mass of humanity, he took a portion from it, set it apart, exercised an unfailing providence over it and kept it in some measure of fidelity to himself by temporal reward and chastisements. The whole history of the Israelites reveals, as it were, a constant fear and anxiety on the part of God, lest the human race should drift from him completely, forget the primordial promises, and so become utterly powerless to profit of the salvation when it should come.

This period from the fall to the Incarnation may be described as the period of merciful kindness—the first mode of God's love. The outstanding feature of it was the "covenant," that is, the pact or agreement between God and the chosen people. That mercy should be extended to rebellious man is a revelation of the extraordinary magnanimity of God. That he should so stoop from the lofty heights of his dignity, should show such condescension as to consent to enter into a treaty of alliance with the race, passes all comprehension. His mercy seems to make him utterly oblivious of the rights of his exalted state. He asks man to strike a pact with him. If they take measures to preserve the memory of him as the one true God and transmit faithfully from age to age the divine promises of Redemption, he agrees to lavish on them the special care of his providence and pour out on them temporal blessings. It was the old covenant. It was imperfect, incomplete, and in it the contracting parties became allied but remained to a large extent strangers one to the other. It was not God's fault. Man lost in sin and as yet unredeemed could not be on terms of perfect understanding with him. Man could not rise to God's views; man was of the earth, earthy: his tastes were not of heaven. There is deep pathos in these words of Isaiah: "For my thoughts are not your thoughts, nor your ways my ways, says the Lord. For as the heavens are exalted

---

[21] Figuratively those three great bands into which the history of man divides itself might be represented as colored the first green, the second red, the third and last white. The first represents the period prior to the Incarnation, the period of hope and expectation; the second, the period of God's sojourn on earth—that of the blood-stained combat by which peace was perfectly reestablished between God and men; the third—pure white—the period of perfect harmony and friendship between the creature and the Creator.

above the earth, so are my ways exalted above your ways, and my thoughts above your thoughts." [22]

With the Incarnation came a great change in the relations between God and men. There appeared the great mediator Jesus Christ. He was eminently fitted to be, as it were, a go-between in the negotiations that prepared the way for a new alliance between the Creator and his creatures. He belonged to both worlds, the divine and the human. He had a perfect understanding of the former; he had full sympathy with the latter. Though God, he had a human heart and could pour out on men the tenderness of a human affection. Separated as he was from them in moral dispositions, he was united with them in the bonds of a common nature. All men were his brethren, and he had therefore the heart of a brother for them. The humanity which he took from them and in which he was one with them was the source of an affection which he could extend to them irrespective of their moral state. It is the second mode of God's love for man and prepares the way for the third.

The great work of Jesus was to effect a final and perfect reconciliation between his Father in heaven and that Father's rebellious creatures. [23] In order to bring it about, he went over completely to the cause of man. He gloried in the title of "Son of man"—that is, *man* simply. [24] He identified himself fully with the lot of his fellows. He gathered up all humanity in himself and reckless of consequences flung himself into combat against all in man that interposed itself as an obstacle to perfect friendship with God. He entered into the lists against sin and death, armed with the forces of his undefiled humanity. "Death and life in wondrous conflict strove." [25] The Prince of Life was slain, but his death swept away all the obstacles to a new and perfect covenant between God and men. "This is my blood of the new covenant," [26] he said. That is, through the shedding of this my blood on the cross, a new testament, that is, a new alliance or covenant, can be struck between mankind and the Father who sent me.

During those last hours with his apostles his thoughts were ever turning to an event not to take place on the night of the Last Supper, not on the day of the Crucifixion, not on the morning of the Resurrection, nor even in the radiant evening of the Ascension, but to an event which was to be the term on which all these were to converge. His thoughts dwelt incessantly on the day of Pentecost. In his parting discourse to his faithful followers he returns again and again to this theme, as if he earnestly desired that their thoughts, like his own, should be directed to it as the supreme event in the economy of Redemption. He said to them: "I go to the Father . . . and I will ask the Father and he shall give you *another* Paraclete, that he may abide with you for ever." [27] It is as if he said: "My work is done. I shall now

[22] Is 55: 8–9.
[23] Rom 5: 10–11.
[24] Cf. J. B. Terrien, S.J., *La Mère de Dieu*, vol. I, p. 87.
[25] Sequence of Paschal Time.
[26] Mt 26: 28; Mk 14: 24.
[27] Jn 14: 16.

return to the Father's bosom. My passion and death will have entitled me to ask him to send his Spirit of love and peace on mankind. In consideration of my merits, the Father will send his Holy Spirit. He, in my place, shall comfort mankind and do so in a higher manner than I. His stay with men will not be transient as mine has been. It will be for all time and the eternity following."

Our divine Lord describes later on some of the activities of this new Paraclete: "But the Paraclete, the Holy Spirit, whom the Father will send in my name, he will teach you all things and bring all things to your mind, whatsoever I shall have said to you."[28] The meaning of the Master's life will not be clear until the Paraclete comes: "But when the Paraclete cometh, whom I will send you from the Father, the Spirit of truth, who proceedeth from the Father, he shall give testimony of me."[29] His life would have failed of its purpose if he were to continue living with them in a perpetuation of the human ties with which he was bound to them, and of the human relations in which he stood to them. That would thwart God's designs on them. These designs could be realized only by the coming of a Divine Person who should converse with them in a divine manner and abide with them in a purely mystical way. "But I tell you the truth: it is to your advantage that I go; for if I go not, the Paraclete will not come to you; but if I go, I will send him to you."[30] The whole period between the Annunciation and Pentecost—the period of the second mode of God's love—was a period of transition, lying between two covenants. Of these covenants Christ's fellowship with men was the consummation of the old and the inauguration of the new. It partook of the character of both, but essentially it looked onward to the new.[31]

That final agreement between God and man was consummated on the great morning of Pentecost. It was the Day of Days—the day of the Great and Final Pact. God's long and merciful pursuit of his wandering creatures reached its term on that tenth day after the Ascension. It was fitting that the long chase should end in a tumult of exultant sound and the flashing of fire, the symbol of the impetuosity of the Divine Charity.

> Now of that long pursuit
> Comes on at hand the bruit;
> That voice is round me like a bursting sea.[32]

---

[28] Jn 14: 26.
[29] Jn 15: 26.
[30] Jn 16: 7.
[31] "He is mediator of a better testament which is established on better promises. For if that former covenant had been faultless, there should not indeed have been sought for a second. For finding fault with them he saith: 'Behold the days shall come . . . and I will perfect unto the house of Israel and unto the house of Judah a new testament not according to the testament which I made to their fathers . . . for this is the testament I will make to the house of Israel after those days. . . . I will be their God and they shall be my people' " (Heb 8: 6–10.).
[32] Francis Thompson, "The Hound of Heaven."

That divine pursuit began when God said to the serpent: "I will put enmities between thee and the woman, and thy seed and her seed; he shall crush thy head, and thou shalt lie in wait for his heel." [33] It ended when "there came a sound from heaven, as of a mighty wind coming, and it filled the whole house where they were sitting. And there appeared to them tongues as of fire, and it sat upon every one of them. And they were all filled with the Holy Spirit." [34] The seed of the woman had fulfilled his promise. The devil had trodden that seed under foot and crushed it into the earth. But there it germinated in the Resurrection, the Ascension and the right to obtain of the heavenly Father the sending of the Second Paraclete. It was but fitting that the Great Woman, to whose seed fell such a glorious victory, should be present at this grand final scene in the great drama of redemption. "All these [i.e., the apostles] were persevering with one mind in prayer with the women, and *Mary the mother of Jesus,* and with his brethren." [35]

With Pentecost is ushered in a new era—the era of the third mode of God's love. A study of the characteristics of this era enables one to differentiate clearly between the role of Jesus Christ and the role of the Holy Spirit in the work of bringing mankind back to God. The difference between the two roles can be summarized in one sentence. To Jesus fell the task of *pacification*—to the Holy Spirit, that of *sanctification.* "For when we were enemies, we were reconciled to God by the death of his Son; much more now that we are reconciled, shall we be saved by his life. And not only so, but also we rejoice in God through our Lord Jesus Christ, by whom we have now received reconciliation." [36] We are therefore reconciled to God by the submission unto death of our elder brother Jesus, but we are saved by his life. We have that life in us when we have in us the spirit of Jesus. In that lies sanctification and salvation, these two being one. The redeeming Christ occupies the stage in the pages of the Gospel and disappears from the scene after the Ascension. Then the "Spirit of Christ" becomes the chief actor in the events that open at Pentecost and will unfold themselves in long succession until the end of time. One has only to peruse the Acts and the epistles to remark the striking changes that followed the accomplishment of Christ's earthly pilgrimage. Prior to that time the Son of man, the mortal Christ, is the radiating center of all influence on souls. After it, the Spirit, whom the Father sent at his request, and whom he himself sends, is the source of all the vital activities in the Church taken as a whole and in individual souls. [37] The Son of man labored and died to merit sanc-

[33] Gen 3: 15.
[34] Acts 2: 2–4.
[35] Acts 1: 14.
[36] Rom 5: 10; cf. 2 Cor 5: 18–19; Col 1: 20–22.
[37] It would be idle to quote texts to illustrate this statement, they are so numerous. The action of the Holy Spirit—called in one place the Spirit of Jesus (Acts 16: 7; cf. 1 Pet 1: 11)—is mentioned over fifty times. A few examples suffice. "The Spirit said to Philip . . . and the Spirit of the Lord caught up Philip" (Acts 8: 29, 39). "The Spirit said

tification for mankind. His Holy Spirit carries out in souls the sanctification merited.

Jesus is the artisan of peace, the great peacemaker between God and man. In his flesh, by his death, he broke down the dividing walls—the "middle wall of hostility" that stood between Jew and gentile and that separated both from God. "For he is our peace, who hath made both one, and breaking down the middle wall of hostility . . . that he might make the two into one new man and might reconcile both to God in one body by the cross, killing the enmities in himself." [38] If one has before one's mind the figure of two states that have been for long years in dissension, the meaning of all this becomes very clear. A perfect condition of things has not been established immediately that the war has ceased and the estrangement between the two parties has been brought to an end. The striking of a treaty is but the beginning of a new and a more perfect condition of things. Christ brought the dissension between God and man to an end. He made peace between the two contending parties by an act of supreme self-sacrifice. Hence it was that the word "peace" falls so naturally from his lips after he had risen from the dead. "Jesus came and stood in the midst, and said to them: 'Peace be to you.' . . . He said therefore to them again: 'Peace be to you.' . . . When he had said this he breathed on them and he said to them: 'Receive ye the Holy Spirit.' " And we read that again, eight days later, "Jesus cometh . . . and stood in the midst, and said: 'Peace be to you.' " [39]

Now when strife has ended much remains to be done. A mere cessation of hostilities between states is an unsatisfactory condition of things. When enmity has ceased, the warring powers have to be drawn close together in the bonds of friendship. The parallel holds in this great drama of redemption. The Son of man had established terms of peace, and in that his work as mortal man was ended. It devolved on the Holy Spirit to strengthen, consolidate and perfect that peace so dearly purchased. [40] Jesus had swept away *misunderstanding*; it remained for the Holy Spirit to create a *perfect understanding*. It is for that he is sent. When a treaty has been struck between two powers, a representative from each is sent to reside close to the seat of government of the other. Christ our chief has ascended to the

---

to him [Peter], 'Behold three men seek thee' " (Acts 10: 19). "The Holy Spirit fell on all them that heard the word" (Acts 10: 44). "And the Spirit said to me that I should go with them, nothing doubting" (Acts 11: 12). "They attempted to go into Bithynia and the Spirit of Jesus did not allow them" (Acts 16: 7). It is significant that in the previous verse, i.e., verse 6, we read: "they were forbidden by the Holy Spirit to preach the word in Asia." The Spirit of Jesus is identical with the Holy Spirit. "And now, behold, being bound in the Spirit, I go to Jerusalem" (Acts 20: 22).

[38] Eph 2: 14-16.

[39] Jn 20: 19-21, 26.

[40] Because of this work of consolidating and perfecting peace between Creator and creature, it is not inappropriate that the Holy Spirit should be presented to us under the image of a dove—the symbol of peace (cf. Gen 8: 8-12). At the baptism of Jesus, the Holy Spirit descends on him in the form of a dove. Here then is a conjunction of the peacemaker and the peace which he merited (Mt 3: 16; Mk 1: 10; Lk 3: 22; Jn 1: 32).

court of our heavenly Father, where he lives, always living to make intercession for us.[41] Keeping the sacred wounds of his flesh ever before the eyes of God, he constantly pleads the cause of humanity at the throne of God. The Creator, on his side, at the request of Jesus, sends his ambassador to represent his interests in the world of souls. That divine envoy is none other than the Holy Spirit.[42]

The full significance of the word "mission" used in connection with the coming of the Third Person of the Most Holy Trinity now becomes manifest. "Mission" means something far more than the mere act of sending. Its consequence is not merely an approach to a certain place, but the taking on of certain definite relations with persons dwelling in that place. The Holy Spirit does not need to come to men's souls, because he is there already in virtue of the divine omnipresence. *"But,"* St. Thomas says, *"a Divine Person is capable of being sent insofar as he exists in someone in a new way."* The Holy Spirit is always in the soul, but when this latter has been justified in the blood of Christ he begins to exist there in a manner entirely different from the former manner. He is now there as a "divine envoy." Having been already in the kingdom of the soul, he now takes up new functions there. He is invested by God the Father with the role of ambassador to the court of man's soul. It is to be noted that Christ as man does not send the Holy Spirit. He does so only as God. As man he can but plead with the Two Persons of the Blessed Trinity, from whom, as from one principle, the Holy Spirit proceeds, that in view of his merits they should send the Holy Spirit to men. Hence it is that he says: "I will ask the Father, and he shall give you another Paraclete."[43] Here Christ is speaking in terms of his humanity, not his divinity. As a divine person, he does not make a request. St. Thomas writes: "A 'mission' implies two things: first, a relation to the person by whom the mission is given, and secondly, a relation to the destination to which the envoy is sent. Now a 'mission' can be predicated of a divine person as implying on the part of the person sent, his having his origin from another divine person and as implying on the other hand a new mode of existing there where he has been."[44] The Father then cannot be sent: such a thing is possible only in the case of the Son and the Holy Spirit. But since it is possible in the case of these Two Persons, it may be asked why the mission to the Church and to souls is so uniformly appropriated to the Third Person only. The reason is that the functions to be performed by the Divine Ambassador have a close analogy with the personal characteristics of the Third Divine Person.

The great aim of a foreign representative in a state is to create in the

---

[41] See Heb 7: 25; "For Jesus has not entered into a sanctuary made with hands . . . but into heaven itself that he may appear now in the presence of God for us" (Heb 9:24); see also Heb 4: 14; 6: 20.

[42] St. Teresa of Avila writes: "It seems to me that the function of mediator between God and the soul devolves on the Holy Spirit" (*Thoughts on the Love of God,* chap. 5).

[43] Jn 14: 16.

[44] *S. Th.* I, q. 43, a. 1 c.

people among whom he resides a deep sympathy with and a strong friendship for his own people. This is precisely the function of the Holy Spirit in the soul. He aims at making that soul love God. His efforts are untiring to generate in it feelings of deep filial affection toward that heavenly Father by whom he, the Holy Spirit, has been dispatched on this very commission. From the very moment of the fall, God had been straining (let the metaphor pass) toward this very consummation. To fallen and unredeemed man he could but extend mercy and kindness. He could love man only with that love which he may bestow on creatures that have but a natural participation of his own perfections. Where man was concerned God could not rest satisfied with this diminished form of affection. He would love his rational creatures with the love friend has for friend, spouse for spouse, and father for child. Jesus has made this possible. God could now set free the torrents of his affection and pour them out on men. He could at last love them with the love he bears toward himself, because by the grace of justification they bear a supernatural likeness to himself. The Holy Spirit is sent in justification, and he, the Spirit of love, labors to impress more and more deeply his own image on the soul—the image of divine love.

St. Paul discloses to us the Divine Envoy at this work, saying: "And because you are sons, God hath sent the Spirit of his Son into your hearts, crying: Abba! Father!"[45] The Divine Ambassador is ever faithful to the interests of the court from which he has been dispatched. He devotes all his efforts to developing in the soul a perfect sympathy with divine things. He strives to make it one with God in aspirations, tastes, ideals. He leaves no means untried to create a perfect understanding between the creature and the Creator. He pours actual grace upon actual grace into the soul in order to impart to it what may be aptly termed "the heavenly mind." He initiates it into the knowledge of divine things. He makes it conversant with the ways, manners, customs and spirit of his native country, heaven. "The things also that are of God no man knoweth, but the Spirit of God. ... But to us God revealed them by his Spirit."[46] The old Greek states declared a perfect alliance of friendship one with another by asseverating they would have the same friends and the same enemies. The Holy Spirit would so transform the soul by his action that it also would come to have the same friends and the same enemies as God, that is to say, would come to love what God loves, hate what he hates, cherish what he cherishes, desire what he desires and, in a word, share all his aspirations. This is the ambition of the Holy Spirit with regard to the soul to which he has been sent. Christ had foretold all this labor of the Spirit of love. He said to his apostles at the Last Supper: "The Paraclete, the Holy Spirit, whom the Father will send in my name, he will teach you all things, and bring all things to your mind, whatsoever I shall have said to you."[47] These words addressed to the apostles have

---

[45] Gal 4: 6; cf. Rom 8: 15.
[46] 1 Cor 2: 9, 10, 11.
[47] Jn 14: 26.

application to all souls called to be saints, that is, Christians.[48] To all the Holy Spirit imparts heavenly instructions with a view to making them ever more and more conformable to what is divine. "The charity of God is poured forth in our hearts by the Holy Spirit, who is given to us."[49]

The third mode of God's love, then, is that by which God is able to love the soul as he loves himself, with a love which is of the same nature as that by which the Father loves his only-begotten Son. The whole economy of God's dealings with humanity was directed toward this objective— namely, that one day the Almighty could look on his fallen creatures and see them not as such, but as beloved children—sons and heirs, "heirs indeed of God, and joint heirs with Christ."[50] It is the Holy Spirit who forms us as God's children and develops in us the love that springs from that relation. That is his "mission" or, one might say, his "commission." He makes us apt for heaven. Without him we could not enter there; without his instruction we could not bear ourselves there as becomes children of God. Christ's Passion won for us the power to be born of God. "But to all who received him, he gave power to become children of God."[51] It is the Holy Spirit who brings us to birth and stamps on our souls the image of God. "Unless one is born of water and the Spirit, he cannot enter the kingdom of God."[52] The Holy Spirit instructs us in the bearing of the sons of God. He imparts to us the divine manner.

The following words aptly recapitulate all the thoughts that have been developed in the foregoing pages. "The glorious and beatifying renovation that we look forward to on the day of resurrection is already being prepared in this present life. It supposes a previous transformation realized here below and is the term toward which souls, renewed by their elevation to the divine and supernatural order, direct themselves. Grandiose mystery, to the enjoyment of which we are all called and the accomplishment of which is to be traced back to the pouring out of the Holy Spirit on the world. The event which marks and inaugurates officially this mystery is well known. On the day of Pentecost the apostles were gathered in a house at Jerusalem, awaiting in recollection and prayer the realization of the divine promise. 'Suddenly there appeared to them parted tongues as it were of fire . . . and they were all filled with the Holy Spirit.' Such was the fact, but it is only a beginning. . . . How often during his mortal life had the Savior spoken of this Paraclete whose task it would be to bring to fruition all the seeds that he had sown in souls and in the world. 'The Paraclete, whom the Father will send in my name, will teach you all things and bring all things to your mind, whatsoever I shall have said to you.'[53] He will console, sanctify, enlighten and strengthen the disciples. In fine, the whole work of Christ is placed in his hands. Being a work of boundless love, it was fitting that it should be attributed to the Third Person of the

[48] Cf. Rom 1: 6.
[49] Rom 5: 5.
[50] Rom 8: 17.
[51] Jn 1: 12.
[52] Jn 3: 5. [53] Jn 14: 26.

Blessed Trinity as being peculiarly his—to that Person who proceeds as the term of the eternal and substantial love of Father and Son. Present in all things, filling all things with his essence and his activity, scattering with creative gesture life and being, sustaining all things and conducting them to their full development, God will exercise henceforth in human souls *a new kind of action* which will begin on earth and be consummated in heaven. Being an operation external to the divine essence, it belongs to the Three Persons. But it is to the Eternal Love that belongs the glory of this action. And as the leaf though appearing on the branch does not cease to belong to the tree and live on its sap, so the supernatural operation of God in souls does not cease to belong to the whole Trinity of Divine Persons, though it be appropriated to the Holy Spirit as his own characteristic operation." [54]

[54] P. A. M. Libert, O.P., *L'esprit du Christ en nous.*

8

The Holy Spirit—the Soul's Delightful Guest

THE preceding chapter has been devoted to a study of the part played by the Holy Spirit in the soul to which he has been sent. The considerations there developed have not exhausted all the meaning contained in this theological expression—"mission" of the Holy Spirit. Much remains still to be said. Having studied this great mystery of faith in the aspect that regards the *action* of the Creator, it now remains to consider it from the point of view of the *reaction* of the creature. It is necessary to have recourse once again to that passage from the *Summa Theologica* of St. Thomas to which reference has already frequently been made. Those few brief and unadorned sentences contain an inexhaustible wealth of meaning. It is also true to say that it demands the sustained, combined and laborious efforts of the theologians of every school to make these close-packed phrases yield up their treasures of doctrine.

The article in question, in the usual calm, restrained, unemotional manner of the great theologian, deals with the multiple aspects of one of the most sublime and most mysterious truths in the whole supernatural system, namely, the mission, and the consequent indwelling, of the Holy Spirit in the justified soul. For the Holy Spirit not only is sent to the soul in the way already explained, he is also said to make it his dwelling. The words of St. Thomas are: "Inasmuch as the rational creature, in virtue of its acts of knowledge and love, attains God by its operation,[1] God, according to that special mode (viz., of the creature's relations to the Divinity), is said not only to be present in the rational creature, but even to *dwell therein as in his temple*. . . . In the very gift of sanctifying grace, the Holy Spirit is possessed by and dwells in a man."[2] What is the significance, what is the import, of this indwelling of God in the soul? The answer to this question will be better understood when the way has been prepared for it by an exposition of certain incomplete and inadequate conceptions of the nature of this great mystery of our faith. What the indwelling is will be more clearly grasped when we have pointed out what it is not.

---

[1] Attention has been already called to the unsatisfactory vagueness of this phrase—"attains God by its operation." The vagueness is only in the English translation. There is none in the corresponding Latin. "The creature envelops God in himself in its operation" might be a more accurate rendering, but it needs a corrective. To envelop would mean literally to enclose perfectly, to take in in its totality the object enveloped. That would mean, in this connection, to comprehend. Now, comprehension of God is possible only for God himself. The creature cannot comprehend God—it can only *apprehend* him. It can apprehend the *totality* that is God, but not *totally*. "*Cognoscit totum sed non totaliter.*" With this corrective applied, "envelop God in its operation" would be admitted as a version of *attingi ad Deum*.

[2] *S. Th.* I, q. 43, a. 3.

The soul in grace reflects the face of God. It is a created likeness of him as he is in himself. In the mysterious processes of the origins of life an analogy is to be found for the relations that are established between the soul and God by justification. As the parent transmits form and features to his child, so God, in an analogical manner, traces a resemblance of himself in the soul that he brings to a new birth in grace. And as the father (speaking figuratively) lives in his son, so might God be said to live in the creature that he has made his child and heir. St. John writes: "Behold what manner of charity the Father hath bestowed upon us that we should be called and should be children of God."[3] "The soul beautified by sanctifying grace is the living image of God."[4] If then there is sought an explanation of the difference between the mode of the presence of the Creator in the creature due to the divine omnipresence and that which is due to the effects of sanctifying grace, it might readily seem to be explained by the existence of this impress of the likeness of God in the soul. By the figure of speech known as metonymy, God could be said to be where his image is, and this would be a manner of presence quite special and different from the ordinary or universal mode of the divine presence in the soul. This would be attributing to God that which properly belongs to the image of God.

In a similar manner, and in much the same sense, God might be thought to be in the soul in the special way signified by inhabitation because of the gifts of inestimable value which he bestows on it in the process of sanctification. "He hath given us most great and precious promises,"[5] says St. Peter. Just as in the foregoing consideration what was proper to the image of God was attributed to God himself, so from this latter point of view it might easily seem admissible that, by a similar transference of meaning, God should be said to be present in the soul in these his gifts.[6]

Again color would seem to be given to this view, namely, that the "inhabitation" is not to be taken in a literal sense, by a turn of phrase that is common in modern spiritual writings and finds its justification in the epistles of St. Paul. Interior souls are taught to find a great aid to close imitation of our divine Savior, and a powerful impetus toward self-effacement in action, in the idea of Jesus dwelling in them. This is a thought that is characteristic of the theology of St. Paul. He prays for the Ephesians that Christ *may dwell by faith in their hearts,*[7] and to the Corinthians he writes: "Know you not your own selves that *Christ Jesus is in you.*"[8] There is a close parallel to this in the epistle to the Romans: "Now if any man have not the Spirit of Christ, he is none of his. *And if Christ is in you,* the body

---

[3] 1 Jn 3: 1; cf. Rom 8: 16–17.
[4] *S. Th.* I, q. 93, a. 4.
[5] 2 Pet 1: 4.
[6] St. Thomas stigmatizes as erroneous the opinion that in grace not the Holy Spirit himself, in person, is given, but his gifts.
[7] Eph 3: 17.
[8] 2 Cor 13: 5.

indeed is dead because of sin, but the spirit liveth because of justification."[9] If in these texts Christ is considered under the aspect of his divinity (though this is not, as seems certain, an admissible interpretation of these passages), then St. Paul is to be understood as merely referring to the doctrine of the indwelling of the Blessed Trinity with special application to the Divine Word. But if Jesus is considered under the aspect of his sacred humanity (and this appears to be the only reasonable interpretation to be assigned to the texts cited), then it is clear that there cannot be question of a physical presence of Christ in the Christian.

Christ is in the Christian inasmuch as Jesus and those bound to him by faith form one Mystical Body, sharing the same supernatural life. The formation of this Mystical Body was the fruit of the Passion. The sacred humanity of Jesus is physically only in heaven, in the Blessed Sacrament, and in the communicant for a short period of time following communion. If he is said to be present in the Christian, then, apart from these few moments following the reception of the Blessed Eucharist, it can only mean that he is there by the influence of his grace. He is said to be in the soul inasmuch as he is exercising in it a formative and assimilative effect. He is there because the action of the grace that flows from him is to change the inner dispositions of the soul and fashion them to a likeness to the dispositions of his own most holy soul. When St. Paul cries out in a well-known passage: "I live, now not I; but Christ liveth in me,"[10] he simply means that the work of sanctification has made such progress in his soul that its every movement has been brought under the control of divine grace and that natural motives and tendencies have been completely eliminated. His words are equivalent to saying that in all that he thinks, determines, speaks and does he is ruled by the Spirit of Christ.[11]

Yet no one of these modes of presence just enumerated verifies all that is implied by the term "inhabitation" or "indwelling." It is clear from the words of Scripture and from the teaching of St. Thomas that it is not a question of a mere moral or figurative presence of the Holy Spirit in the justified soul. For instance, in the epistle to the Romans may be read the words: "The charity of God is poured forth in our hearts by the Holy Spirit who is given to us."[12] In this text there is a clear distinction drawn between the effect, namely, created charity attributed to the Holy Spirit, and the cause, that is, the Holy Spirit himself; and both the one and the other are stated to be *possessed* by the soul. St. Thomas develops this thought and seems anxious—if we judge by the manner of his phrasing—to leave no room for doubt that he understands "indwelling" in the literal

[9] Rom 8: 9–10; cf. 2 Cor 5: 17.

[10] Gal 2: 20.

[11] It is significant that in these texts and in all similar ones—with one doubtful exception (2 Cor 13: 5)—St. Paul uses the words "Christ Jesus" and not "Jesus Christ." This points to the conclusion that in the context in each instance he is thinking in terms of the Mystical Body and the union of Christ and Christians in that Body. The presence means that union. The union is a question of vital influence based on faith and perfected by charity (cf. Prat, *Théologie de Saint Paul*, vol. 2, pp. 359–362).

[12] Rom 5: 5.

sense of the term. There is perceptible a kind of iteration, a turning back on and a resumption of his words that is unusual with him and is a departure from his customary concision and brevity. He says: "It is only when we can freely use and enjoy a thing that we are said to have it; but it is by reason of sanctifying grace that we can have the fruition of the Divine Persons. However, in the very gift of sanctifying grace the Holy Spirit is *possessed by*, and dwells in, a man. Hence the Holy Spirit is given and sent."[13] There can be no doubt that for St. Thomas the indwelling is understood to mean being present in a place, in a way which is real, substantial and physical.[14] Although those modes of presence which derive their nature from the action of God on the soul, either in the work of ordinary conservation or in the production of effects of grace, can be very intimate, they can never verify the idea expressed by the term "inhabitation." A person may be present in a place and yet in no sense be said to dwell there. Travellers are successively present under many roofs but dwell only at home. God is present in all things by essence, presence and power. He can be in a still more intimate way even in sinners, enlightening their intelligences and moving their wills by actual graces. But he "inhabits" exclusively the souls of the just.

All the inadequate views of the mystery of the indwelling are inadequate because those who hold these views consider that the particularity of the divine presence, due to grace, is based on the special nature of God's action on the soul in the work of justification and sanctification. But the mode of presence consequent on sanctifying grace is what it is, not because God is effecting in the creature a work of surpassing power and goodness, but because of the energy that results in the soul from this work. The soul is not merely a passive recipient of God's action. It does not receive it as the marble receives the stroke of the sculptor's chisel. It develops a vitality of a supernatural kind as God's work on it progresses. It reacts to the action of God. It develops life under that divine action. Habitual grace gives to the soul a power of reaction which makes it capable of holding God vitally—of possessing him—of having him as its own. It is not in virtue of the action of God but of the consequent reaction of the soul that the latter is made the temple of God.[15] If, for instance, the marble on which Michelangelo worked developed life as well as form under the strokes of his chisel; and if, instead of a lifeless statue, a living thing of radiant beauty emerged from the shapeless block on which his genius wrought; and if that living thing of beauty, the

---

[13] S. Th. I, q. 43, a. 3 c.

[14] The term "physical" is opposed to "moral." A ruler, for instance, is said to be morally present where the effects of his power are felt. He is physically present when he is there in his own person.

[15] Botanists tell of a flower which, when a certain substance is placed on it, folds its petals around that substance and then absorbs it into itself. Assimilation completed, the plant again unfolds its petals. Divine grace endows the soul with a quality which bears an analogy to that virtue in the flower which enables it to envelop the foreign element in the embrace of its petals. Grace enables the soul to enfold the Holy Spirit in its embrace.

perfect reflex of the artist's mind, recognizing in the artist the author of the life and beauty that it possessed, were to enfold him in its embrace in an act of loving recognition and gratitude, we would have an image of what is meant by saying that it is in virtue of the soul's power of reaction given by grace that God is said to dwell in the soul. Of course, the comparison falls short of the reality as every comparison must, for though the statue clasped the sculptor in its embrace, it is but by a figurative use of language that the artist would be said to *dwell* in its arms.

To seize the full import of what is meant by the "inhabitation" of the Holy Spirit in the soul it is necessary to consider it in its relation to the whole supernatural system. To consider the mystery of the indwelling by itself in an isolated manner is necessarily to expose oneself to a vague and incomplete notion of it. To understand the supernatural system, it is necessary to have a clear and accurate knowledge of what that system is meant to lead to—in other words, of man's supernatural destiny. Of course, every Christian knows that he is destined for heaven. All know that heaven is a place of everlasting bliss. But it is quite another thing to know in what the life of heaven consists and what relation, if any, it bears to the life here below. Not a great number realize the internal and intrinsic connection that exists for the just between the life here and the life hereafter. As a child one is taught to think of earth as a place of trial and heaven as a reward of the trial successfully borne. This idea is true as far as it goes. It is one that appealed to St. Paul himself. "Know you not that they that run in the race, all run indeed, but one receiveth the prize? So run that you may obtain it. And everyone that striveth for the mastery refraineth himself from all things; and they indeed that they may receive a corruptible crown, but we an incorruptible one."[16] The Christian life presents itself to the imagination of the Apostle as a stern conflict to which is assigned a glorious reward, if one emerges victorious.[17]

The notions of contest and reward attached to success in contest are familiar to us. They are invested with a multiplicity of associations derived from the experiences of ordinary life. In the struggles which we witness, the prize or premium is something of a nature totally distinct from that of the efforts put forth to win the prize. A man, for instance, gains the supremacy in a struggle that calls forth vigor of mind or strength of body and is awarded some valuable object in gold or silver for his success. The bestowal of a disc of precious metal is an ordinary way of rewarding prowess in intellectual or athletic contests. This is regarded as a normal thing, and such rewards are greatly coveted by the contesting parties. Yet there is no natural or intrinsic relation between the premium and the effort it rewards. An object of gold or silver has no affinity to a human activity of mind or body. Now, by association of images, notions of reward derived from earthly trials of skill and endurance are transferred to the spiritual arena. Life is regarded as a struggle in which the Christian soul armed with

---

[16] I Cor 9: 24–25.
[17] Cf. Eph 6: 15–17; I Thess 5: 8.

grace contends against the seductions of the world, the onslaughts of Satan and the uprisings of sensuality. God is looked upon as the impartial arbiter of the contest, who, it is true, desires a successful issue for us and furnishes us with the means to come forth triumphant from the struggle. Heaven is looked upon as a reward which bears proportionately the same external relation to the factors that make for success in the Christian combat as the trophies of gold or silver bear to energies of intellect or limb. This is a view of things which needs correction.

In the spiritual field of combat the connection between praiseworthy action and its reward is not external, arbitrary or conventional. It is internal, intrinsic and the outcome of the efforts which have earned it. Meritorious action in the supernatural sphere is action inspired by divine charity, that is, love of God. Every action done for the motive of pleasing God merits a reward. And that reward consists in an infusion of grace and charity—a further infusion of the supernatural vitality from which sprang the meritorious act. If a man contending with another in a race of speed and being successful were rewarded by an increase of the physical powers which give him victory, one would have an image of what takes place in the world of grace. Successful action in that world is "grace-full" action. It is rewarded by a further infusion of grace, the effect of which is to make possible, normally speaking, action still more vigorous with the vitality of grace. The reward of grace-full action is more grace. It always remains a reward freely given by God, the arbiter in the spiritual combat—for grace is not generated from within by meritorious action; it is always infused from without.

As on earth the reward of each act done in charity is more grace, so the recompense of a whole life lived according to God's plan is yet more grace, but grace that now has flowered into its final state, in the "light of glory." The light of glory (which is God's reward to man for having lived the good life) is simply the full evolution or the perfect fruit of grace, just as the flower or fruit is the final issue of the vital and fecund activity of the plant. The recompense of a life truly Christian is not something fundamentally different from the Christian life itself, but that very life carried to the point of its final development. Grace, as it is said, blossoms into glory. "The exercise of the theological virtues (i.e., faith, hope and charity) constitutes a life of a sublime kind ... and the recompense of this life presents itself in the normal development and the crowning perfection of the present existence which postulates this recompense and tends toward it, of itself." [18]

The life of grace then is substantially the same during time and eternity. The existence of the blessed in heaven bears to the existence of the just on earth the relation of the perfect to the imperfect, the relation of the stage of full and final development to the stage of growth and progress. To know the nature of anything properly, it must, Aristotle tells us, be studied in its perfect state. [19] To gain a knowledge of the vital force and the properties of

[18] *Vie Spirituelle,* vol. I (October 1919–March 1920), 84.

[19] Aristotle, *Politics,* bk. I, chap. 2. Nature implies complete development, as the nature of a thing, e.g., of a man, a house, or a horse, may be defined to be its condition when the process of production is complete.

the seedling we must study it in the perfectly developed plant that is the seedling come to maturity. The inhabitation of the Holy Spirit in the soul is not something in the supernatural life that is peculiar to earth; it belongs also to heaven, only in a more perfect form, according to the words of our Lord to his disciples at the Last Supper: "In that day [of eternity] you shall know that I am in the Father, and you in me and *I in you.*" [20] This must be so since the "inhabitation" is one of the essential elements of the supernatural life. The indwelling of the Holy Spirit in the soul on earth is a direct consequence of grace; the indwelling of the Holy Spirit in the souls of the blessed is a consequence of the light of glory. The former is, in its essence, the same as the latter, but with the limitations and restrictions that cling to the life of faith.

Here below we harbor within us the Divine Guest, whom we must contemplate confusedly through a glass. In heaven we shall behold him within us unveiled—"face to face." [21] Pope Leo XIII points out this truth in his great encyclical on the Holy Spirit. He writes: "This wonderful union, which is properly called indwelling, differs only in degree or state from that with which God beatifies the saints in heaven." [22] The beatific vision is the culminating point of the supernatural life infused into us at baptism. The beatific vision has as its immediate and proper effect the "indwelling" of the Blessed Trinity in its perfect and final form. The indwelling of the Holy Spirit in the souls of the just on earth is the beatific vision in embryo. To grasp what is implied by the former, all that is needed is to study that mode of presence of God in the soul which is the consequence of the beatific vision. From a doctrinal study of the "indwelling" in its perfect state can be gathered a clear notion of what it is in its initial and imperfect state.

To expound in simple language, free from technicalities, in what the beatific vision consists is not very easy. But the difficulty of this exposition should not deter one from trying to give to the ordinary reader as clear a notion as possible of the wonderful destiny that awaits those who, dying in the state of grace, are admitted to the kingdom of God. The difficulty in this matter is somewhat diminished by the fact that each one can find in his own intellectual activity a faint image of what takes place when God is seen intuitively in the beatific vision.

The formation of the idea in the ordinary processes of thought furnishes us with an analogy from which we can rise to some apprehension of what is meant by seeing God face to face. From an analysis of what is involved in acquiring a clear idea of any object of thought, we can dimly perceive what is implied in the soul's seeing God.

We are commonly said to "grasp" a thing when it is properly understood. The term "grasp," which everyone uses quite naturally, though metaphorical, expresses accurately what takes place in the acquisition of knowledge. The metaphor is drawn from the act of closing the hand on

[20] Jn 14: 20.
[21] 1 Cor 13: 12.
[22] Encyclical *Divinum munus,* May 1897.

an object and thus making it one's possession. When the nature of a thing is perceived by the mind, that is, when the intellect has seen what the thing is, that thing becomes truly "present to" and "in" the mind. A teacher says that he is trying to get things into the heads of his pupils—this is another way of expressing the same notion. A master in any art is said to "possess" his subject perfectly. That means to say that the objects of his particular branch of study, in their ultimate structure, in their properties and in their mutual relations, are in his intelligence. They are there, of course, not in their material concrete reality, not in that form of existence which they have as lying under his eyes or as taken up in his hands. Nevertheless, when a thing is understood, it has a true existence in the mind. It exists in one manner outside the mind: it exists in another manner in the mind. That is clear even to a person unversed in philosophy, because it is implied in the ordinary turns of speech. "To apprehend" is simply to lay hold of, to seize, to grasp, to get a grip of by the mind—"apprehend" being a word of Latin origin similar in meaning to these ordinary English terms.

The existence of a thing in the mind as compared to its existence outside, might seem, in hasty consideration, to be a very shadowy and unsubstantial kind of existence. The statue or picture in the artist's mind might be thought to be not so valuable as the same statue or picture existing in the materials that the artist or painter makes use of. The statue or picture might seem to be "present" in a more "real" way in the exhibition hall than in the artistic faculties of its author. This, however, is not so. Every true artist feels the limitations imposed on him by the material on which he labors. He knows (and this causes in him a species of artistic frenzy and despair) that the masterpiece, as existing in his mind, can never be realized in matter in its full perfection.

Now, in the acquisition of knowledge we have a reversal of the process observable in creative art. In artistic production the object existing in the artist's mind passes from the ideal mode of existence (that is, the existence in thought and imagination) to the material mode of existence and suffers in its passage a certain diminution in reality. In the act of understanding, on the other hand, the object passes from the material world into the ideal world. That which was present in matter and continues to be present there under the limitations imposed by matter passes into the spiritual world, the world of intelligence, and is there freed from all the limitations of material existence. The picture on canvas is fixed and definite: it can never have any more perfection than it has as it issues completed from the hands of the artist. It cannot develop any further beauty or acquire any more perfection of form or coloring. The masterpiece as it exists in the artist's mind is capable of finding ever more and more perfect expression. It may give birth in picture after picture on the same theme, each bearing a closer resemblance to the thought which gives it origin. The picture is more "really" present in the artist's mind than it is in the pigments and the canvas, because it is present in a more vital way and endowed with an immense dynamic energy.

When a mathematical principle expressed on a printed page passes, when studied, into the mind of a man gifted with mathematical genius, that principle becomes instinct with a kind of life. It begins to originate and effect new combinations between what were hitherto scattered items of mathematical knowledge. Were a man perfect in the science of mechanics, the bridge constructed in his thought would be completely perfect. Before being made actual in terms of steel and masonry, it preexists in the mind of the engineer. There it is free from all the flaws and limitations it carries with it in the world of matter. These limitations spring from the defects inherent in the materials that the constructor has to employ in building.

Now all this is to show that a thing existing outside the mind, in the world of things, can enjoy a higher though different existence in the mind by which it is properly understood. And because the mind lays hold of the object, seizes it, draws it into itself and bestows on it its own spiritual mode of being, the word "grasp" is used to designate the act of cognition. The term "see" is commonly used in the same sense, by a figure of speech based upon the act of bodily vision. The activity of the intellect in apprehending its object is likened to vision because it bears a certain analogy to the action of the eye in seeing. Owing to the vitality of the visual faculty, a colored object effects in the animated organ of vision a likeness of itself. It is in virtue of that similitude in the living organic faculty that the object is seen. It becomes present in the eye in the act of vision. In a somewhat similar manner the object of the intelligence becomes present in the intelligence and is vitally held, possessed or grasped by it, in virtue of the act of intellectual vision. The mind lays hold, as it were, of its object, in the intellectual act of seeing what it is, that is, in understanding it. The mind "seizes" or "grasps" its object in "seeing" it.

In this intellectual process of apprehension we have a faint parallel with what takes place in the beatific vision. If, instead of created things, God himself, in the full and glowing splendor of his reality, is the object that is presented to the human mind for its contemplation; if, moreover, that uncreated object becomes present *in the mind* in all the reality that it has *outside the mind,* then in this one has an idea of what takes place in the vision face to face. *For beatitude is nothing else than the spiritual possession of the divine reality.* It seems to us that a thing could not be more fully in our possession than when we hold it firmly grasped in our hands as our own. Yet this possession, from the point of view of perfection, falls short of that which is realized when an object in all its physical reality—in all the reality it has—becomes present in, and therefore possessed by, the intellectual faculty.[23]

---

[23] The following passage from Maritain will shed further light on this exposition: "Knowledge," he says, "draws all forms of things, all the good of things, into our soul, but stripped of their own proper (i.e., extra-mental) mode of existence and reduced to the condition of being objects of thought. Present in us, grasped as it were in us, but according to a mode of being essentially incomplete, they demand a further complement. They generate in us forces of gravity, that is, the desire to enter into relation with

The intellect, in "seizing" or "grasping" its object, does not hold it in its concrete, extra-mental reality. It holds it in, and by means of, an idea only. The object in its physical reality eludes the grasp of the intellect. In heaven it is otherwise. There the vision of God by the soul consists in the soul laying hold of and taking into itself that reality which is God. It apprehends God literally, and by this act God in person becomes present *in the soul*, not merely *to the soul.* An object that is understood is present to the mind but in its physical reality is not in the mind; but God, when seen in glory, becomes physically present in the soul. It is in this respect that there is a profound and fundamental difference between the effect of the act of vision exercised under the influence of the light of glory and that exercised under the influence of the natural light of the intelligence in the act of intellectually apprehending an object here on earth. In ordinary earthly knowledge it is but the idea of a thing, its mental image, its species or ideal form (as the philosophers call it), that is actually in the mind. If God were present in the beatified intellect only in this way, there would be no beatific vision. For no mental created form, no idea produced by a created intellect, no matter how perfect, could reveal God or make him present to the mind as he is in himself. Nothing short of God himself can express or represent God adequately. Any created mental image of the divine must necessarily fall infinitely short of representing the divine uncreated reality. If then we were limited to knowing God in the very same way as we know the things about us here below, that is, by means of ideas of them, we should never come to know God personally—know him in the same way as he knows himself.

There would be a manifold incompleteness in that knowledge of God. Our knowledge of things about us, though necessarily abstract, can be adequate. We can really know these things in their own nature by means of the ideas we derive from them. But the ideas which we could naturally form of God would necessarily be all drawn from created material things —and though we submit these ideas to a process of purification and "infinitation," still they could give us nothing but a poor, indirect and analogical notion of God. If then a creature is to apprehend God as he is in himself, that is, in his own nature and not merely in the effects of his creative power, God himself in his own being must be in the intellect. The divine essence itself must fulfill with regard to the creature's intellect the role of idea. In other words, if we are to enjoy the intuitive vision of God (see God as he is in himself), God himself, in all his reality and not in a representative form, no matter how perfect, must be present in the soul as completely and as really as the idea of a thing we understand is in our mind. The soul cannot see or grasp or hold or possess God (all these

---

these objects in their own proper mode of existence, of possessing them no longer in idea but in reality. Love, taking its rise in the soul (from knowledge), impels the soul toward a real union (as opposed to a merely ideal union) which the intelligence left to its own resources cannot procure except in case of the vision of God" (*Les Degrés du Savoir,* chap. I, p. 14).

expressions mean the same thing) unless *God himself* is the image in which God is seen or "seized" by the intellect.

"Dearly beloved," writes St. John, "we are now children of God; and it hath not yet appeared what we shall be, but we know that, when he shall appear, we shall be like to him, because we shall see him as he is." [24] These words of the apostle demonstrate that the beatific vision consists in our seeing God after the manner in which God sees himself. That vision of God by himself constitutes God's possession of himself, possession of all that is worth possessing: all truth, all good, all beauty. By that vision God is in possession of all the divine riches—all the divine resources, all the wealth of God's kingdom. We are heirs to God's estate. "Heirs of God, and joint heirs with Christ." [25] It is in the seeing of God that we enter into our inheritance, that we possess our property. The only adequate idea or image of God—equal to the Godhead itself in all things—is the Word of God, the Second Person of the Blessed Trinity, "who," as St. Paul says, "is the brightness of his glory and the figure of his substance." [26] Since the Word of God can be called the effulgence, the flashing forth, the eternal revelation of the splendors of the Divinity, the aptness of the words of Scripture—"in thy light we shall see light" [27]—becomes clear. Though it is the divine essence itself, fulfilling the role of idea, that God is seen in the facial vision, this role is, by the law of appropriation, attributed to the Word [28] of God: "The Son," writes the Venerable Libermann, "gives himself to our soul in his *essential light,* by means of which we grasp the Divinity in its essence and so face to face." [29]

To give a yet clearer understanding of all this, a further point of difference must be noted between the presence of the idea in the mind in the natural act of comprehension and the presence of God in the soul in the beatific vision. The idea in which we perceive an object is not to be understood as something that is substantively distinct from the intellect in which it exists. It is not as distinct from the intellect, for instance, as the ink used in writing is from the pen with which one writes. It bears much the same relation to the intellect in which it inheres as health does to the body which is healthy. The idea is an intellectual condition of the mind as health is a corporeal condition of the body. Or again, to use another illustration, the taste of an orange is not the orange; it has not an existence independent from that of the orange. The taste cannot be separated from and exist apart from the orange. If the fruit is destroyed, the taste of the fruit is destroyed with it; whereas the seeds can be extracted from the fruit and the fruit remains essentially what it was. Now, the idea is to the intellect in much the same relation as

[24] 1 Jn 3: 2.
[25] Rom 8: 17.
[26] Heb 1: 3.
[27] Ps 36: 9.
[28] The term "divine word" is equivalent to the "divine idea," which is the adequate intellectual expression or enunciation of *what God is.*
[29] Ven. Libermann, *Ecrits spirituels,* p. 16.

the taste bears to the orange, and not in the relation that the seeds bear to it.[30] God's presence in the soul in the intuitive vision is not to be understood in the former of these two modes, but in the literal sense in which one substance is in another substance and distinct from it. As literally as the pen is held by the hand that writes with it, is God held and possessed by and in the soul that sees him intuitively. The possession is without comparison more perfect in the latter case than in the former.

There is no parallel in nature to the closeness and intimacy of this union between the creature and the Creator—it is far closer than that which exists between the child in its mother's womb and the mother that bears it. In heaven the union between Mary and the divinity of Jesus Christ is far more intimate than was her union with the sacred humanity when the Word was made flesh in her womb. The fervor of possession enjoyed by the mother who clasps her infant to her bosom is but a feeble reflex of the fervor of possession enjoyed by the soul in bliss as it clasps God to itself in that spiritual embrace which is the act of intuitive vision. We can form no idea of what it means to have one spiritual substance in another and possessed by that other; for such "in-ness" is possible only to God. Only he can be *in* and *possessed by* a spiritual being. Such a union cannot exist between angel and angel. Our mind does not embrace the idea in it, because, as has been explained, the idea is not a substantive thing distinct from the mind. The mind cannot embrace the object external to itself in the extra-mental world in the concrete reality it has in that world. It "grasps" or "apprehends" its object (in the literal sense of apprehend) only in the idea it has of that object. But in heaven the soul can and does actually embrace the Idea in which it sees the Divinity, because that Idea is nothing else than the Divine Substance itself or, by appropriation, the Living Word of God.[31]

When by the act of intelligence which the soul is able to elicit by aid of the light of glory (which is nothing else but divine grace in its final perfection) God is caught in the embrace of his own creature, the will of the creature surges up in a great wave of love for, and delight in, and satisfaction with the Infinite Good thus made present in it and constituted its possession. These two acts—the act of vision and the act of love—constitute infinite beatitude, for they reproduce in finite measure in the created spirit the very life of the Blessed Trinity itself. That life expresses itself in the intuitive vision of, and infinite satisfaction in, the divine

---

[30] In the language of philosophy, the relation of the taste to the orange is the relation of accident to substance: the relation of the seeds to the orange is the relation of substance to substance.

[31] Cf. Maritain, *Les Degrés du Savoir,* chap. 1: "By the Beatific Vision the soul becomes God 'intentionaliter' (that is, according to the mode of being proper to an intelligible object), not substantially. But it is united to him by a real union (*unio secundum rem*) since it is by the infinite essence of God itself actuating the intelligence in the intelligible order and without the aid of any intermediate form, that the soul holds him and sees him. The intelligence supernaturalized by the light of glory is thus as it were the hand by which the blessed hold God."

essence—the Infinite Good. In heaven, God, in the fullest as well as in the most accurate sense of the term, inhabits, that is, dwells in the soul. The inhabitation is the immediate consequence of, and results from, the acts of the intelligence and the will exercised on the Godhead. *The indwelling of God in the soul in heaven is due to the vital acts of knowledge and love that the soul, strengthened by the light of glory, is enabled to elicit. The indwelling is to be assigned, then, not to the action of God on the soul, but to the action of the soul on God, in knowing him and loving him.* Similarly, the indwelling of the Holy Spirit in the soul during its time of trial in this world is based on and due to the acts of the soul exercised on him.

For all that is verified in the "state of glory" in heaven can be applied proportionately to the "state of grace" on earth. Here on earth we are in the condition of wayfarers who have not yet arrived at their journey's end—that end being the life of the Blessed Trinity to be lived by us in a finite degree. As every forward step on a journey is a partial arriving at the goal, so that life of the Blessed Trinity lived by the soul in heaven has some beginning for us here below. While awaiting the facial vision, we have to be content with the dim vision of faith. "We see now through a glass in a dark manner." [32] But imperfect though this vision is, it is, nevertheless, a vision, and a vision of nothing less than the Divinity itself. The human reason, even if raised to an incalculable degree of perfection along the lines of its own natural capacities, could never know anything of the intimate nature of God. It could never see him except externally, that is, in the works of his hands. But when the same intellect is vivified by the divine infused virtue of faith, it has this power of knowing God in his own inner nature and life. Of course, the knowing of God here and the knowing of him hereafter present a difference.

In heaven we know him clearly, because we know him by an idea which is an adequate expression of him. On earth we know him only indistinctly, because in apprehending him we are obliged to use ideas which have a human origin. It is to be remarked that in the most consummate natural knowledge of God our ideas would not only be derived from created things, but would always remain ideas of created things. In the knowledge of faith, our ideas of God, though formed *from* created objects, are not *of* created objects. They are ideas which are of God himself in his own reality, though, of course, they must reveal him very darkly and inadequately. For instance, we derive the ideas of fatherhood, sonship, nature, personality, etc., from the objects that fall under our experience and then, enlightened by faith, apply them to God. To express the inner life of God to ourselves we are obliged to use these terms. We know that they do not attach to God in the very same sense as they do to created things. We know that they may be used in reference to him only in a proportionate manner and purged of all the limitations and imperfections with which they are verified in creatures. We only know that whatever is implied of perfection in these ideas is applicable to God in an eminent and infinite manner. God is a person, but

---

[32] I Cor 13: 12.

supereminently a person. But in spite of the inadequacy of these ideas it is the Godhead itself—the Divine Substance, though robed and disguised in these veils of earth—that faith contemplates through these earth-woven veils.[33]

Were God seen clearly with undimmed vision, it would be impossible not to love him. It is because there is this full and clear vision in heaven that love goes out necessarily and indefectibly from the soul to God. But when the Divine Being comes to us in the wrappings and disguise of faith, the brightness and attractiveness of the infinite good is concealed from us. It is clothed in the material garb of human concepts, and consequently love does not follow with inevitable necessity on this vision. We can know that infinite loveliness belongs to that object which is present to our understanding, but for us the loveliness is hidden beneath earth-born ideas. Not being unveiled to us, it does not exercise its absolutely compelling spell on us. We must walk in the obscurity of faith. Our trial consists in loving what we do not see, in stretching out our hands in hope toward what is not seen.[34]

God is in everything, as was pointed out, because wherever anything is, there God must be. But when the creature enjoys a merely natural existence it can never realize God's presence in it. Man, endowed with reason, may know by reasoning that God is in the depths of his being; but he can never realize that presence. God is present in the soul which has faith without charity. His presence in it is more intimate than it is in creatures in whom there is no vestige of supernatural life. He is in the soul that has the faith not only as sustaining that soul in existence but also as producing in it the infused supernatural virtue of faith. In the soul in which charity is dead but faith and hope linger, God is present in a mode which lies between the mode of mere omnipresence and that which is named inhabitation and is distinct from both. When the soul is in sin but still preserves the infused virtues of faith and hope,[35] it can continue to know God as he is in himself, God as the source and author of the supernatural life. God, as the God not of philosophy but of revelation, remains under the gaze of the soul, but that gaze is dull, unheeding, cold and uninterested when faith is divorced from charity. God himself is present *with* the soul but not present *to* the soul. It is just as when in a crowded apartment our eyes rest on individuals there present who mean nothing to us; we see, in a certain sense, without seeing.

---

[33] By reason we could know God only in those attributes that are manifested in the works of creation. By faith we know the very inner nature of God. Our *mode* of knowing in each case is the same; *what* we know is not the same. The content of the object of knowledge in the two cases is different. In both cases, however, we have to use ideas drawn from created things. But never could we, through any knowledge of God acquired by our unaided reason, come to apply to God the ideas of paternity, sonship, divine procession, one nature communicated to Three Distinct Persons, etc. These words stand for notions drawn from created objects, but unless taught by faith, we should never know that they find their application in describing the inner life of God.

[34] Cf. Rom 8: 24–25.

[35] These virtues in such a soul are said by the theologians to be "formless"—that is, not informed (animated) by the life of charity.

On such occasions the act of vision is merely physical: there is no soul contact or interest accompanying it. It is only when, among the crowd, our glance lights on one in whom we are interested or to whom we are bound by the bonds of affection, that we can be said, in the full sense of the term, to see the person on whom we fix our eyes.

We see not only with the organ of sight but, in a sense, with our heart and soul as well. Or again, to change the figure, one with whom we are not on friendly terms may happen to find himself for a time in our own home; yet he would not be said to be dwelling with us and sharing our life. This is what happens, in a certain way, in the case of the sinner and God. The Divine Being is in the soul devoid of charity, by essence, presence and power. He is there in a more perfect way than he is in creatures devoid of intelligence or in the souls of infidels, for he comes, in a certain sense, under the gaze of the intelligence, informed as it is by faith. But he is seen as a stranger is, or as an enemy. The soul that sees him holds itself apart and stands aloof from him. God and the soul are from one point of view quite near, but they are, in the realm of supernatural life, very remote one from the other. "The Lord is far from the wicked." [36] They are as near and as remote as two persons standing side by side in a crowd and completely indifferent to each other. There is a spatial or local nearness, nothing more. There is no sympathy, no mutual interest, no love of friendship linking the two together. God does not dwell in such a soul.

But when, following on the infusion of sanctifying grace, there is a "mission" of the Divine Persons to the soul, all is changed. [37] "The charity of God is poured forth in our hearts by the Holy Spirit who is given to us." [38] The Second Person of the Blessed Trinity imparts to the intelligence a participation of his own personal character—*notitia spirans amorem.* He who is the living knowledge of God impresses on the soul that mode of knowing God which generates the desire of drawing closer to that infinite good which is being revealed. The Word of God gives to the soul's glance that animation and that penetration which makes God, from being present *to* us, become present *in* us. The eye of our soul rests now, not on a being to whom we are indifferent, but on One in whom understanding excites interest. The Holy Spirit, in his turn, impresses on the soul the stamp of his personal character, which is love.

In virtue of the mission of these Two Persons, God is contemplated with interest and cherished [39] with love. The soul is no longer passive under the presence of God in it, as are all created things which do not enjoy sanctifying grace. The soul reacts to the presence. God now receives as

---

[36] Prov 15: 29.

[37] In the order of efficient causality, the Blessed Trinity precedes sanctifying grace in the soul; in the order of material causality, their presence follows sanctifying grace. The soul is "disposed" by grace for their presence.

[38] Rom 5: 5.

[39] Attention is drawn to the etymology of the word "cherished." It is the same as the Latin *"carus,"* from which is derived the word *"charitas"*—divine love. It is a word suitable to describe the appropriate effect of the Holy Spirit (who is called *"Charitas Dei"*) in the soul.

well as gives. He is laid hold of and enveloped in the activities of the creature's intellect and will. These faculties, through the infused divine virtues of faith and charity, are endowed with the energy to attain God himself in their acts. God begins to dwell in the soul as one to whom in person the soul cleaves in the bonds of intimate knowledge and affection, no longer as a stranger. *It is, then, in virtue of the activities that the will and the intellect are enabled, through grace, to exercise on God that his presence in the soul becomes indwelling.* And this is the explicit teaching of St. Thomas. He says: "Because a rational creature by knowing and loving (by the knowledge and love that flow from sanctifying grace) attains to God himself, it comes to pass that God according to that special manner of presence (the mode by which what is known is in the knower and what is loved is in the heart of the lover) is said not only to be present in the rational creature but to dwell in it as in his temple."[40]

The infused virtue of charity does not suffer the limitation of faith. By the intelligence operating through faith we tend to impose on the object of our contemplation the limitations inherent in our mode of understanding; by the will operating through charity we tend toward the object loved as it is in itself in its own mode of being. "This same God caught by the glance of faith in obscurity and as it were at a distance—since for the intelligence there is distance where there is not intuitive vision—is seized by love immediately in himself—love as such uniting us heart to heart with that very Person who is hidden in the veils of faith."[41] What faith sees is God, but it sees him enveloped in the forms of the human understanding and obscured by these forms. But the will embraces that object presented to it by the intelligence, and it is the "Veiled God" that it embraces. Seeing by faith is like gazing on a person hidden in the folds of some thick, dark, shapeless and unbecoming vesture, which precludes all possibility of forming a definite mental image of the beauty of form and feature that is hidden under the thick disguise. Therefore, though the object presented to the intelligence through faith is God, the Divine Being himself, still that Being remains at a distance from the intelligence. But charity gives immediate contact with God, for it tends toward what is seen, not after the manner in which it is seen, but as it is in itself. It holds the reality.

God is more intimate to our heart than to our head—that is, in this world. Here below he is united much more perfectly with will than with intellect. Hence the preeminence of charity over the other two theological virtues. "And now there remain faith, hope and charity, these three; but the greatest of these is charity."[42] The directness and immediacy of the

---

[40] *S. Th.* I, q. 43, a. 3. The words that immediately precede those quoted throw further light on the subject. He says: "Beyond and above the common or ordinary manner in which God is in all things [i.e., by presence and power], there is a singular and special manner which belongs exclusively to the rational creature, in which God is said to be present as what is known is present in the knower and what is loved is present in the lover."

[41] Maritain, *Les Degrés du Savoir,* chap. 1, p. 24.

[42] 1 Cor 13: 13.

union with God effected by charity is further shown by its being the one theological virtue that survives death. Faith and hope disappear with vision, but charity abides in heaven substantially the same as it was on earth. "Charity never falleth away; whether prophecies shall be made void, or tongues shall cease, or knowledge shall be destroyed. For we know in part, and we prophecy in part. But when that which is perfect is come, that which is in part shall be done away." [43] A profound knowledge of theology will not effect the indwelling of God in the soul: love alone will do this.

In faith, the dark mists of ideas of created origin interpose themselves between the intellect and its divine object. In the case of charity, no such obstacle exists. It enfolds God in its embrace—or, rather, the will informed by charity does so. Of course, charity does not cause God to be present in the soul as if he were not there already prior to its operation. God is present, by his immensity, in all things; he is present in a more perfect way where there is faith, even though love is absent, than he is in other things. Wherever God is present, he is necessarily present as God and, therefore, in the totality of his being, which is indivisible. *Charity does not make God present, but it completely transforms the nature of the universal presence which the soul shares with all creatures. Under the influence of charity what was a presence of immensity becomes a presence that is an indwelling.* It effects that God, from being a stranger and unobserved, becomes a friend, a welcome guest, a spouse. It transforms the mode by which God is in irrational things to that by which he is present in a dwelling which is lovingly constructed for him and in which he finds himself "at home." [44]

Charity transmutes a merely spatial presence into a vital presence: it changes a closeness of proximity into a closeness of affection. It changes a presence of God in the soul, which was natural, into one that is supernatural and a presence that gave merely human existence into one that imparts a similitude of the existence proper to God. Charity brings it about that a presence that was energetic and effective in the natural order only becomes energetic and effective in the supernatural order. It commutes juxtaposition into intimate union. In the beatific vision God becomes present in the soul in a real, substantial, physical[45] manner; he is held and possessed by the soul through the act by which the intellect strengthened by the "light of glory" is enabled to see God unveiled. He is embraced by the soul in the act of the will which follows this intuitive vision. On earth God "indwells" in the soul when the human intellect strengthened by faith contemplates him in his own nature and the human will informed by divine charity lovingly clings to him whom the soul beholds in faith.

God dwells in the soul in grace, because the soul by its acts of faith and love builds a spiritual tabernacle around him. He is enveloped by and in

---

[43] 1 Cor 13: 8–10.
[44] God is "at home" more or less perfectly in the soul according to the degree of its charity.
[45] In all this matter, the word "physical" is to be understood in its strictly etymological and philosophic sense. It is derived from the Greek word *"physis,"* meaning "nature."

these acts. One recalls the ecstatic words of St. Peter on Mount Tabor: "Lord ... let us make here three tabernacles, one for thee, and one for Moses and one for Elijah." [46] What were wild and incoherent words on the part of Peter on this occasion find a literal fulfillment through the wonders wrought by divine grace. By faith and hope and charity the soul constructs a tabernacle in which God, the Holy Spirit, may dwell. It is a living tabernacle, and its fabric is woven of materials in which are resplendent the green of hope, the white of faith and the royal red of divine charity, and thus

> The smallest portion of this edifice,
> Cornice or frieze, or balustrade or stair,
> The very pavement is made up of life. [47]

It is not, perhaps, fanciful to see in the tabernacle that Moses was commanded to construct for the ark a material symbol of this living tabernacle reared by the activities of divine grace. God dwells with much contentment in this new and immaterial tabernacle because it not only houses him, it also enfolds him in knowledge and love. It shelters him and worships him. One does not "dwell" in an abode to which one is not bound by ties that are enduring and affectionate, ties such as the homestead twines around the hearts of those who are born and spend their lives therein. These ties of affection exist between God and the soul which he by grace makes his dwelling or his home. Unlike the rooftop under which we are born, God's home is a living thing, which can respond to the love that its "Indweller" bears to it by an affection which reciprocates the affection which is extended to it. It is in virtue of the divine charity that springs from sanctifying grace that this living receptacle of God is not a mere abode in which he happens to be present, but a house which it is his delight to make his permanent dwelling.

The Holy Spirit, Divine Charity Subsistent, is the source of all the effects of charity, and it is to him, therefore, that is appropriated the grace of the "indwelling." According to the extent we lend ourselves more perfectly to his operations in us, more flexibly to the movements that he impresses on our spirit, more ardently in love of God, the more we begin to realize the great fact that God is within us, not merely as creator, ruler and judge, but as guest, friend and lover. "For the Spirit himself giveth testimony to our spirit that we are children of God." [48] The indwelling, as being an effect of love, is distinctively appropriated to the Holy Spirit. It is he who is said to inhabit the soul, and, because of this, he is rightly named the "Soul's Delightful Guest."

---

[46] Mt 17: 4.
[47] Newman, *Dream of Gerontius*.
[48] Rom 8: 16.

9

Finger of God's Right Hand

WITHOUT a realization of the fact of the indwelling of the Holy Spirit in the souls of the just and some understanding of the properties, the purpose and the effect of that indwelling, the Christian will have but a very inadequate notion of his sublime vocation. If, among the multitude of Christians, there are so many who walk in a manner unworthy of their high calling, is it not in large measure due to great ignorance of, and to a consequent failure to appreciate, the great dignity and the wonderful privileges which become theirs when they are "born of water and the Holy Spirit"?[1] If they clearly understood and, with that understanding, habitually adverted to the dignity with which they are invested as members of Christ and sharers of his prerogatives, what strength they would find in this intimate realization of what they truly are in the eyes of faith, to resist the allurements of the world, repress the assaults of the flesh and defeat the wiles of Satan. If so many of the faithful live in habitual neglect of God, offend him with but scant compunction and offer only a feeble resistance to the forces of evil, is it not to be attributed, to a considerable extent, to their incomprehension of the relations in which God wills to stand to them? To walk in the path of rectitude demands courage, perseverance and, at times, positive heroism. A dutiful regard for the sovereignty of God, accompanied by a dread of his displeasure, may secure us against straying from the straight and narrow way. But if we are to walk with ease in it and to find the inclination of our will in harmony with our duties, a filial love for God must draw us toward our appointed goal. Without that tender affection we shall endure a perpetual conflict in ourselves as we are torn between what the law of God enjoins and that to which our tastes incline us.

That freedom of movement toward the divine and the absence of all servility in our attitude of obedience to God are, in Scripture, attributed to the action of the Holy Spirit in the soul. This is insinuated by the Apostle, saying, "Where the Spirit of the Lord is, there is liberty."[2] A man is said to be a slave of passion or of sin when, dominated and controlled by evil desires, he is withdrawn from his rightful allegiance to what is his true good. There is still the taint of slavery on him when, laboring under a strong affection for what is but an apparent good and a real evil for him, yet, through fear of consequences, he resists its appeal and adheres to the law of righteousness. He is unshackled completely when his native impulse

[1] Jn 3: 5.
[2] 2 Cor 3: 17.

is all toward what God dictates, when his desires and aspirations are in harmony with what makes for his ultimate good.[3] It is the Holy Spirit, who is the love of God, in person, who impresses this affection for the divine good on the will of man. It is he, whose name—Holy Spirit—implies a rushing forth, a secret, invisible, mysterious, impulsive motion onward, who imparts to the soul this strong, easy and unfettered movement toward God and what is of God. All spiritual experience teaches that the service of the Lord grows easy as love for the Lord grows strong. It is, on the other hand, very burdensome as long as fear, rather than affection, prompts one's activities. If men find it hard to have an inspiring love for their Father in heaven, it is because they understand him so little and, above all, remain so ignorant of his yearning love for them.

Nothing so calls forth affection as the practical experience of another's loving devotedness. There are no joys in life that surpass the joy of knowing that one is the object of deep regard on the part of another—especially if that other is one who cannot be won unless by what is truly lovable. Now God loves the soul in grace with an ardor which is more than a reflex of, for it is an actual participation of, the ardor with which he cleaves to his own transcending loveliness. When faith is poor and weak in the Christian, he has but a very dull perception of this, and, in consequence, his attitude to God is cold. It is in striking contrast to the attitude of God toward him. The Almighty manifests a desire to nestle in the soul he has created, and the soul shows itself cold to his advances or, rather, uncomprehending in face of them.

The average Christian, when the mercy of God is extended to him, has little more comprehension of what takes place than that the burden of his guilt is removed, the danger of eternal loss is avoided, and, if new sins are not incurred, an eternity of contentment is secured. The problems presented by life on earth would not prove so harassing and exasperating for men did they have a more adequate understanding of the supernatural. It is only love for God that can render light the burden of existence and mitigate its pain. That love would come easier to men, if, acquiring a more profound knowledge of the mysteries of their faith and of the purposes of God in their regard than is commonly possessed even by those who are thought well instructed, they realized what the Holy Spirit aims at doing in the soul when he takes up his residence therein. Marvellous and happiness-giving consequences flow from the divine indwelling in the measure in which the Christian cooperates with the action of the Blessed Trinity in the interior of the soul.

For the presence of God is in no sense an inactive presence—neither is it one which is merely transient. It is permanent, loving and enduring. As far as God is concerned, it is proof against all vicissitudes. The initiative in the rupture of the union established between the Creator and the creature is always taken by the creature. God has no desire to quit the soul he has made his dwelling. Quite the contrary. He leaves with reluctance and only

---

[3] Cf. St. Thomas Aquinas, *Summa contra Gentiles*, bk. IV, chap. 22.

when driven from his earthly house by the soul's lapsing into mortal sin. It is with sorrow that the Blessed Trinity utters the fateful words, "let us go forth hence," when their temple has been defiled and profaned by guilt. But as long as the soul submits to the divine commandments, God is willing to abide in it. He remains there for no selfish object. He does not sit enthroned within in cold majesty and merely to be the recipient of the homage and worship of his creature. Neither does he come so close to us for the single purpose of stimulating us by his presence to avoid evil and to accomplish those acts that are meritorious of eternal life. A passing and intermittent contact with the soul would suffice to enable it to elicit acts of a supernatural kind. The Holy Spirit, being God, is essentially active and energizing, and if he elects to be within us in a constant fashion, it must be with a view to exercising in the soul a sustained activity or series of activities. The Holy Spirit, being the gift of God, comes to give rather than to receive. It is in the creature's interest, not in the Spirit's own, that he knits with it that close relation which comes of the indwelling. From the moment that the Third Person of the Blessed Trinity takes up his abode in the soul he is preoccupied with one project alone—a project at which he labors incessantly. That project consists in actively molding the soul of man to an ever closer resemblance to its God. That loving toil inevitably comes to a happy and successful issue, unless it is marred and thwarted by the resistance of the creature.

Justification is the first step in that process of transforming the soul to a supernatural likeness with God. It is the initial effect of the coming of the Holy Spirit into the sanctuary of the spirit. At his entry not only is the guilt of sin canceled, but the soul's sinful state itself is changed. The Holy Spirit brings, not merely a sentence of pardon and the assurance on the part of God that the debt incurred by sin is remitted, but an active and energetic influence to change what was unjust into just, what was scarred and disfigured into something flawless and comely, what was dark and foul into something bright and glowing. Change marks his coming. Through it the sinner, from having been a sinner, becomes just and a friend of God. There is here something far more than a condonation of fault: there is a veritable physical transformation effected in the soul. The justified sinner is not merely one who has turned from sin and whose guilt has consequently been overlooked, but one who has shed the very nature of a sinner. He is not merely *legally justified*; he is made positively and *actually just*.

In human tribunals the judges may, on a plea for mercy and an avowal of regret on the part of the repentant culprit, arrest the course of justice and forego punishment of the crime. But when the accused leaves the court, he leaves it still a criminal freed not from guilt, but only from the chastisement of guilt. The judges can declare him innocent; they cannot make him innocent. They have no power to effect an inner change in him. The followers of Luther, in a strange incapacity to realize the extent to which God's action can affect the soul he has made, fail to see in justification anything more than a legal imputation of innocence. They surround God's tribunal of mercy with the same limitations which belong to human courts of justice. In their system of justification the sinner remains a sinner, but God chooses to hold him guiltless. But God's arm is not thus shortened.

When the Holy Spirit takes up his residence in the soul, he does more than repute the sinful creature guiltless; he makes the creature be guiltless. The guilt is not merely glossed over; it is purged away. "And it shall come to pass, that every one that shall be left in Zion . . . shall be holy . . . if the Lord shall wash away the filth of the daughters of Zion . . . by a spirit of judgment."[4] These are the words of the Old Testament, and in the New Testament we find St. Paul addressing the Corinthians in the following terms: "And such [that is, stained with sin] some of you were. But you are washed, but you are sanctified, but you are justified, in the name of our Lord Jesus Christ and the Spirit of our God."[5] The cleansing of which the Scripture speaks does not affect merely the surface of the soul. It penetrates to its very depths and, while purifying, transforms. In the beginning, when the Holy Spirit moved over the waters of chaos, order and light marked his passage. When he passes over the soul of the infant newly baptized or of the sinner who has quitted the ways of sin, beauty and life replace the chaos and the lifelessness caused by sin. His passage is the signal, as well as the cause, of a new spiritual creation. The inspired writer says: "Thou shalt send forth thy Spirit and they shall be created, and thou shalt renew the face of the earth."[6] St. Thomas attributes a spiritual signification to these words of the Psalmist.[7] This creation is more than a calling forth of things from the womb of nothingness. It is an imparting of life to what was dead. In the symbol of faith, recited at Mass, the Third Person of the Blessed Trinity is saluted as "the Spirit that imparteth life." *"Credo in Spiritum Sanctum, Dominum et vivificantem."*

The soul thus raised or recalled to life (if there is question of one who having been justified had relapsed into sin) is, by the operation of the Holy Spirit, made the friend of God, bound to him by the bonds of an affection which is mutual. The sinner, made by his sin hostile to God, finds his inner dispositions changed and becomes a lover of God. The virtue or power of loving God, which had been destroyed by sin, is restored by habitual grace. And this wonderful conversion is wrought by the Holy Spirit. He is the artisan of that understanding through which God becomes dear to the soul and the soul dear to God. "The charity of God," says St. Paul, "is poured forth in our hearts by the Holy Spirit who is given to us."[8] It is true that this radiance of heavenly beauty imparted to the soul by grace, and the power of loving God which is its first consequence, is an effect in the creature that must be assigned to the Blessed Trinity itself as its productive cause. Nevertheless, it remains an effect which has a special claim to be appropriated to the Holy Spirit, as its source and origin. For that which by

[4] Is 4: 3, 4.
[5] 1 Cor 6: 11.
[6] Ps 104: 30.
[7] *Summa contra Gentiles*, bk. IV, chap. 21.
[8] Rom 5: 5.

123

grace is wrought in the creature reflects in an express manner the distinctive character of the Third Divine Person. He is divine love, that is, the love of and for God, personified. As all reflected light is a participation of the sun's light, so all love for the Divine Beauty is a participation of what the Holy Spirit is in person, namely, the love of the uncreated beauty of the Godhead.

In the measure in which the soul loves its God, in that measure it is patterned on the Spirit who proceeds from Father and Son, by way of love. St. Thomas says that the charity by which we yield ourselves to the attraction of God and are drawn to him in affection represents, or shadows forth, the Holy Spirit.[9] The Holy Spirit may truly be called God's ambassador, bringing peace, healing, and friendship to the soul that has been estranged from its Maker by sin. His special function is to make man and God friends after having been enemies. He does this by taking away all the obstacles to that friendship which exist in man's soul and establishing in their place the dispositions themselves of friendship. In transforming by his presence the created spirit, he imparts to it that quality which makes it an object of deep affection for the Father and the Son. God is like all lovers in this, that he abides in thought and affection in the person who is dear to him. The Latin equivalent of "dear" is *"carus,"* whence is derived the word *"charitas"*—that is, "dearness." Charity, as has been said already, is an effect proper to the Holy Spirit. He makes us dear to God and, thus, brings it about that God dwells in us. St. John writes with his usual theological insight: "And in this we know that he abideth in us by *the Spirit* which he hath given us." [10]

Christians do not dwell as they ought on the immense advantages that they may derive from the intimate friendship which the Holy Spirit is eager to establish between them and himself, as God. The word eagerness may be justly employed in this connection because all the advances are initiated by God, and the gift of love is proffered by him to his creature. "In this is charity, not as though we had loved God, but because he hath first loved us." [11] So speaks St. John the Evangelist. God wants the creature to love him and wants, too, that he himself should be empowered to love that creature ever more and more; he is ever ready with those gifts which, by giving the soul a closer resemblance to God, make it possible for God to love the soul more dearly. That possibility is opened to him when the soul responds with warmth to the gracious and tender overtures of the Creator.

Coldness of heart and dullness of comprehension as to the designs of God in their regard are too common with many Christians, who are, otherwise, faithful enough in the accomplishment of their duties and the exercises of their religion. Is this not due, perhaps, in considerable part, to their inattention to the exact meaning of the terms used to express the relations between God and those whom he has justified? They hear the phrase "friend of God," and they make use of it themselves but are prone

[9] *Summa contra Gentiles*, bk. IV, chap. 21.
[10] 1 Jn 3: 24.
[11] 1 Jn 4: 10.

to attach to it a vague or figurative meaning. Too often, expressions which set forth in language theologically exact the tender and intimate relations established between the soul and God, by the grace of Christ, are taken by the faithful to be but poetical modes of speech, become conventional in the treatment of spiritual themes. Because of this they frequently remain all their lives on the margin of the world of wondrous mysterious realities to which they are given access by the *tessera* of the faith. They miss much which sheds light on the perplexing problems and much which would marvelously lighten the burden of existence here below. A Christian will ill comprehend the experiences of life unless he grasps what it is that God chiefly wants him to get out of, and through, life on earth. He runs the risk of having his soul numbed, his vital *élan* checked and his heart crushed by the bitter trials and disappointments of existence, unless he knows where to draw on the resources of strength that God has liberally provided for Christians in their hard struggles in the arena of time.

It is only those who rely wholly on the assurances of their heavenly Father and take his words literally who realize how true it is that "to them that love God all things work together unto good." [12] Christ meant to be taken at his word when he stated that the yoke the Christian life placed upon man's shoulders was sweet and its burden light. [13] If his followers so often complain that they find it neither the one nor the other, it is because they do not use, or even become conversant with, the means he has placed at their disposal for the lightening of the burden. Most people would probably find it easy, as the apostles found it easy, to bear the trials and difficulties of life with a measure of cheerfulness, if they had the comfort of Christ's presence by their side and the voice of his encouragement in their ears, when struggling to conform to the exactions of the Christian code. When Jesus was about to leave his disciples and apostles, he promised them that he would not leave them deprived of the comfort they got from his presence. He assured them that he would send them "another comforter" (these are his words), who would more than substitute for him. "And I will ask the Father, and he shall give you *another Paraclete* [that is, consoler], that he may *abide with you for ever.*" [14] This pledge was redeemed on the morning of Pentecost. On that day Jesus sent One who is prepared to fulfill perpetually, with regard to all the redeemed, the most exacting duties of friendship. God the Holy Spirit is the divine friend of the human souls to whom he is sent.

Jesus sends his Holy Spirit to us in order, among other purposes, to banish from our life on earth that which constitutes one of the great pains of our present existence. The term which the Savior selects to name the Holy Spirit that he was to send to his disciples—a term that bespeaks the tender and almost homely concern of Jesus for the painful lot of his followers in this world—manifests that consolation and comfort and strength and encouragement are envisaged as being not the least among

[12] Rom 8: 28.
[13] Mt 11: 30.
[14] Jn 14: 16.

the effects that flow to the soul from the presence of the Third Divine Person within it.

There are few things so hard for man to bear as loneliness and isolation. Man is not made to live alone. "The man," says Aristotle, "who lives in isolation, if the cause of his isolation be natural and not accidental, is either a superhuman being or low in the scale of civilization."[15] In a world which is ever hostile to Christ and will always hate his followers as it hated him, the Christian necessarily suffers a certain measure of ostracism. The words of the Divine Master addressed to his apostles in the first instance have application to all who, in the ages to come, were to embrace their teaching. "If the world hates you, know you that it hath hated me before you. If you had been of the world, the world would love its own; but because you are not of the world . . . therefore the world hateth you."[16] It is scarcely necessary to point out how literally these words are being fulfilled in every age, including our own "enlightened" one. A kind of social and even political outlawry is bound to be the fate of the individual or the group that gives an uncompromising adherence to the principles of Jesus of Nazareth. This hostility is not confined to the limits of that "world" which is, so to speak, officially the enemy of Christ. Even in the bosom of Christian circles, those who show an unflinching and whole-hearted loyalty to the teaching of the Savior meet with an opposition which hurts more than does the opposition of the enemies of the Christian name. In addition to this enforced estrangement from much in that world in which he has to work out his existence, the Christian has to bear the loneliness that, with the advance of years, is the common lot of mortals. Death and other causes tend to thin the ever narrowing circle of one's friends and acquaintances. It often happens that men, when they reach an advanced age, have the sensation of being cast by the waters of life high and dry on a barren, lonely and loveless strand, while the tide sweeps past them and onward on its unheeding course. How frequently the pathos of this abandonment shows in the eyes of the aged whose contemporaries have vanished year by year!

Jesus has provided for the comfort of lonely hearts. Did Christians but develop some realization of the proximity of God to them and of the intimacy which the Divine Guest within wills to share with them, no sense of loneliness at any period of their earthly pilgrimage would find access, at least, to the inner regions or their consciousness. If men, by God's help, have been able to preserve sanctifying grace in their souls, they need never be alone, even though earth and every person on earth slip away from them. When it comes to a human creature, neither to love nor to be loved by anyone, then existence has turned to dust and ashes. The disciples of Christ need never experience this dread starvation, this withering of their powers of affection, seeing that they may, by grace, possess within themselves in the closest intimacy a Person who, by the Word of Truth, has

[15] Aristotle, *Politics*, bk. I, chap. I.
[16] Jn 15: 18–19; cf. Lk 21: 17; Mk 13: 13; Mt 10: 22; 24: 9.

been declared to be preeminently a consoler—a Person who may be loved without limits and who repays every mark of affection by more than the hundredfold in warmth of tenderness. The power of loving of the most devoted of human hearts is almost insensibility in comparison to the capacity for loving that belongs to the Person who is love personified.

All that love demands is that it be given free scope to express itself. The affection of the Holy Spirit for the soul he inhabits and adorns is not only strong and ardent, it is doubtlessly faithful as well. A great poet has styled the Savior of men "a tremendous lover." The words, with meaning reinforced more than a hundredfold, are applicable to the divine love of which the human love of the heart of Jesus is but a created reflection. The affection of creatures, however devoted, is subject to vicissitudes. This is not so with the affection of God for the sanctified soul. However broken the faithful may be by the trials and disappointments of life, however disfigured by time and hardship, they can always feel secure of the "loyalty" of God. They need never experience misgivings lest they may appear ill-favored in the eyes of their loving God, if only they are careful to preserve divine grace in their hearts.

The Holy Spirit has not only an infinite capacity for friendship. He has, as well, an infinite power to make his friendship effective for the consolation and comfort of those he loves. In the great trials of life, notably in the bereavement caused by the death of those dearest to us, how impotent we find the well-meaning efforts of our friends to touch our grief with healing. These themselves feel, with a sinking heart, that their words of sympathy, though sincere and heartfelt, are utterly powerless to reach the source of sorrow—the darkened soul itself. When the soul is burdened with a great sorrow, nothing can bring alleviation and strength except that which can penetrate and change the spirit of man. This no created friend can do. This the Divine Friend alone is capable of doing. How frequent an experience it is to find the faithful who, when faced with an overwhelming calamity, which should normally paralyze and crush them, manifest a courage, calm and resolution, traceable to no natural source. The origin of the mysterious peace, confidence and what is almost buoyancy that Christians so frequently find themselves possessed of when the loss of those on whom they depend envelops all the future in a somber darkness is the Paraclete, the Comforter. They themselves, if unskilled in interior things, may trace this unexpected power of bearing up, which is accorded them, to the prayers of others and to their own. They are partly right in this. But these prayers are rather the occasion than the cause of what they feel.

Their turning to God in their distress has provoked the inner, mysterious and direct action of the Holy Spirit on the substance of the soul itself. It is not on odd occasions only, as in times of great crises, that Christians would experience this potent, strengthening influence of the Divine Friend within them, but perpetually, as if they but trained themselves to constant, loving attention to his presence. St. Thomas writes in this connection: "It belongs to the very nature of friendship that a man should take delight in the society of his friend and find in him relief in all anxieties, hence it is that in our distresses it is to our friends we, in a special manner, have recourse for consolation. Inasmuch as it is the Holy Spirit who makes us friends of God and makes God abide in us and us in God, it follows that it is through him, the Third Person of the Blessed Trinity, that we find joy in God and comfort in all the trials and adversities of life. Because of this the Savior names the Holy Spirit, Paraclete, that is, Comforter."[17]

The Spirit of Jesus not only consoles hearts, he enlightens minds as well. Mutual communication of secrets is a characteristic of friendship. Most men find it difficult to carry alone the burden of some important piece of knowledge. It is a profound relief to share the burden with one who is loyal, devoted and trustworthy. What has found its way into the heart of one's friend only can be scarcely counted as having left one's own, so closely bound in one are those who are knit together in the bonds of a true friendship. The Holy Spirit is laden with all the secrets of God— secrets not only of surpassing interest in themselves but of great import for the creature. "For the Spirit searcheth all things, yea, the deep things of God . . . the things that are of God no man knoweth but the Spirit of God."[18] These deep things of God the Holy Spirit is all eagerness to communicate to the soul, as is the tendency of friendship. Unfortunately, the creature, too often, is a listless and inattentive listener, and the accents of the Spirit fall on deaf ears. Nevertheless, even the most heedless catch, at times, something of the divine whisper. Those who are better disposed and are more exact in satisfying the obligation of the divine friendship are favored with many an insight into the mysteries of the supernatural life. To none other than the Holy Spirit are to be attributed those sudden illuminations which, at times, cast a flood of light on the mysteries of faith and on the words of Sacred Scripture.

When the meaning of the sacred text is laid bare in this manner, there is a deepening of faith in, and a strengthening of attachment to, the doctrine and person of Jesus. The soul becomes, as it were, more malleable to his teachings when, through the radiance shed on them by the Spirit of God, the mysteries of religion are lighted up, their inner harmonies are disclosed and their correspondence with all the needs and aspirations of the human heart are revealed. A great love for them follows. Their appeal tends then to make their moral consequences and exigencies appear less difficult and onerous. When the faith is deeply loved, its moral obligations are borne with greater ease and buoyancy.

During three years Jesus shared the divine secrets with the inner circle of those he drew about him. "No longer do I call you servants, for the servant does not know what his master is doing. But I have called you friends, for all that I have heard from the Father I have made known to you."[19] But because their knowledge of what he so painstakingly communicated to them remained largely superficial, that knowledge did not

[17] *Summa contra Gentiles,* bk. IV, chap. 22; see Jn 14: 26.
[18] I Cor 2: 10–11.
[19] Jn 15: 15.

render them strong when the hour of trial came. On the other hand, the intoxication of soul caused by the revelation of Pentecost rendered them indifferent to persecution and death. It was not that new truths were given them but that new light was shed on the old truths taught them by Jesus, as, at the Last Supper, he had said would be: "The Counselor, the Holy Spirit, whom the Father will send in my name, he will teach you all things and bring to your remembrance all that I have said to you."[20] For the mysteries illuminated for them by the Holy Spirit, the apostles conceived an attachment proof against the menace of death.

The Holy Spirit not only explores the secret things of God; with the same unerring insight, he sees into the things of human life. He knows fully life's problems and their correct solution. He knows its dark issues on eternity and how they are to be found. With a divine destiny to be worked out by use of divine means and by the exercise of actions of more than human merit, man is exposed to serious risk both of error and failure in the conduct of his life.[21] Man is called to the beatific life of God, that is, to live for all eternity like God. To attain this goal it is incumbent on him to live as God already here on earth. It is only by life-activities of a divine texture that he can merit an unending divine existence hereafter—in other words, enjoy the beatitude of God. To live and to have the life-activities of God one must become like to God through spiritual perfections that generate this resemblance. St. John points out that life in heaven postulates this likeness. "We know that when he shall appear, we shall be like to him, because we shall see him as he is."[22] The likeness that is to be then in the hereafter demands the beginning of that likeness now in the present.

The spiritual gifts that induce this resemblance and render the creature apt to act in a certain way, divinely, are all given by the Holy Spirit. "Now he that confirmeth us and that hath anointed us is God, who also hath sealed us and given the pledge of the Spirit in our hearts."[23] St. Thomas points out that this anointing of the soul, of which the Apostle speaks, has as its purpose to impart to man a supple ease in executing actions of a meritorious perfection.[24] The Holy Spirit not only gives us the grace of justification, he also moves us to right action by enlightening the intelligence as to the course to adopt and imparting strength to the will to accomplish what has been revealed as the proper thing to do. He does this by a continual flow of actual graces to the soul. Hence it is that St. Paul could say with justice that the children of God, that is, Christians, are guided by the Spirit of God. "For whosoever are led by the

---

[20] Jn 14: 26.

[21] "In the intellect there reigns a certain darkness and ignorance which brings it about that, as is said in the Epistle to the Romans (8: 26), we 'know not what we should pray for as we ought.' The perpetual variation of circumstances and the imperfect knowledge of ourselves that we have, make it impossible for us to know what makes for our good. So we read in the Book of Wisdom (9: 14): 'For the thoughts of mortal men are fearful and our counsels uncertain'" (S. Th. I, II, q. 109, a. 9).

[22] 1 Jn 3: 2.

[23] 2 Cor 1: 22.

[24] Summa contra Gentiles, bk. IV, chap. 21.

Spirit of God, they are sons of God." [25] It is the prompting of the Holy Spirit, and not a spontaneous movement of his own will, that inclines the spiritual man to action. But those who allow themselves to be swayed by natural and, especially, selfish reasonings in the determination of their conduct render themselves inapt for this interior, divine guidance. To be led by the Holy Spirit, one must be willing to be docile to him and attentive to his promptings.

But the action of the Divine Guest of the soul is not wholly, or even mainly, restricted to giving counsel for the right ordering of life; he labors interiorly upon the soul itself, molding it and transforming it so that it should become a more fit abode for a divine person. God is essentially good and is ever in activity to impart his own perfections to subjects disposed to receive them. The action of the Divinity on the soul does not cease once that sin has been purged away. All the Creator's dealings with his rational creatures are directed toward their sanctification. Justification takes place in an instant. Sanctification is a process that is extended over the entire period of the soul's union with the body. It consists in this: God, who is the chief agent in the process, imparts himself to the soul in ever-increasing measure, according to how the soul's power of receptivity develops. To the Holy Spirit is appropriately attributed the beginning, the continuance and the crowning of this mysterious process. All the activities that are concerned with the sanctifying of the rational creature are rightly considered to be peculiarly his, by reason of his personal characteristics. He is the subsistent sanctity of God because he is the subsistent love of God—sanctity being nothing else than love of the divine essence.

Now, as pure light, if there were such a thing, tends with its whole being to diffuse light, and as a living source of heat, if such a thing could be, radiates warmth, so the divine energy of the Holy Spirit continually pours itself forth in imparting sanctity to the created spirit in which he dwells. [26] As one, by drawing down thick blinds, can exclude the midday sun, so, unfortunately, may the creature place an impenetrable obstacle between itself and the sanctifying, beneficent rays that stream from the source of all holiness. The obstacle shuts off the rays; it does not cause them to cease to be. The barrier removed, the Holy Spirit at once exercises his function as the "Spirit of Sanctification." In us he is truly the source of charity by which we, in imitation of God, love the Divine Good. "The charity," says St. Augustine, "which according to the Apostle is diffused in our hearts by the Divine Spirit [27] is not the charity by which God loves us, but that by which he makes us lovers of himself." [28] The Holy Spirit initiates us into the blissful experiences that attend the growing love for God. Religion is

[25] Rom 8: 14.

[26] This is the comparison used by Dionysius the Areopagite. Like all comparisons, it is imperfect. The living source of heat would act necessarily. God, in diffusing his goodness, acts freely.

[27] Rom 5: 5.

[28] St. Augustine, *De Trinitate* 5.17.

regarded by many, who practice it faithfully enough, as being mostly a code of strict and irksome morality. The harshness and austerity of feature that the faith wears to such persons would melt, did they realize that faith is an opportunity given to poor mortals of enjoying the blissful romance of falling ever more completely in love with God. Death would be robbed of its terrors were it regarded—and the Christian may so regard it—as but the happy ending of an intoxicating courtship in which the soul is the wooed and God is the wooer.

God's love for the soul grows in accordance with the soul's growth in attractiveness for him. It is the Holy Spirit who imparts this attractiveness which wins the favoring regard of the Almighty. He does it by giving ever more and more grace. The gifts of God, it is true, are distributed in varying measure. To some, more is given, to others, less. But nevertheless, in the case of the individual, the only impediment to his own growth in a beauty that charms God is his own resistance to the action of the Divine Artisan of spiritual perfection. The name "Divine Artisan" is one not unsuited to designate the Third Person of the Blessed Trinity. In the hymn *"Veni Creator Spiritus,"* he is styled "Finger of God's Right Hand." The idea underlying this designation is found in the writings of the Fathers of the Church. By them he is likened to an artist delineating on the canvas of our souls the features of God. By a figure still more expressive he is compared by them to a divine seal impressing on the created spirit the divine resemblance, when that spirit becomes by perfect docility to the divine will as melted wax under the hands of the worker. "True God," says St. Cyril of Alexandria, "he imprints himself invisibly on the souls which receive him, as a seal on wax, and thus communicating his own likeness to our nature, retraces therein the beauty of the divine archetype, and restores in men the image of God." [29]

Actual graces and habitual grace are, by the Holy Spirit, pressed into service for the furtherance of this enterprise. By actual graces he communicates supernatural light to the intelligence and breathes supernatural energy into the will. He thus disposes the soul to the state of justice, or, if it is justified already, he aids it to put forth actions becoming its state and meriting an advance in supernatural nobility. To the soul prepared by actual graces, the Holy Spirit imparts a participation of his own life, through the infusion of sanctifying grace. The giving of this great and most precious gift of God [30] is that on which bears, and toward which is made to converge, every action of God on his rational creatures. In justification the soul receives, with the forgiveness of sin, a participation of the nature of God. This participation is made more and more abundant according to how one is disposed for it by an increasing fidelity to the divine will. The work of actual grace might be likened to the application of heat to the hardened wax to induce in it that soft condition which makes it capable of receiving the clear impress of the seal. Sanctifying grace is the instrument

[29] St. Cyril of Alexandria, *In Ioann.* 17.
[30] See 2 Pet 1: 4.

which, with delicate yet potent pressure, the Holy Spirit employs to stamp a divine form on the soul rendered receptive to his touch.

Now the form or figure of the seal that the heavenly author of sanctity aims at impressing on the soul resembles God, through being fashioned or, to continue the metaphor, graved on the model of the divinized features of the soul of Jesus. The created sanctity of the Savior is the perfect human expression of the holiness of the invisible God. As the Word, he is "the brightness of the Father's glory and the figure of his substance,"[31] the adequate divine expression of the divinity. As man, because he has received the plenitude of grace—all of it that can be given to a creature in the present order of providence—he is the created human expression of the divinity, forged to that likeness by the Holy Spirit himself. As the artist casts in metal the features of the person with whose image coins or documents are to be stamped, so the Divine Spirit casts in the mold of the human soul of Jesus an image of God. Having done this, he forthwith proceeds to stamp the souls of men with the divine likeness set in the human materials of the sacred humanity.

This language, though figurative, expresses with accuracy the truths of the Christian faith that have the Incarnation as their center. Sacred Scripture assigns the formation of the body and soul of the Savior to the Holy Spirit. "And the Angel answering said to her [that is, Mary]: "The Holy Spirit shall come upon thee, and the power of the Most High shall overshadow thee. Therefore, the child which shall be born of thee, shall be called the Son of God."[32] It was the handiwork of the "Finger of God's Right Hand" that made that creature of flesh and blood, the Son of Mary, stand forth before man, a living, breathing ideal of a human-divine perfection, flawless even in the eyes of God. It devolves on the Holy Spirit, having formed the head of the regenerated human race, to proceed to the formation of the members.

As living members of the Mystical Body of Christ—the formation of which gives effect to the Redemption—men must have in them the Spirit of Jesus and retrace in themselves his spiritual features. The work of him whom Christ sent to complete his mission consists in creating in men that likeness to the Son of God by which their predestination is fulfilled. "For whom he foreknew, he also predestinated to be made conformable to the image of his Son, that he might be the firstborn among many brethren."[33] The Holy Spirit, present in souls, labors to effect in them that transformation by which they gradually shed their resemblance to their first father Adam and take on the form and features of the New Adam, Jesus—taught in him, "to put off the old man who is corrupted according to the desire of error, and put on the new man, who according to God, is created in justice and holiness of truth."[34]

The soul of man is destined by God to be clothed with a resemblance of

[31] Heb 1: 3.
[32] Lk 1: 35.
[33] Rom 8: 29.
[34] Eph 4: 22–24.

the Divine. It is created to become like to God, as God is in his own nature. This resemblance is achieved in the measure in which the soul is molded to the form of the soul of Jesus, which, as divinized by grace, is the most perfect created effulgence of the divine perfections that can be. On the eve of his death the Savior said to Philip: "He who sees me sees the Father." [35] Hence to be like him is to be like God. When our humanity, in its thoughts, judgments, decisions, ideals and actions, is like to his, then we reflect the divine excellence, fulfilling that injunction which, at first hearing, strikes with dismay: "Be ye perfect, as your heavenly Father is perfect." [36]

Jesus, having finished his career on earth, commissioned the Holy Spirit to change the redeemed into the likeness of the Redeemer. Hence all that are sanctified can be called "his [that is, the Paraclete's] workmanship created in Christ Jesus." [37] Under the continual infusions of the divine grace merited by the Passion of the Son of God, the Divine Spirit is ever shaping souls to the character of the Son of man. Under the action of the Divine Artisan, the features of Jesus show ever more and more distinctly in those who make progress in sanctity. They become continually more Christlike. It is, to use another comparison employed by the Fathers, as when, under the patient chiseling of the sculptor, the human features and the human shape of the model emerge from the formless block of marble. So from the human soul, which has been shapeless and formless by sin, is hewn, by the Divine Sculptor, a living image of the Christ. Each fresh infusion of sanctifying grace brings its own touch of perfection to the work, helping to make the resemblance more striking. Each time that the creature, responding to the impulse of its Divine Guest, performs an action into which it casts all the fervor of charity which its actual spiritual condition allows of, it makes a step forward in the process of sanctification—it grows in resemblance to Jesus. [38] The act it elicits in charity merits an increase of divine grace. This implies a further participation in the divine life, as that life is meant to be reflected in humanity.

The Holy Spirit, with a divine joy and satisfaction, draws upon the inexhaustible ocean of the grace of Christ, the head of the Mystical Body, and gives to the soul in the full measure that has been merited. Dwelling in our inmost being he is, without ceasing and unwearyingly, moving us by the stimulus of actual graces to perform supernatural acts and then bestowing on us the complement or increase of sanctifying grace thus merited. In this consists the process of sanctification. Growth in perfection or holiness is simply growth in habitual grace. With the development of this latter goes the increase in likeness to Christ and so in likeness to God. The more closely the soul resembles God the more closely is it united to him.

[35] Jn 14: 9.
[36] Mt 5: 48.
[37] Eph 2: 10.
[38] Cf. *S. Th.* Ia, IIae, q. 52, a. 3.

Christ as man was at the summit of this created resemblance to God because of the immense grace with which his soul was flooded. Hence he is the model of all human perfection. He is the model which the Holy Spirit has before his eyes as he works at bringing the soul to its perfection. As we grow in likeness to the Incarnate Son of God, the more perfectly and fully we share his prerogatives. As the work of sanctification progresses under the deft touch of the Holy Spirit, increasing spontaneity, conviction and tenderness penetrate the soul's accents as it murmurs, Abba, Father, when speaking to its God. "For the Spirit himself giveth testimony to our spirit that we are children of God." [39] The more truly filial our attitude toward our heavenly Father, the more fully we participate in the inheritance of Christ and the more fully we enter into our condition as adopted children of God. Because, as St. Paul tells us, "if we are children, we are heirs also, heirs of God and joint heirs with Christ." [40] It is the sanctifying grace poured into our souls by the Holy Spirit that gives us this co-heirship with Christ, making us children of God. It remains to consider the nature of this mysterious gift of the Third Divine Person, which bestows such astonishing prerogatives on the human soul.

[39] See Rom 8: 16.
[40] See Rom 8: 17.

10

Born of Water and the Holy Spirit

IT is not without significance that the stream of woe which has caught all mankind in its flood had its source in what might be called a tragic misconception.[1] Disaster befell the race through Adam's pursuing something he already possessed: "You shall be as Gods," said Satan to the first man and the first woman. Blind to the fact that already, through grace, they were *as gods,* they reached out after a vain mirage of the divine resemblance conjured up before their imaginations by the lying archfiend. Under his words was concealed a mocking irony. Deceived, our first parents, in seeking to grasp an empty phantasm, lost the possession of the divine reality which they already possessed. They blinded themselves to the fact that they held what they looked for. God had given them already in the present what the devil held out to them as yet attainable in the future. St. John Damascene writes: "The end, in view of which God created us— an end which is the apogee of our elevation above the conditions of our nature—was to deify us by imparting to us a resemblance to himself. He had no other purpose in our creation than to deify us by bestowing on us a share in the divine light (in which he stands revealed to himself), and not by some inconceivable metamorphosis of our nature into that of God."[2]

Our faith teaches us that the purpose of the incarnation of the Son of God was to restore to us what had been forfeited in Adam's fall. It was to make us (at least, essentially) what he had been, in his relation to God.

St. Thomas in his measured language, so free from rhetorical emphasis, uses even bolder and more direct terms to express the same thought. Pointing out in what the restitution of fallen man consisted, he says: "If the Son of God became man and underwent circumcision in the flesh, it was not for his own sake but in order to make us 'gods' by grace and to merit for us circumcision of the spirit."[3] In this he follows closely the mode of expression employed by St. Augustine. "God," said the great bishop of Hippo, "became man that man might become God."[4] That these formulas do not overstate the reality is proved by the tenor of the language that the Holy Spirit employs to express the same mystery of faith. In the first epistle of St. John are to be read the following words: "Whosoever is born of God, committeth not sin; for his seed abideth in him, and he cannot sin, because

---

[1] Reading the history of mankind from the supernatural point of view, one can discern this initial misconception working through all the subsequent aberrations of the human mind in the sphere of religion.

[2] St. John Damascene, *De Fide Orthod.,* bk. II, chap. 12, quoted by J. B. Terrien, S.J., *La Grâce et la Gloire,* vol. 1, p. 52.

[3] *S. Th.* III, q. 37, a. 3, ad 2.

[4] St. Augustine, *Sermon* 128, quoted by Terrien, *La Grâce et la Gloire,* vol. 1, p. 52.

he is born of God."[5] "His" in this text refers to God, and the term "seed" is equivalent to "germ of the divinity." The phrases of St. John are an echo of those of St. Peter, the infallible head of the Church. The great apostle writes: "Love one another earnestly, being born again not of corruptible seed, but incorruptible."[6] Elsewhere this birth is shown as a restoration to a condition that had once been the condition of man but had been lost. Addressing himself to the Colossians, the Apostle of the Gentiles says: "Lie not one to another, stripping yourself of the old man with his deeds, and putting on the new, *him who is renewed* unto knowledge, according to the image of him that created him."[7] The word "renewed" marks a return to a pristine state from which man had fallen. The nature of that state is revealed as consisting in man's being in the image of his Creator.

That this image or likeness was something other than that which belonged to man as merely endowed with freedom and intelligence is made clear by the words of St. Paul in another context. In his instructions to the Romans, he writes: "For whom he [i.e., God] foreknew, he also predestined to be made conformable to the image of his Son, that he might be the firstborn among many brethren."[8] Evidently the resemblance to God with which man, born of God "by water and the Holy Spirit,"[9] is clothed bears an analogy to the resemblance which the Son of God, born of his heavenly Father by an eternal generation, has to that divine source from which he proceeds. Man is reborn to the image of him "who is the brightness of God's glory and the figure of his substance."[10] A divine restraint and sobriety mark the phrasing which God makes use of when referring to the favors which he, in his infinite generosity, bestows on his rational creatures. Understatement and not overstatement characterizes the divine utterances. This springs even from the necessities imposed by the nature of the themes dealt with. Human concepts and human speech must falter and break down when called upon to bear the weight of expressing the wondrous counsels of God in man's regard. Human language is wholly inadequate to render the marvels of God. Regeneration, renewal in the Holy Spirit,[11] born of God,[12] begotten of God by the word of truth,[13] created after the likeness of God,[14] created new in Christ[15] (for that is the significance of the words, "a new creature")—such are the restrained terms which the Holy Spirit makes use of to unveil to our minds the wonders wrought in the depths of our being by the grace and charity that he pours forth in our hearts.[16]

It is sanctifying grace that transforms the soul of man, makes of him a being newly created and forges in him a likeness to the Son of the Most High. A study of the nature and properties of the mysterious entity that is capable of such marvelous effects imposes itself, if one is

---

[5] 1 Jn 3: 9.
[6] 1 Pet 1: 22–23.
[7] Col 3: 9–10.
[8] Rom 8: 29.
[9] Jn 3: 5.
[10] Heb 1: 3.
[11] See Tit 3: 5.
[12] See 1 Jn 3: 9.
[13] See Jas 1: 18.
[14] See Eph 4: 24.
[15] See 2 Cor 5: 17.
[16] See Rom 5: 5.

to have even a dim idea of the generosity of God to man and the magnificent "ambitions" that God permits himself to conceive on behalf of his elect. Since habitual grace is the bond that unites us to God—for the whole economy of the Creator's dealings with his rational creatures is directed toward imparting to them these most great and precious promises;[17] since the whole vast organization of religion is but a means to make the treasures of divine grace accessible to men; since the sole end of life on earth is to attain to and develop in sanctifying grace; it is easy to understand what a hazy and bewildered notion of life's meaning man will have, unless he has some understanding of that inner life of the soul which is imparted by grace and to the growth of which man's years on earth are meant to contribute. *Without an adequate notion of grace there cannot be an adequate notion of Catholicity.* For the Catholic system is not merely a means to right living, much less an ingenious contrivance to help us to evade the unpleasant consequences of wrong living. The Church with its system exists primarily for the communication of grace to the souls of men.

Divine grace ushers us into the realm of the supernatural. This latter term has repeatedly appeared in the foregoing pages, and it is now the occasion to unfold its meaning. As the form of the word implies, it signifies what is above or beyond or, better, outside of the range of nature. Above nature means superior to the whole natural created order, matter as well as spirit. It is what lies outside of the aptitudes, the exigencies, and the powers—even when indefinitely increased in their range—of all things created, when these have nothing but their natural resources to draw upon. Let the will and the intelligence of him who is supreme in the created spirit world undergo a development, everlastingly increasing the range and the force of his spiritual faculties—still, a development confined within the limits of what the intellect and will could naturally reach to—nevertheless, even when raised to these dizzy heights, the created spirit would yet fall infinitely short of attaining to the lowest degree of the supernatural. This being so, it is to be expected that words descriptive of realities outside of the Godhead will convey but an imperfect notion of the realities of the supernatural system. Such words, however, when stripped of what they imply of the imperfect, can give a true, if analogical, notion of what cannot be properly expressed in human language.

As the effect of habitual grace on the soul can be likened to the modification produced in a substance by a quality inhering in it, grace can be defined as something pertaining to the nature of a *quality.* An example will illustrate the sense of this word taken from the vocabulary of philosophy. A worker in wood will be conversant with the qualities of the different timbers he makes use of in his art. He will not employ the same kind of timber for flooring a room as for roofing a house. It is the quality of the timber that determines whether to apply it to one rather than the other

---

[17] See 2 Pet 1: 4.

object. The quality establishes a certain disposition in the wood which renders it adaptable for one purpose and not for another. It does not make the wood to be wood, but it makes it suitable for certain purposes and not for others. Transparency is a quality of ordinary, good glass, but not all glass is suitably transparent, letting the rays of light through without interrupting them in their passage. Transparency does not make glass to be glass, but it is that disposition or quality in the glass which allows the relatively free passage of the rays of light. A quality presupposes a substance which it modifies. It does not change it into a different substance; it simply so disposes the substance that it is well or ill conditioned in itself or aptly or inaptly disposed for the exercise of its proper activities.[18] Moral goodness, for instance, is a quality in a human being. Where it is found, certain definite principles of action and ways of acting can be looked for and expected confidently. The like principles, and actions of a similar type, will not belong to a man who has not goodness in him.

Now, grace is a reality, which, though it cannot be properly or rightly called a quality, yet affects the soul in which it inheres in somewhat the same way as a quality affects the substance which it modifies. Though grace makes the soul good, it would be erroneous to regard the goodness which it imparts as equivalent to that which would result from the possession of the natural moral virtues in a harmonious balance and combination. *"Grace-fullness" and mere ethical goodness are not the same thing.* Even if there were question of actual grace, which is a help given us by God to avoid evil and do good, it would be a mistake to look upon the right action which it inspires and aids as nothing more than action conformable to the laws of reason. What is done under the inspiration of actual grace is certainly in accord with reason, but it tends toward the attainment of a perfection which is greater than mere rational perfection. Where there is question of habitual grace, it would be a still greater error to consider the goodness which is its effect to be merely of a moral or ethical kind—mere uprightness in a rational sense. Grace does far more than simply make the soul righteous.

When grace inheres in the soul, it raises it to a condition of being which transcends all the limits of nature and natural good. It is not a purely moral entity. It is a real physical supernatural quality inhering in the soul, not making the soul simply good, but making it, in a sense, divine. By it, according to the words of St. Peter, we are made "partakers of the divine nature."[19] "Grace to you and peace be accomplished in the knowledge of God, and of Christ Jesus our Lord, by whom he hath given us most great and precious promises, that by these you may be made partakers of the divine nature." These inspired words of the head of the apostolic college are the utmost effort that has ever been made by human language to express the inexpressible. No paraphrase or analysis can equal their power to give man an understanding of the destiny to which he has been called.

[18] Gredt, O.S.B., *Elementa Phil.*, vol. I, p. 154.
[19] 2 Pet I: 4.

They open up perspectives of dazzling splendor. They point to heights of attainment that are of overpowering sublimity.

The word "nature" is the key to the theological explanation of what sanctifying grace is and what it effects. The nature of a thing is not quite the same as the essence of that thing. The essence is what determines the degree of existence which a being enjoys; the essence gives that being its position in the hierarchy of existing things. The higher the essence, the more perfect is the existence enjoyed. Man exists in a more eminent way than the animal, and the animal in its turn holds a higher place in the scale of being than the plant. On the other hand, the angelic existence is more perfect than that which is human, because the angelic essence is nobler than that of a creature composed of matter and spirit. Nature is the essence of a thing considered under a particular aspect. It is the essence viewed as the source of the activities proper to and characteristic of each being. According to the nature of a thing so shall be its activities. Human nature constitutes an individual a man and is in him the root principle of the activities that are specifically those of man. For instance, because the Son of God Incarnate had a human nature, he could exercise all the operations of mind and will and sense that are proper to man. Like other men he could reason, judge, will, adore, pray and feel emotions of joy and sorrow, pain and wonder. Similarly it is the possession of the divine nature that makes him to be true God and capable of exercising those activities that are exclusively proper to the Divinity—as, for instance, all works that demand the putting forth of omnipotence.

When, then, we are said to participate in the divine nature, it means that, in a mysterious manner, that perfection in God which makes *him what he is* and which is the root principle of the operations that belong specifically and exclusively to the Divinity is ours in a limited and created measure. St. Thomas, speaking of habitual grace, says: "That which exists substantially in God, that same perfection exists in the manner of an accident in the soul that participates in the divine goodness." [20] That which is in God is in the soul, with this difference; it is substantially in God and is identified with the divine being, whereas, in the soul, it is found as a quality, inhering in it after the mode of being proper to an accident. Its absence from the human soul leaves that soul substantially unchanged. But by its presence the soul becomes capable of reflecting the inaccessible perfections of the Godhead.

Every activity that is in accordance with the nature of a being carries that being onward to the goal of its perfection. Virtue is, according to Aristotle, the disposition that belongs to a thing that is perfect, and a creature is perfect when it is such as its nature demands that it should

[20] *S. Th.* I, II, q. 110, a. 2, ad 2. In philosophical language, an accident is a modification of a substance but does not enter into the constitution of the substance. It is something which can be present or absent without the substance being essentially affected by the presence or absence. Whiteness, for instance, is an accident of bread. Bread, while still remaining bread, can be white or brown. A man remains a man whether he is short or tall, white or black, learned or unlettered.

be.[21] Man is by nature rational and, speaking philosophically, he would be perfect when, by growth in virtue, he would come to be habitually reasonable in all his conduct. Every reasonable decision and action flowing from such a decision tends to make man perfect, in that it contributes to the development of the habit of acting according to reason. Acts of justice lay the foundation of the habit of justice, acts of prudence build up the virtue of prudence, and acts of temperance aid a man to acquire the power of unfailing self-restraint. On the other hand, deliberate acts governed by passion, prejudice or impulse bring about the deterioration of the rational creature. Reasonable activity goes to perfect a man; unreasonable activity goes to corrupt a man. Now had man been created for a natural destiny and not for a supernatural one (as is historically the case), his final end would be the full and stable possession of the cardinal virtues. Equipped with reason and will and aided by God, he would, by the exercise of actions according to reason, that is, by actions according to his nature as a reasonable being, have been able to attain his goal. But, in fact, man was created for a supernatural end and bidden to tend toward this end by actions that serve to bring him to this higher goal of endeavor appointed to him by God. He is bound to tend to his final end and to reach it by his own actions.

A supernatural perfection cannot be forged out by any but supernatural acts. It is only by the exercise of supernatural actions that man can progress toward and merit a supernatural final perfection. From the nature that was his as man could spring nothing but natural acts, that is, acts according to reason. By these, indeed, he could achieve perfection; but it would be a perfection contained within natural limits. To act supernaturally and thereby to make for and merit a supernatural perfection, man needs a new nature or, rather, a quasi-nature, which should be in him the permanent source of supernatural activity. A supernatural destiny calls for a nature which shall be a veritable super-nature. God supplied this need. In predestining man for an end to which his natural powers, no matter how evolved and perfected, could never bring him, the Creator equipped him with a species of super-nature, to be in him the perennial spring of actions utterly beyond the force of mere rationality to effect.

"Supernatural" is a compound word. Its sense becomes somewhat clearer if it is broken up into its elements. "Super" means above, or beyond, or outside the range and scope of something. "Nature" has already been defined, as that which in any creature is the radical principle of the activities that are proper and exclusive to it. Man being supernaturalized means, then, his being endowed with a permanent inner principle of activity by which he is able to exercise activities invested with a quality greater than human; that is, with a quality with which he would be utterly unable to clothe them, if left to his own native powers. "Just as," writes St. Thomas, "creatures move, in virtue of the nature in them,

---

[21] Aristotle, *Lib. Physic.* 7, quoted by St. Thomas in *S. Th.* I, II, q. 110, a. 3, and II, II, q. 23, a. 7.

to the conquest of their final end determined for them by their Creator, so, too, in the supernatural order, God infuses a 'form' or 'nature' into the soul, by which it is able to exercise those operations which put it in possession of its final supernatural end which is divine." [22] In other words, the function that rational nature would discharge for man in the conquest of his final natural end, had he been created for such an end, that same function belongs to grace in the soul's achievement of an end which is divine. Grace gives a new nature, by which man becomes, literally, a super-man.

Taking the word "accident" in the philosophic sense above, *grace is accidentally what God is substantially*. It is, according to the words of St. Thomas, an accident "which is a certain likeness to the Divinity shared in by man." [23] When, therefore, the rational creature is said to participate in the divine nature, it does not mean that a part or fraction of that reality which is God himself is given to it, to be added, as it were, to its substance. [24] There can be no fractioning in the ineffable unity, simplicity and spirituality of the Divine Being. What the phrase "participate in the divine nature" does mean is that there is wrought in the creature, by the action of God, a perfection which bears a resemblance to, is modeled on, and has its source and principle in the divine nature itself. The divine nature, not the divine essence, is stated to be the fount of grace, for reasons to be given a little later. The participation in the Divinity imparts proportionately and in a finite manner to the essence of the soul what the divine nature gives to God in an infinite way. Grace is in the creature a real, physical, not simply moral, imitation of a perfection which is found in God in an infinite degree. By it man does not become the divine nature; he does not become God; he becomes "deified," or "deiform." What the Almighty enjoys in virtue of the divine nature with which he is identified, the rational creature enjoys in a certain finite limited manner by reason of the participation of the divine likeness given by habitual grace.

Bearing a resemblance to the divine nature is not the same thing as bearing a resemblance to the divine essence. Though nature and essence in God are the same identical reality, the notions corresponding to these terms are formally distinct. All creatures and all created perfections reflect and, consequently, bear a likeness to the divine essence and divine perfections which are their prototype. Everything, substance and accident, insofar as it exists, is a participation of God, as the supreme, infinite, unlimited source of existence. The purpose of creation was this communication by the Creator to his creatures of his own goodness in varying measure and degree. God is infinitely desirable; created things in their finite way imitate this desirability—this perfection. Existence is an excellent thing, and all the works of God's hands enjoy, each, its own measure of existence. The multiplicity of creatures and that distinction of things, each from each, which gives the universe its refreshing variety, was deliberately intended by

---

[22] *S. Th.* I, II, q. 110, a. 2.
[23] *S. Th.* III, q. 2, a. 10, ad 1, and I, II, q. 112, a. 1.
[24] Cf. Froget, *De l'Habitation*, p. 289.

the Creator. "For God called forth things from nothingness in view of sharing his own being with them and having it made visible by them. A single creature could not by itself sufficiently shadow forth the Creator's perfection, hence existences were created in great number and variety, so that the perfection not imaged in one, might be set forth in another. Hence that goodness or perfection of being, which, in God, is of utter simplicity and unity, is broken up and multiplied in creation." [25]

The essence and the perfections of God are communicable and communicated, by the very act of creation, to all things that are. The inanimate world exists with an existence which is, in a far off way, like to the existence by which God is. The life of plants reflects his life. The movements and the sensibility of the animal world are a pale reflection of him who produces all change without undergoing any. The intellectual life of man is a still more express image of the fount of all life and being. Man's free will suggests the boundless freedom of God; his intelligence, capable of assimilating all the universe of sense to itself, resembles that creative intelligence which contains in an eminent and causal manner all the reality of the universe. The intellectuality of the angel still more purely mirrors forth the intellectual life of the Divine Being. The justice, the wisdom, the power, the freedom, the kindness, the mercy—the very being of God—are projected on the screen of creation in images which do not distort or falsify these attributes, though they must necessarily figure them forth very inadequately. [26] Since, then, all things that are bear a likeness to God, whence comes the necessity of invoking a new entity, as distinct from the act of creation, to impress this likeness on creatures? If grace but gives a resemblance to God, what more does it effect than the creative act itself?

The answer to this question illuminates the inner constitution of this mysterious entity infused into the soul in the act of justification. There are perfections in God which by reason of what they imply are of themselves communicable to creatures; over and above these there is a perfection which, of itself, is incommunicable to creatures in the ordinary course of creation. This is because that perfection is proper and exclusive to God himself. It is a perfection which is specific [27] to God and consequently incapable of being shared by any other. Man shares with the animal movement and sensibility; he cannot share rationality with any being that is not human, be that being angel or brute. Rationality is specific of him and is incommunicable to any being outside humanity. So too in God there is a perfection in which no creature as such can share. Nothing outside the circle of the Divinity can have access to it naturally. Goodness, truth, freedom, life—all these can be found in nature and in nature's God. But no measure, however finite, of that perfection in God, of which there

---

[25] S. Th. I, q. 47, a. 1.

[26] Cf. Maritain, Les Degrés du Savoir, pp. 27, 28; also Terrien, La Gloire, pp. 94–96; and Froget, De l'Habitation, pp. 289–291.

[27] The word "specific" is used here in a purely analogical sense; it is not properly applicable to the Deity.

is question, can be found within the whole realm of created being, embracing the spirit world as well as the world of matter.

Everything in nature, it is true, bears the impress of God, but of God as Creator; it reflects him not as he is in himself, but as the work reveals the worker. In much the same way as a painting discloses to us its author as an artist and not as a man, so, in a certain sense, the participations of the Divine Being found in creation mirror forth their divine source as Creator and not as triune God. Creation reflects the *power* of God, not the *nature* of God as such. God would still be God, though he never created. It is not necessary to him to have formally that perfection which is signified by the term "Creator." It is absolutely necessary to him to have that perfection which makes him to be God. Through creation we can know him. "For the invisible things of him, from the creation of the world are clearly seen, being understood by the things that are made, his eternal power also and divinity." [28] But through this visible world we can know him but partially, inadequately and analogically. "We can know him only in part, because God reveals to us in his works only those perfections which belong to him as supreme cause, and the others that logically flow from them." [29] Creation does not reveal to us God in the intimacy of his divine nature. It shows forth the artist of infinite power and intelligence; it does not give us a glimpse of the person, or persons, of whose being this artistic power is but an aspect. It does not introduce us into the intimate, personal life of the Blessed Trinity.

When, therefore, the soul is said to participate in the divine nature by sanctifying grace, there is question of a participation of something in God that transcends all the perfections of the Almighty which are made visible to us in the created universe. To find the exemplar and archetype of that similitude of himself which he communicates to the soul by grace and which is beyond the whole order of nature, God has to leave behind him all those perfections which are realized in him under the aspect of Creator, penetrate into the very inmost recesses of his own being, and eventually come face to face with that dazzling, blinding, glowing center from which issue forth those two fiery streams of divine activity in which the inner, proper, exclusively divine life of God expresses itself. In his search into himself for what he is to give to creatures in the supernatural order, God does not pause until in himself he comes into the presence of that which makes him to be God and which is not his wisdom, nor his omnipotence, nor his justice, nor any of those other attributes by which he is made known to us by reason. [30] To find the archetype of that perfection which the

[28] Rom 1: 20.

[29] *S. Th.* I, q. 32, a. 1.

[30] See Maritain, *Les Degrés du Savoir*, pp. 27–28. All the names by which we name God, while designating one and the same ineffable, simple, and indivisible Reality, are not synonymous. They signify the perfections which preexist in God in a condition of sovereign simplicity, after the manner in which these perfections are shared in and diversified in creatures. God is Substantial Goodness, as he is Subsistent Truth and Subsistent Being, but the idea of goodness or of truth or of being, even if it subsisted in a pure and absolute "imparticipated" state, would not be God.

Holy Spirit pours forth in the soul when justifying it, it is necessary to make one's way into that inner sanctuary, that Holy of Holies of the Divinity, where the Father, by the intuitive comprehension that he has of himself, engenders the Son and where from the Father and the Son, as from one unique principle of infinite love of the Divine, proceeds that personal love which is the Holy Spirit. That which we conceive in God as the radical principle, the source from which issue those two streams of divine activity which we call the divine processions, that is the excellence in himself of which he undertakes to form a similitude, a finite reproduction, in the essence of the human soul, when he transforms and elevates it by grace.

The analysis, therefore, of the phrase "participating in the divine nature" consists in determining what are those operations of the Godhead characteristic of it and naturally incapable of being shared in any form, by any creature whatsoever. While sharing intellectuality with his creatures, God cannot (again speaking according to the order of nature) impart to the created intellect the range and sweep that belong to his own. The adequate and appropriate and proportionate object of the divine mind cannot be the object of human apprehension. Man, like God, can see with his intelligence, but he cannot see what God sees. It is in the object (and in the measure in which it attains that object), which is the term of the intellectual operation in God, that lies the difference between the divine intellect and the created. The angel's intuitive glance explores only that realm of reality which its own form reveals, and it cannot transcend the limits of that revelation. The object of the angelic glance, no matter how piercing that glance may be, remains finite. The angelic vision cannot fix the infinite reality itself. What is impossible for the intelligence of the angel cannot be possible for the weaker intelligence of man. What constitutes the Divinity in itself—that simple, infinite reality by which God is God—can lie bare to the penetrating intuition of God himself only. The intellectual, adequate comprehension of the Divinity, the adequate expression in the form of a mental word of what is disclosed to that comprehension, and the movement of the will to clasp to itself the measureless beauty contemplated and expressed in that word—these two operations are exclusive to God and are the supreme form of the activity to which the divine nature extends itself.

No created intellect can gaze on the face of God. No created will can share in that kind of love with which God loves the divine goodness itself. "No man hath seen God at any time, the only-begotten Son who is in the bosom of the Father, he hath declared him."[31] The "divine nature," after our way of conceiving things, is that essential, necessary principle in God in which the divine processions have their source. The intellectual expression of what the Divinity is—and the movement of love which, in its resistless tide, bears with it all the energy of divine loving—is as proper to God as it is for man to seize the essences of material things, or for the angel to comprehend, in one intuitive glance, his own reality. A newborn infant

[31] Jn 1: 18.

is very remote, in intellectual power, from the highest of the angels. Yet the distance between these two minds, though so great, is finite. The distance between the intellectual power of him who is supreme in the angelic hierarchy and the intellectual power of God is infinite. It is a greater impossibility for the grandest intellect that God has created, or might create, to see what is the proper object of the vision of God than for a man born blind to have an exact notion of color. God as he is in himself is utterly and incalculably outside of the range of all created vision—even if that vision were to be continuously perfected and strengthened during all eternity. Yet at baptism there is infused into the soul of the child a power that enables the soul and its faculties to bridge, in a measure, this infinite gulf between the vision of man and the vision of God.

The simplicity and ease with which the Almighty achieves this wonderful thing fills the soul that is strong in faith with an emotion that is a commingling of admiration, exultation, awe and abasement. The child born of water and the Holy Spirit is touched with infinity. For the human intellect reinforced, through grace, by a participation of the divine energy of knowing and loving the Divine has given to it as term of its exercise the very same term as is assigned to the highest act of comprehension on the part of God. The Holy Spirit is the link between the creature and the Creator. Through him man is enabled to touch God. For by grace in this world and by the flowering of grace in the next, that is, by the light of glory, the soul of man can tend toward the vision of, and the love of, God himself. It is true that the soul, though it contemplates and loves the "all" that God contemplates and loves, does not see with the completeness of God what it does see. It grasps in a finite and limited manner what God grasps in an infinite way. But it is the very same object that is laid hold of by created and uncreated intelligence. The creature is really and truly given to share in what constitutes the actual and exclusive life of God.

Grace is not, in consequence, a mere ornament or beautification of the soul, cleansing it of its impurities and perfecting it in its own line of possible and indefinite development. It does not consist in a mere rectitude of the will; still less is it a purely legal imputation of justice. It is a real, physical, formal communication of the divine nature, by which the soul and the soul's powers are endowed with a certain, divine quality. The essence of the soul is modified by it, and so are its faculties. They are given aptitudes which could never naturally belong to the creature and which belong naturally only to God. The purpose of grace is to effect a spiritual union—a union, at first affective, and ultimately real, between the soul and God. Sanctifying grace is a preparation for a good of a supreme kind. It is the premise of the "Gift of gifts." It is a preparation for the communication of the Holy Spirit coming in person into the soul of the just, accompanied by the Father and the Son, and uniting himself to that soul, in an ineffable manner, as object of its knowledge and love. To put us in possession of God, here below, in a real though obscure way, while awaiting that hour in which we can contemplate him face to face—that is what constitutes the essence of grace and gives it its value. Hence it is that our "deification" comprises a twofold element: one created, the other uncreated. The created element serves as a sort of connecting link between God and the soul, adapting the latter for the indwelling of the Divine Persons. Such is the function of grace. The uncreated element in justification constitutes the term of our aspirations and the summit of our perfection; it is that supreme good, the enjoyment of which, even in its initial stage, is a foretaste of heaven. It is the Holy Spirit himself giving himself to us, coming to dwell in our hearts, according to the words of the Savior: "If anyone loves me, he will keep my word, and my Father will love him, and we will come to him and make our abode with him." [32]

Grace endows the soul with a kind of divine aptitude for divine operations. It enables it to elicit those acts by which it is empowered to tend toward and, in its measure, enter into and share that intimacy which exists between the Divine Persons themselves. St. Thomas writes: "It is evident that God loves with a special love those whom, through the Holy Spirit, he has made lovers of himself. But the Beloved dwells in the heart of the lover as is the rule of love. Hence it must be that, through the Holy Spirit, not only God dwells in us, but we in God. As is said in Scripture: 'he that abideth in charity abideth in God, and God in him.' " [33] This mutual inhesion, an image of the divine *circuminsession*, was looked forward to by the Savior as the fruit of his Passion. At the Last Supper he said: "I pray that they also may be one, as thou, Father, art in me, and I in thee, that they also may be one in us." [34] This contact with God does not consist in the mingling of the essence of the soul with the divine essence. That would mean the corruption both of the divine and the human. It is by and through its faculties that the soul is able to lay hold of and possess God. It is united to him through the activities of the divine infused virtues of faith, hope and charity residing in the intellect and will. Grace modifies the substance of the soul; the divine virtues that issue from it have their place in the soul's faculties. Grace is, in final analysis, a kind of super-nature given to angels and men and added to the nature received in their creation; or rather—it is that nature itself transmuted, transfigured, lifted above itself, and endowed with energies of a divine character. This super-nature is imparted in order that it might be in them the adequate principle of operations apt to attain to the Blessed Trinity itself, in acts of faith, hope and love.

[32] Jn 14: 23; cf. Froget, *De l'Habitation,* p. 295.
[33] *Summa contra Gentiles,* bk. IV, chap. 21, quoting 1 Jn 4: 16.
[34] Jn 17: 21.

11

The Spirit of Adoption

SANCTIFYING or, as it is more commonly called in the language of theology, habitual grace creates a veritable tie of nature between God and the soul. It constitutes a basis on which reposes a "oneness" in thought and in affection which binds creature to Creator in the bonds of a true, mutual sympathy. It is the teaching of theology that the infused virtue of charity—the characteristic expression of the vitality of sanctifying grace—establishes us in the friendship of God. Furthermore, St. Thomas teaches that the love which is the love of friendship demands and springs from a "certain community of life." "*Omnis amicitia,*" he writes, "*fundatur super aliqua communicatione vitae.*"[1] Community of life is but a very poor rendering of the meaning contained in this phrase, "*communicatione vitae,*" employed by the great theologian. For it implies a companionship, almost a fellowship, in the great and high adventure to which a man's life energies are consecrated.

Man, by grace, participating in the nature and, therefore, in the vitality of God, is empowered, thereby, to live a life which, in its characteristic and specific activities, bears a resemblance to the life of God. In that sense there is, through grace, initiated a life for man which has features that resemble those of the life of the Creator as lived in the inner circle of the Divine Persons. Now likeness in the source of vital activity is not, in itself, the formal, adequate reason of friendship. All men share the same human nature. Their specific activities are the same. All are endowed with sensibility and reason. Many of them pass their days together in the same circumstances and surroundings and are, moreover, bound to one another by ties of blood. And yet, all this does not prevent them from, at times, entertaining feelings of violent hostility toward one another.

A great part of human history is a record of angry and sanguinary conflicts between peoples often closely allied by ties of blood. Hence, a oneness or community of nature, though it is the necessary condition of friendship, still does not, of itself, create bonds of friendship between peoples or individuals. The love of friendship exists when two, being of the same rational nature, are drawn together by a resemblance which is not merely in the nature that is common to the two but in something profound in the way of life's purpose—in something which shapes and determines in a particular and decisive way the activities in which the common nature expresses itself. That is rightly considered to be a man's life which absorbs his interests, in which he takes special delight and at which he aims as the

---

[1] *S. Th.* II, II, q. 25, a. 3; and q. 23, a. 1; cf. Aristotle, *Nic. Ethics,* bk. VIII, chaps. 3 and 4.

goal to be striven for in the use of his reason, his will and, even, his emotions.[2] That is his life which mainly, and above all else, calls his manly powers into play.

The "oneness," or community of life, which is the characteristic mark of friendship consists in this: that two, in many accidental respects unlike, are one in being enamored of the same ideal, to the attainment of which they consecrate all their deliberate energies and which they make the supreme objective of their existence. The same absorbing interest—not in life merely but in that which has become the passion of a life; in that which being made an end to attain gives life its particular features and direction; in that which decides its definite and sustained orientation; in that which, finally, exercises a dominating influence on the thoughts, aspirations and decisions of the soul—effects a "oneness" between two persons and creates between them that warm "sympathy" which fuses their two lives into a unity. "Friends," writes Aristotle, "seek the society of their friends above all else in that particular pursuit in which the existence of each is most truly centered and which seems to both to be the only object worth life's efforts. . . . Friends, wishing to live a common life with their friends, do those things together and share those occupations in which they consider that this common life of theirs is most fully realized."[3] It is this concentration of purpose on the attainment of some good of a reasonable kind which each desires the other to arrive at, and the conquest of which they will to be the fruit of their united efforts—it is this that brings about that affective identification between two in virtue of which the friend becomes another self. The good that is jointly sought is desired by each for the other with the same eagerness with which it is sought for himself.

Instances of such close ties between human beings are furnished in those groupings which men instinctively form among themselves to promote some ideal of a social, political, artistic or, above all, of a spiritual kind. When a man, by some secret stirring within, finds himself urged on to devote his energies to the realization of some good in one or other of the spheres mentioned, he, following the social bent of his nature, seeks out another or others who are moved, or capable of being moved, by the same ideal. Gladly they consort together to talk over and discuss all the aspects of what has become their common purpose in life: eagerly they desire to resume these conversations where they have left off and, by the interchange of fresh and newly-developed thoughts, discover more perfect ways of compassing their common objective. They separate after such meetings with minds and hearts inflamed by their mutual contact, to pursue with still greater understanding and energy what has become the exclusive interest of their lives. Each meeting deepens their mutual consciousness that the good they aspire to is an object of as much preoccupation to the one as to the other. With the strengthening of friendship grows

[2] *S. Th.* II, II, q. 179, a. 1.
[3] *Nic. Ethics*, bk. IX, chap. 12.

the conviction that the interests of one are wholly the interests of the other. The same aspirations to share, the same ideals to pursue, the same objective to gain, it is all this that makes oneness in the life of friends, draws them together in frequent intercourse and causes the energies of their several existences to flow in the same direction and in a common channel.

Can community of life in this sense exist between God and his creature? Can the Creator and the work of his hands have a common ideal in existence? If the love of friendship exists between them, it must necessarily be possible. "Persons," writes St. Thomas, "who have the same end in view, must in some way be united insofar as they tend toward that end. Men in a state, for instance, are bound together by the bonds of civil concord, to achieve the good of the state. Soldiers in battle act in unison to gain the victory which all aim at. The final end toward which man is directed by the aid of God's grace is the vision of the divine essence—a vision proper to God himself. This supreme good is willed infinitely by God, for it is loved infinitely by God. Man cannot reach this goal, therefore, unless he is one with God, through harmony of will. This harmony of will is the effect of love. For it is the mark of friendship that friends should love and hate the same things, rejoice and be sad for the same reasons."[4]

The object toward which all the energies of God's being are directed, the goal of existence for him, lies in the seizure of all that is real by an act of intellectual vision, in the full, adequate, reposeful possession of it, and in the happiness that results from that repose in the supreme object of all possible desire. God's tendency—a tendency which is not a movement toward a good yet distant, but an indefectible cleaving to a good eternally possessed—is toward living life to the utmost by exercising the highest act of life possible. His objective is to live absolutely and infinitely. His aim, his ideal—an ideal eternally actualized—is beatitude, which St. Thomas defines as the highest good of an intelligent nature.[5] In face of this dazzling vision of life—this infinite ideal—God is all aglow with a loving and beneficent desire to inflame all rational creatures with an ambition of, and an enthusiasm for, what he himself enjoys. As a man possessed by a high purpose is restless until he has communicated the ardor with which he himself is aflame to all whom he hopes to influence, so God would have us enamored of that high object, to the possession of which all the energy of the divine being is consecrated. And when man, giving free scope to the development of grace in his soul, devotes himself to the exercise of the infused virtue of charity, in which the vitality of grace manifests itself, he responds to that appeal of God and makes common cause with him.

Divine charity cannot be in us by nature, nor can it be acquired by the natural powers, but only by the action of the Holy Spirit, who infuses it into us—he who is the essential love of the Father and the Son, and the

---

[4] *Summa contra Gentiles*, bk. III, chap. 151.
[5] *S. Th.* I, q. 26, a. 1 and a. 2; I, II, q. 3, a. 4.

participation of whom is created charity in us. Grace is a participation of the divine nature; charity, by appropriation, is a participation of the Holy Spirit. Charity in the soul is a created image of the Love Divine. It is in the Holy Spirit that God loves the divine beauty. The Holy Spirit is sent by the Father and the Son so that we, in our turn, might through him be enamored of the same divine beauty. According to how that loving attraction develops, the creature becomes, speaking figuratively, inflamed with God's enthusiasm and, united with God and sustained by his friendly and ever ready help, bends all its energies toward the conquest of that beatitude to which its Divine Friend beckons it. This conquest becomes the absorbing passion of the life of the creature that is responsive to the interior action of the Holy Spirit.

The soul in which the Holy Spirit's action is not hampered, as he pours out in it the divine charity of which he is the source, readily comes to consecrate all its endeavors to the attainment of an ever fuller vision and an ever deeper love of its God. God to be seen and to be loved becomes the whole preoccupation of existence for such a person. Life has no meaning except as spent in tending toward that goal. To live for such a one is to know and to love God. It is easy to understand that, when this view of life and life's purpose is gained, contact between the soul and God becomes easy. There is a deep sympathy because there is a profound understanding between the two. Both the One and the other are enamored of the same ideal. In the appeal or attraction exercised by this objective—namely, the divine beatitude—is found the tie which binds the created to the uncreated in the bonds of friendship.

Necessarily this beatitude becomes the constant theme of their communings with each other. The lives of all the saints illustrate the truth of this. The burden of that familiar intercourse with God, which is called prayer, is the life of God, which the soul wishes to share in and to enjoy, in constantly increasing measure. The saint thirsts after the life of God. The soul, knowing God's interest in this very thing, knowing that God desires beatitude for it proportionately as he desires it for himself, will eagerly pray to God about the means by which the sublime end of God's life and of the creature's may be realized. It will converse with him, too, about the measures to adopt in order to surmount the obstacles that oppose themselves to the attainment of its goal. And as friends part after their conversations with each other, inflamed with fresh ardor to pursue their common purpose and with renewed courage to combat the obstacles that oppose themselves to its realization, so the soul quits its intercourse with God always burning with a greater desire of beatitude and with a firmer resolve to dare all in its attainment. This friendly communing with God on a topic of common interest is what mental prayer should be, at least in its initial stages. The soul in grace, when with God, should, as becomes friend with friend, rejoice in God's infinite happiness; it should, as well, be firmly convinced that God wishes for it the happiness he himself enjoys, more ardently than it wishes it to him. The spirit of friendship—and real friendship is established by the Holy Spirit between God and man—

demands that the soul should have a clear consciousness of this consoling truth, namely, that in this mutual contact of Creator and creature, God is solely preoccupied with the friendly object of enlightening the soul as to the steps it is to take in order to make its way to the position in which its divine lover stands, and of giving it the strength it needs to make that arduous journey, in spite of the repugnances of fallen nature.

As friend encourages friend when they meet together, so God gives to the soul that strives in prayer to enter into his views and to espouse the same ideal an incessant stream of actual graces which make it to be more and more exclusively possessed by the ideal of true beatitude—of that beatitude which God has called the creature to share with himself. The community, or "oneness," in that which constitutes the goal of life's endeavor—the essential condition of true friendship—is, in this way, realized between God and man. For he destines men effectively to the pursuit and attainment of the beatific vision by the grace which he gives them in an unfailing supply. The creature becomes dear to God when it flings itself generously into the conquest of that which God himself prizes as the supreme good. God delights in seeing man, spurred on by the forces of graces liberally given, pressing forward ardently and breathlessly to the divine union. "I press toward the mark, to the prize of the upward call of God in Christ Jesus." [6] Such are the words of St. Paul. Comprehensible are the felicitations bestowed when the goal is reached. "Well done, good and faithful servant . . . enter thou into the joy of the Lord." [7] It will be as when friends stand clasped hand in hand, when victory has crowned their united struggle for the conquest of an objective that has called forth their highest and best endeavors.

It is clear from all that has preceded that it is not merely a moral resemblance with God that follows on justification. The just man is something more than an image of God, considered under the attribute of his righteousness. All created realities, as has been pointed out, are broken gleams of the one central fiery source of all reality. The goodness of the good man, supposing that there were for mankind no elevation to the supernatural condition, would reflect God's goodness in the same manner as any other created reality reflects the divine reality. *But, by grace, man's justice does more than reflect; it shares the nature of God's justice.* It is of a divine and not merely a human texture. The human element in it is not, of course, eliminated or corrupted. There is no absorption of what is of man in what is of God. That would be the gross and monstrous error of pantheism. The human does not disappear before the onrush of the divine; it is simply sublimated and endowed with a more than human potency.

Through the operation of the Holy Spirit in the justified soul, there is produced there a physical reality endowed with the properties of the intimate nature of God. The nature of God—itself undergoing no change or diminution—is reproduced in the created spiritual substance. One

---

[6] Phil 3: 14.
[7] Mt 25: 23.

shrinks from the attempt at illustrating this mystery by an example drawn from experience, for all such comparisons will, necessarily, under some aspect or another, be misleading. The most serviceable illustration is perhaps taken from light. It was the one habitually employed by the great doctors of the Church. A mirror exposed to the sun's rays becomes, itself, a source of radiance and illumination without, thereby, taking from or adding to the illuminative power of the sun. It participates in the sun's power to dazzle and illuminate. So the soul exposed to the action of the source of all grace and charity, namely, the Holy Spirit, becomes illuminated and becomes charged with the radiance and the power of the Divine Being. The physical reality produced in the soul by the Spirit of Sanctification endows it with the aptitude to be associated hereafter in the blissful life of God and with the capacity of being able here, in time, to perform supernatural acts that are, at once, a preparation for and a meriting of that divine life.

It goes without saying that as long as man sojourns on earth the intimate nature of God can be reproduced in him only in a very imperfect manner. It can never, as long as we are in the flesh, reach its final evolution and perfection. The intimacy of earth, however close, can never reach the intimacy of heaven. The energies, therefore, given by grace cannot have their full play in this world. The most perfect perception of God given in the highest mystical states, while being true as far as it goes, remains necessarily enigmatic. The most perfect vision of God that man can have while he is in the body is the clearest vision of what he is not. "We now see through a glass in a dark manner, but then, face to face. Now I know in part, but then, I shall know even as I am known." [8] So speaks St. Paul, who was ravished to the third heavens and whose gaze penetrated further into the secrets of the supernatural world than did that, perhaps, of any other man who has ever lived. The glass through which we see God is both thick and darkened. What is more, its lines tend to impose their own contours on the divine form which shows through in such dimness. St. John of the Cross constantly teaches that the more the created elements which enter into the formation of the concepts of faith affect our spiritual vision, the less pure is our perception of God. Whereas, on the other hand, the less these elements obtrude themselves on our line of vision, the more perfect is the view of God conveyed by them.

Though love, unlike intellectual sight, does not contract its object to its own measure in laying hold of it, nevertheless, it suffers because of the infirmity of sight. The love of heaven, because God is seen there face to face, is of a totally different quality from that of earth—though it is the same in essence. "Charity never falleth away." [9] By grace it is God himself—in the full stature of his being, in the richness of his nature, in the plenitude of his triune personality, who is loved—not a diminished image of him contracted to human measure. *Our intelligence must think God*

[8] 1 Cor 13: 12.
[9] See 1 Cor 13: 8.

through its own forms; our will can love God in his own form. But in spite of this, as has been said, the will is trammeled and cramped in its exercise, because the intellect reveals the beloved to it in such an obscure and unsatisfactory manner. Love feeds itself by gazing; and faith, at its best, offers a sight of God vague in the extreme. It is as when the outlines of some object at a great distance become indistinct and dissolve because of the very intentness of the gaze in which we strive to trace them with definiteness and decision for our own satisfaction of seeing. The outlines will become for us firm and clear and definite only when grace receives its final consummation in glory and faith yields place to the vision face to face. There at last love can fully satisfy itself with gazing.

But, in spite of its imperfections, grace, the moment it is given, bestows a right and a title to the inheritance of God. "Regeneration" is a term frequently applied in the New Testament to the process of justification.[10] For the sacred writers, being justified consists in being born anew, and this second birth is of God.[11] The words of St. John give admirable precision to the statement of St. Peter so frequently referred to, in which the chief of the apostles says that the faithful are, by grace, made to participate in the divine nature. In conception and birth the infant derives its nature from its parents. In the second and mystical birth, the neophyte takes his supernature from his heavenly Father. The direct consequence is that the "newly born"[12] (the words are St. Peter's) of water and the Holy Spirit are entitled one day to enter into the inheritance of God. It is as when the firstborn to the owner of a great estate becomes heir to the property by the very fact of his birth. From his father he receives with his nature the title to the domain. What is more, when the neophyte reaches the age when he can distinguish between good and evil, choose the right and reject the wrong, he can, by exercising activities in accordance with the life of grace in him, accomplish acts which will have a twofold effect. They will merit an increase of the inheritance that awaits his coming of age, and they will give him as well a partial acquisition of it, before that coming of age; he comes of age when, through entry into heaven, he has attained "unto the perfect man, unto the measure of the age of the fullness of Christ."[13]

Every act that proceeds from the deliberate will, under the influence of the infused virtue of charity, merits an increase in the degree of beatific vision that is to be the lot of the members of Christ. At the same time, such an act makes more perfect the union between the soul and God, within the limits of the development set to that union on this side of the grave. Hence the Savior stresses the importance of every moment of life, saying: "Lay up to yourselves treasures in heaven, where neither the rust nor the moth doth consume."[14] These words plainly indicate that the followers of Jesus may, if they are responsive to the promptings of grace in their decisions and

---

[10] See Jn 3: 4–7; Tit 3: 3–5; Jas 1: 18.
[11] See Jn 3: 7.
[12] 1 Pet 2: 2.
[13] Eph 4: 13.
[14] Mt 6: 20.

their acts, increase constantly the value of the heavenly possessions which are to be theirs after death. Not only that, but, if the exercise of the infused divine virtues of faith, hope and charity becomes so habitual that a sustained and permanent disposition is created in the soul by means of which its deliberate acts spring spontaneously and almost instinctively from, and are informed by, these virtues, the way is prepared for that experience of God within us which is a real foretaste of the bliss of Paradise. Examples of this anticipated experience of heaven—always, of course, within the realm of faith—are frequent in the lives of God's saints on earth.

Here below, those regenerated through the merits of Christ are in the condition of heirs. As yet they cannot exercise all the functions which will devolve on them when, passing from the state of heirdom, they become proprietors. But just as those who are destined to succeed to large estates begin, before they are of age, to associate with their fathers in the management of affairs, perform acts which bear on that management, and develop a personal interest in the extent and the possibilities of enlargement of the family property, so, too, the justified, if they use the super-nature that is in them, are gradually drawn more and more into the intimacy of God and become privileged to share his mind. To his apostles, the Savior said at the Last Supper: "I will not now call you servants, for the servant knoweth not what his lord doth. But I have called you friends, because all things whatsoever I have heard of my Father, I have made known to you." [15] Growth in intimacy with God is attended by a gradually perfected initiation into his secrets, his plans, his designs and his "preoccupations." The great "preoccupation" of God remains as always that the inheritance of heaven should be for his chosen creatures as well as for himself. He cherishes as his heirs all to whom he has given grace. "For the Spirit himself giveth testimony to our spirit, that we are children of God, and if children, heirs also; heirs of God and joint heirs with Christ." [16]

Faith is the novitiate of vision. Its acts are as the heir's imitation of, and initiation into, the acts that the same heir, become proprietor, shall be called on to exercise. These acts are the very acts in which the life of God himself, that is, of the One God in Three Divine Persons, exercises itself. "Dearly beloved," says St. John, "we are now God's children, and it hath *not yet appeared what we shall be. We know that when he shall appear we shall be like to him, because we shall see him as he is. And every one that hath this hope in him sanctifieth himself, as he also is holy."* [17]

God is from all eternity proprietor of the heavenly estate. At death, those who are purified will be called to share that proprietorship with him. The same privilege will be extended to all those who die in the state of grace when their period of purgation is terminated in Purgatory. It is the intuitive vision—the vision of God in which he is seen as he sees himself—that puts the soul in possession of the supreme good, namely, God

[15] Jn 15: 15.
[16] Rom 8: 16–17.
[17] 1 Jn 3: 2, 3.

himself, the possession of all possessions. On earth God can be seized only in and through faith and, therefore, he is held very incompletely and imperfectly. The soul enjoys him in hope, not in complete attainment. It is in the state of "looking for the blessed hope and coming of the glory of the great God and our Savior Jesus Christ." [18] This hope in which the Christian lives is not wavering or timid. He can, with unshaken confidence, "glory in the hope of the glory of God." [19] While awaiting the revelation, he is admitted to close friendship with almighty God. He can embrace the Lord in charity—even if, always, what he loves is obscure for him. Or, to use another metaphor, just as the infant not yet come to the use of reason has, nevertheless, the faculties of knowing and willing—faculties which, in process of time and in the ordinary course of development, will function of their own native capacities; and as the same child, when it begins to reason, is not acquiring some new faculty, but only putting to exercise one which has, in an undeveloped state, been his from the beginning; so too, when the soul shall enter into glory, it shall not be acquiring new powers but shall simply be bringing into full play powers which were latent in it from its initiation, by grace, into the supernatural life, that is, from the moment of its regeneration.

Though grace is a "creature," it presents many points of difference from all created things that, actually or possibly, come under the study of natural reason. As to its mode of existence, it is inferior to all created substances because it is not a substance. It has not an independent existence in itself. It cannot stand alone, as neither color, nor taste, nor figure can stand by itself. It demands a subject in which to inhere and to sustain it in being. It cannot exist isolated from the spirit of the angel or the soul of man. But, in modifying the soul in its essence and its faculties, it endows them with a force and a power which enable these faculties to transcend, in their exercise, everything in the whole range of reality outside of God. Though habitual grace is an accident, it differs fundamentally from all other accidents in its origin. Quality, quantity, action and the rest of the nine categories into which Aristotle divides non-substantial reality, all emanate from the created substance itself, either as properties naturally flowing from it or else as emerging from its potentiality under the action of external causes. The virtuality of the accidents produced or, rather, "educed" in this latter fashion preexists in the causes which call them forth. Therefore there is nothing in any created substance that is not capable of coming forth from it in the ordinary course of nature, or which is not capable of being called forth in it by the energies of an external created agent.

Now, there is no being in nature that contains in its potentiality the least element of grace. [20] There is no created energy that can call it forth. It does not exist in the tiniest degree in the whole vast possibilities of all created reality. Were all the natural forces of the worlds of angels and of

[18] Tit 2: 13.
[19] Rom 5: 2.
[20] See St. Thomas Aquinas, *Quaest. disp. de potentia*, q. 3, a. 8, sol. 3.

men marshalled together and combined in effort, they would prove utterly and absolutely powerless to call forth a spark of divine grace in a spiritual substance. God alone can be its cause.[21] The divine nature itself is the exemplary cause, while the life and death of Jesus are the meritorious cause, of this mysterious entity. But to be *efficient* cause of it—that is reserved to God himself inalienably. With no creature, not even with the sacred humanity of his divine Son, can he share this principality in the causation of grace. It is only as instruments that creatures can be employed in the process of "deifying" the soul. The humanity of Jesus, and the sacraments instituted by him, are instruments in the hands of the Holy Spirit in this work.

St. Thomas likens the action of God in infusing grace into the soul to the act of "creation," while pointing out that the word is not quite applicable in this connection. Grace in its genesis is like creation in this, that it does not come to be out of preexisting conditions. But the production of grace in the soul is unlike the act of calling beings from nothingness in this, that the act of creation terminates in a subsistent thing. Whatever is created is something having an independent existence of its own. Grace has not this independence in existence. It is an accident, not a substance. Accidents are not created; they are, rather, "con-created," [22] coming into being with the substance which they modify. Yet grace, though an accident, does not come to be with the creation of any substance that has come from the hands of God in the course of creation. It cannot then be said to be "con-created" like all other accidents. God produces grace in the soul, making use of the soul itself in the production of that effect. It is not evolved out of the substance of the soul as other accidents are. God, directly using his supreme power, causes the soul to be modified by a form which gives it a divine quality. All creatures are completely subject to his irresistible action. He can make them to be as he chooses. Their existence and the modifications of that existence are wholly at his bidding. Hence, he can, by an act of his omnipotent will, cause the soul to be modified by the quality of divine grace, without this quality needing to be preexistent in, and apt to be called forth from, the soul's natural potentialities. This aptitude of the creature to be elevated to an act, such as it could in no wise attain to by its own natural resources, is called in theology *potentia obedientialis*— obediential potentiality.[23]

These precisions having been given, it remains true to say, however, that Sacred Scripture favors the term "created" in speaking of justification. St. Paul writes: "For we are his [God's] workmanship, *created* in Christ Jesus." [24] And again: "Put ye on the new man, who according to God, is *created* in justice and holiness of truth." [25] Elsewhere the Apostle of the

---

[21] *S. Th.* I, II, q. 112, a. 1.
[22] St. Thomas Aquinas, *Quaest. disp. de veritate*, q. 27, a. 3.
[23] See R. Mulard, O.P., *La Grâce*, pp. 326–327.
[24] Eph 2: 10.
[25] Eph 4: 24.

Gentiles warns his disciples that nothing they can do of their own native resources is of any avail toward being in the grace of God, and that to enjoy such a favor they must be, in a sense, formed or created afresh. "For in Christ Jesus neither circumcision availeth anything nor uncircumcision but a *new creature*." [26] The same form of expression is employed in the epistle to the Corinthians: "If then any be in Christ a *new creature*, the old things are passed away, behold all things are made new." [27] Nor is this mode of expression peculiar to the writings of St. Paul; in the Catholic epistle of St. James one reads: "For of his own will hath he begotten us by the word of truth, that we might be some beginning of his *creature*." [28] The recurrence of this term in its various modes is not without significance. It disputes, with the words generation and regeneration, the place of predilection in the verbal armory of the sacred writers. Perhaps through the usage of it, the Holy Spirit wished to carry back men's minds to the first fair dawn when the soul, after having been created by God, was robed in the glittering garment of original justice. The term would then be intended to convey a veiled and gracious assurance that the original fairness and splendor, lost in the prevarication of Adam, were being restored in the bath of waters prepared by the blood of Christ and impregnated with the virtue of the Spirit of Sanctification.

[26] Gal 6: 15.
[27] 2 Cor 5: 16.
[28] Jas 1: 18.

12

The Principles of Supernatural Growth

THERE is no living creature that can, at one stride, attain to the fullest development of which it is capable. The animate creation, throughout its whole extent, is submitted to the law of growth and progress, at least during a portion of its existence. The qualification "at least during a portion of existence" is inserted because, in the natural order, a process of decay and retrogression normally sets in before life reaches its term. To achieve their perfection and to attain to the end appointed to them by nature, the beings endowed with life are equipped with powers or faculties by which they can promote their own development. This is manifest in the plant and in the animal kingdoms. The law finds a more perfect expression still in the realm of rational creatures.

No child of human parents is born a man. He comes into the world furnished with the nature and the faculties through which he can achieve his manhood. The phrase "self-made man" is one that is familiar, in a narrow and restricted sense. All men in a certain true sense are meant to be self-made men. Were there no creation in the supernatural order, God would intend that each human being should, by his own activities, make himself a man, that is, achieve himself. Self-realization, in the sense of the perfect evolution of his manhood, would have been the task enjoined on man, in the supposition of creation in the natural order. To this self-expression—stripped of all egotistical implications—God would lend his sustaining power and would, by his providence, cooperate in its achievement.

It is scarcely necessary to remark that the acquisition of virile strength, balanced physical energies and a stature exhibiting neither excess nor defect is but an aspect—and the least important aspect—of this growth into manhood. It is in the soul rather than in the body, in the reasonable faculties rather than in those of sense, that lie the vital elements that are to germinate into human perfection. Growth in age, strength and stature does not make the man. Development of firm and constant rational control over the tendencies and impulses he finds in himself, and over the active and passive contacts into which he is drawn with his fellows—this is what makes him truly a man. The moralists speak of this as the acquisition of the moral virtues.

The etymology of the word "virtue" is illuminating. There are two Latin words to translate the English word "man," "*homo*" and "*vir*," but they have not quite the same signification. "*Homo*" means anyone who has human nature. It connotes that initial provision with which each one sets out on the high adventure of life, toward the goal of completion. That initial provision is human nature with its multiple faculties, among which hold preeminence the faculties of the intellect and of the will. *"Vir"* denotes the finished product issuing from the right usage of these powers. *"Vir"* means the human being who is a man—all that a human being should be. He is that when he is "vir-tuous." Virtue, derived from *"vir,"* is what makes a man good and his actions excellent.[1]

To know the truth—and in that knowledge to discern what is right and good in reference to oneself and to others and then to adhere unswervingly to that good—that constitutes the end of the law of growth to which human nature, had it no supernatural destiny, would be submitted. By means of his intellect, endowed with the knowledge of the first principles, which contain all truth in germ; and by his will, with its native inclination to what, in judgment, choice and act, is becoming for human nature; man could forge his own perfection and so work out his own destiny. By his own acts, by the right usage of what he would find in himself, he could achieve himself. St. Thomas writes: "Man, according to the capacities of his nature, is perfectly equal to the attainment of a goal of achievement, to which he has an innate tendency. By his own native powers he can bring himself onward to that final perfection, which consists in such contemplation of the divine as is possible to man, confined within the natural range of his reasonable faculties. It is in this contemplation that the philosopher places human happiness."[2] This happiness would be the normal consequence of the acquisition of the moral virtues that go to constitute the perfect or "accomplished man." It would constitute the final end, had man been created for a natural and not a supernatural destiny.

Truly admirable is the skill with which God, when he raised man to the supernatural order, appointing to him a supernatural goal, shaped the gifts of divine grace to the mold of human nature. In his work of surpassing love and generosity he shows a tender, delicate and divinely respectful consideration for the essential constituents of human nature itself and of its characteristic activities. In imparting to man a supernatural life, God takes extreme care that it should preserve a close analogy to the natural life which it transforms and sublimates. The first infusion of habitual grace is a birth to a new life, at once human and super-human. It is a life such as a man may live and yet could not, of his own human powers, attain to, or even pretend to. And just as the child when it derives its nature from its parents is not yet a man—a *vir*—but is destined to forge himself to manhood through the interplay of moral forces during his earthly career, so too the child of God as it issues from the waters of baptism is not the complete man of God but is destined to that manhood as the consummation of life's efforts. The catechumens, as they came from the bath of regeneration, were, for St. Peter, *"Quasi modo geniti infantes"*—"as new-born babes."[3] Their souls vivified by grace, they are saved only "in hope."[4]

---

[1] Cf. Aristotle, *Nic. Ethics*, bk. II, chap. 6.
[2] *Quaest. disp. de veritate*, q. 27, a. 2.
[3] I Pet 2: 2.
[4] Rom 8: 24.

According to the normal working out of God's plan, the investiture with grace is not followed by an immediate transportation to heaven. The reception of life in the supernatural plane, as in the natural, is but the launching of the creature on a career of effort and achievement. The bestowal of grace is not the ending but the beginning. The Christian who would be quite content with being in grace and would have no ambition or make no effort to grow in grace is but a fainéant and a malingerer. Such an attitude is base and even absurd. It is as if a person were content to contract his mind and limbs to the measure of the cradle during his entire existence. When God makes a person a Christian, he by no means dispenses him from the effort to be a man. The law of progress holds sway in the world of grace as in the world of nature. The child of Adam, had he been left with merely the resources and powers of nature, would have been obliged to achieve a life wholly regulated by reason. The newly-born of water and the Holy Spirit has the obligation of winning his way, through the harsh experience of everyday existence, to a life entirely controlled by faith. Faith is not alien from reason: it is reason endowed with a divine penetration. The daily stress that a man is submitted to, if he is not to prove traitor to the principles of reason and faith in his decisions and acts, is what God places in man's way in order that man may achieve himself. This stress is the perpetual ever-recurring cross of which Christ speaks. "And he said to *all:* 'If any man will come after me, let him . . . take up his cross daily and follow me.' " [5]

Christ was a man—not *homo* only, but *vir.* He was a man in the received sense of that expression. He would have his followers be men, not babes or cowards or sluggards. He would have his followers leave behind them the weakness, inconsequence and irresponsibility of childhood and set before themselves the goal of supernatural manhood, to be attained by praiseworthy effort. St. Paul is the faithful interpreter of the Master's intentions when he urges the Ephesians to bend their efforts to arrive "unto the measure of the age of the fullness of Christ." [6] God is merciful to the fainthearted and unambitious—to those who, having little insight and no idealism, acquiesce in remaining unshaped, unwrought, undeveloped and unspiritualized by life. But his esteem and regard are extended to those who, responding to his high ideal for them and impatient of what does not become a man, seize upon earthly circumstance, whether harsh or kind, in order to make of it an instrument by which they may be forged to the resemblance, in thought and conduct, of him who answered to all the requirements of complete and perfect manliness. When the Church brings to a favorable conclusion her inquiry into the moral and spiritual worth of a candidate for the honor of her altars, her verdict is equivalent to a proclamation to the world, that the person whose cause has been examined was, in very truth, "a man."

It is in accordance with God's exceeding regard for us that he should

[5] Lk 9: 23.
[6] Eph 4: 13.

make the attainment of the final end of the supernatural life an achievement on the part of man himself. God's life, to be captured and enjoyed by man, is meant to be both the reward and the resultant of human endeavor. One may ask how this thing can be, since there is such a disproportion between the human and divine. No road will bring a traveler to the end of his journey except the road of which the end itself forms the final part. A divine objective to be reached by personal effort postulates activities which are themselves divine. It would seem that man, being such, cannot rise above action which is purely human. This would be so, were man left to his native resources. God has provided for the difficulty. Appointing a divine goal as the final end of man's strivings, he furnishes man with the means apt to carry him on to that goal. St. Thomas, with his habitual incisiveness and clarity, develops this theme in a passage found in his study of the virtues considered in their general aspect. "It is to be noted," he says, "that the final good for man is of two kinds. One of these[7] is quite commensurate with his nature as a reasonable being. But the second kind of final good, or end, appointed to man surpasses the powers of attainment and the native requirements of mere humanity. . .".[8]

Everything tends toward its final end by the putting forth of its own operations. There ought, moreover, be a consonance between the means and the end.[9] Hence, man, being destined for an end which is above nature's range and exigencies, must be furnished with perfections which, in their capacities, surpass the principles and the perfections proper to human nature. This could not be unless God were to infuse into his rational creature principles of activity essentially superior to the ones belonging to it by nature, and added to these latter. The principles of operation appropriate to man as such are the essence of the soul and the rational faculties of reason and will. The intelligence is equipped from the start with those first principles of knowledge which contain in germ full intellectual development. The will has an inborn inclination to that "good" which is the completion and the crown of nature.[10]

If, then, man is to be in a position to posit acts which gain for him, and lead him on to, that final end which is the very life of God to be lived in a participated fashion by him, he must have infused into him, first, grace, which imparts a higher nature, and then, principles of action, in harmony with that superior nature and the end toward which it gravitates. These principles of action are none other than the theological virtues of faith,

[7] In the actual historical state of humanity, this end is but hypothetical. Man has been, "de facto," created for a higher than natural end.

[8] *Quaest. disp. de veritate,* in comm. a. 10.

[9] The meaning of this familiar axiom might be made clear by pointing out that it is equivalent to stating that "not anything will purchase anything else."

[10] In the natural endowments of will and intellect is contained the seedling which is capable of expanding into the complete perfection of the ethical man, along the path of the formation of the acquired virtues. These faculties call for nothing to be superadded to them in order that man might be able to reach his perfection through their operations. This, of course, is to be understood in the hypothesis of a creation in the natural order (see Billot, S.J., *De virt. infusis,* 2d ed., vol. 1, p. 117).

hope and charity. Faith sheds light on certain supernatural truths, which, in the supernatural sphere, fulfill the same role as, in the natural order, is fulfilled by the principles that are known instinctively or naturally. Hope and charity move and incline the will to the acquisition of that supernatural good which the human will, left to itself, would have no inclination to seek. And just as the natural principles need to be completed by certain acquired virtues if man is to reach the perfection proper to him, so, too, must the regenerated soul receive from the divine influence other virtues, namely, the infused, which perfect it in view of those actions by which it is to force its way onward to the goal of eternal life.[11]

The normal human life is made up of a certain number of years. Every moment of deliberate activity throughout the extent of those years is meant to play its part in securing man's growth in supernatural stature. He does not, like the angel, reach his destiny at one stride. The consummation for him is the outcome of what should be an unbroken series of decisions and acts.[12] With a growth of years should go an advance in wisdom and grace—that is, a continual progress in faith, hope and charity.[13] The formation of the complete natural man is a time process and usually a protracted one. The close analogy between the life of nature and that of grace has been frequently referred to. The very difference between them stresses the analogy. Both have a maturity to aim at. But whereas, in the natural order, once this peak point has been reached there sets in a process of retrogression and decay, there is no necessary and inevitable decline in the supernatural life. It can always wax stronger and stronger as long as the years on earth endure. Its development can be commensurate with the whole term of mortal existence, and the maturity it then has reached will last for eternity. The Venerable Libermann writes in this connection: "The soul, in order to receive the divine into itself and to fulfill God's will, must keep itself united with God. This is done by faith, hope and charity. Here it is not a question of transient or occasional acts of these virtues, but of a life of faith inspired by hope and charity. In this world the soul tends (that is, ought to tend), unceasingly, toward God and adheres to him by the *habitual* application of the theological virtues to all its conduct, even to the details of that conduct. If God has made us for the purpose of being united with himself, it follows that every act in which this union with God is not exercised or aimed at is a lost act and useless. It is only in aiming at this union, in and through its actions, that the soul finds its happiness; for it can be happy only when it is practically in line with the purpose for which it has been created."[14]

---

[11] St. Thomas, *Quaest. disp. de veritate*, in comm. a. 10.

[12] St. Thomas says *à propos* of this: "The Angels, who occupy a degree in being superior to man, win beatitude by a single movement of a meritorious nature. Men, however, attain to it by a succession of such movements. These constitute what is termed merit" (*S. Th.* I, II, q. 5, a. 7).

[13] Cf. Lk: "And the child grew and waxed strong . . . and . . . advanced in wisdom and age, and grace with God and man" (2: 40, 52).

[14] *Ecrits spirituels*, p. 12.

It is for man's great glory and merit that he can be the artisan of his own perfection. God has placed in his hands the instruments by which he can create that most perfect of all works of art, a human life wholly super-naturalized. The beneficent Creator has given his creature the talents by which he can carve out a fortune for himself and acquire "a living" which shall resemble "the living" that is enjoyed by God himself. These talents have been mentioned already. They are none other than the infused virtues, theological and moral.

They are given the name infused in opposition to the acquired virtues, which latter are the fruit of man's endeavor and can be developed by his own acts. Man is the author of the acquired virtues; God alone can be the source of the infused. It is only by him they can be imparted; their very existence can be known only through his revelation. The three theological virtues of faith, hope and charity hold pride of place among the virtues divinely given. Their existence is explicitly mentioned in Sacred Scripture. "And now there remain faith, hope and charity—these three: but the greatest of these is charity." [15] These are the words of St. Paul. The Council of Trent is no less explicit. It teaches that, in the act of justifi-cation, man receives, at the same time as pardon of his sins, the virtues of faith, hope and charity, through Jesus Christ—of whom he becomes a member. [16]

Not only is our knowledge of the existence of these three virtues due to divine revelation, not only have they in God their unique and exclusive origin—they have this as their special characteristic, namely, that their activities are exercised on God himself, in his own nature and triune personality. Other virtues may have God as their *objective,* that is, while being concerned with creature things, such as human dealings and human passions, they may serve to forward a man on his way to the divine goal of life. A Christian, who, in a Christian spirit, occupies himself with the transaction of business or with the regulation of his own passions and impulses can, in so doing, grow in perfection and be brought closer to God. So that, in these cases, while being occupied with things of a created nature, the Christian has still, in his actions, God as his objective. But where there is a question of the theological virtues, God is not merely the *objective* which is aimed at. He is the *object* about which they are con-cerned. [17] The distinction may be made clearer by a homely example. When a devoted mother is using imagination and hand and eye in the fabricating of dainty garments for her child, her attention and her industry are necessarily riveted to the careful execution of the work on hand. But the little one remains all through the chief and ultimate interest. But when the mother holds in her arms and presses to her bosom the child arrayed in all the finery she has lovingly worked for it, then the tiny person held in the maternal embrace is the direct object on which thought, affection and

[15] 1 Cor 13: 13.
[16] *Conc. Trid.,* session 6, chap. 7.
[17] St. Thomas Aquinas writes: "The theological virtues have God not only as their *end,* but for their direct *object . . .*" (*Quaest. disp. de virtute,* in comm. a. 12).

caresses are lavished. In a somewhat similar way, faith, hope and charity fix the activities of the soul on the person of God himself, as One to be "devoured" by the eyes of the soul and enveloped in its affections.

Faith gives us an acquaintance with God and the things of the spiritual world. It does for that world what reason does for the material universe. The knowing of God with the knowledge imparted by the gift of faith is utterly beyond the natural powers of angels and of men. The vision of God and divine things given by faith is the beatific vision in embryo. The inchoation of a thing and its consummation belong in essence to the same order of reality. Without faith it is impossible to please God; without it all access to God is barred. St. Paul writes: "But without faith it is impossible to please God. For he that cometh to God must believe that he is and is a rewarder to them that seek him." [18] He addresses himself to the Romans in parallel terms: "We have access through faith into this grace, wherein we stand, and glory in the hope of the glory of God." [19]

This necessity of faith springs from the very nature of things. God himself cannot override it once he has created man for that final end, which is identical with the final end of God's own life—namely, the intuitive contemplation and love of the Divine Essence. [20] A man would be powerless to direct his steps toward the goal appointed to him by God unless he had some knowledge of that goal. The apostle Thomas, in the dullness of his understanding where supernatural realities were concerned, moved this difficulty when told by Jesus at the Last Supper that he and the others were destined for the same goal as the Master himself. The puzzled apostle said: "Lord, we know not whither thou goest, and how can we know the way?" [21] The objection would be well grounded and eminently reasonable were the speaker altogether in ignorance of the term of the life of Jesus and of his own. Like many another Christian, Thomas was, by a strange paradox, blind to the vision he enjoyed. Jesus said to him and to the others: "Whither I go you know, and the way you know. . . . I am the way and the truth and the life . . . if you had known me, you would without doubt have known my Father also . . . and you have seen him . . . he that seeth me, seeth the Father also. How sayest thou [to Philip], 'Show us the Father?'" [22]

To set oneself in movement toward an end presupposes, then, some idea, at least, of the end. The perception must be attended with a real desire of what awaits one as the term and crown of endeavor. But the dim perception of a distant goal would not be sufficient to set the wise man in movement toward it, however ardently it might be desired. He would never embark on this great and arduous enterprise of ultimately seeing

---

[18] Heb 11: 6.

[19] Rom 5: 2.

[20] Faith is the first step in man's salvation, the foundation and root of all justification. In its absence it is impossible to please God and to attain to the fellowship of his children (cf. *Conc. Trid.*, session 6, chap. 8).

[21] Jn 14: 5.

[22] Jn 14: 4–9.

God face to face unless he had reason to have strong hopes of eventual success. It is only a foolish person who would venture on an utterly hopeless undertaking. It is only hope of success that inspires effort. The desire of the final end implies love of it, because there is no eagerness for what is not loved. "Hence," St. Thomas concludes, "arises the necessity of the three theological virtues of faith, hope and charity if the soul is to be duly equipped for the realization of its destiny, which consists in making its way, in perfect freedom and by deliberate choice, to its final supernatural end. Faith reveals in God, to be seen and possessed in the reality of his own inner being, the supreme goal of life. Hope is the virtue through which man relies, for the successful prosecution of his enterprise, on the help that God guarantees to give him. By this virtue he looks to God unfalteringly for eternal beatitude and all the means useful and necessary to reach that beatitude. Finally, charity inspires the soul with a sovereign love of him, who is supremely the object of love."[23]

Since man's ultimate perfection consists in living the life of God in heaven and since each stage of the growth of a living thing is a promise or imperfect form of its final development, it follows that the divine life must, already in time, be lived in some measure by every regenerated soul. "The rule of action for the justified," says St. Thomas, "is the divinity itself as participated in by man, in a certain fashion. He is therefore bound to act, no longer as becomes a mere man, but as becomes one who is, as it were, made God by participation in the divinity."[24]

To fare toward the goal of his supernatural destiny man must live a divine life humanly. It is the function of the infused virtues to enable him to do so. They do not of themselves impart a facility in the exercise of this divine-human activity. In this lies the chief distinction between the natural, or acquired, virtues and the supernatural, or infused, virtues. The acquired virtues do not impart to us the power to know and to will. They perfect our powers of knowing and willing. We may choose the right or the wrong, be temperate or intemperate, just or unjust; we may follow the path of the coward or of the man of courage. The choice between these opposing courses is open to us. It is a dangerous power to be able to follow wrong courses.

It would be a good thing for us to protect ourselves against this danger. We do so by acquiring good habits. The aim of these is to form certain strong and fixed dispositions, in the will and in the intellect, by which these powers receive a definite bent toward what is right. By the frequent exercise of acts of justice, for example, a man's will loses the tendency to do unjust actions and achieves a constancy and facility in doing deeds that are just. Such deeds become, as is said, second nature to him; that is, they proceed from his will with something of the spontaneity of the activities that spring from nature. It is natural for man to will. It is not natural for him to will rightly in an indefectible manner. When the moral virtues are

---

[23] See St. Thomas, *Quaest. disp. de virtute,* in comm. a. 12.
[24] *Sent.* III, d. 34, q. 1, a. 3.

developed, it becomes quasi-natural for him to elect the right constantly and with ease. It is natural for man to reason. It is not natural for him to arrive always at prudent conclusions as a result of his reasoning. He does so only when his intelligence has acquired the virtue of prudence. The acquired virtues are the result of the repetition of acts. They come slowly, as a rule, and gradually. One becomes just by continually acting in a just manner. But once the good habit is formed, there is no longer felt a difficulty in accomplishing acts that are in accordance with it. The temperate man, as Aristotle teaches, performs deeds of self-control with facility and delight.

No such ease of action necessarily accompanies the divine habits which are infused into the soul with grace. The acquired virtues presuppose the power of acting reasonably. The infused virtues do not presuppose the power of acting divinely, they bestow it. Suppress them and supernatural action becomes an utter impossibility.[25] They do not give a certain definite inclination to faculties already existing and which might be inclined in a contrary direction. Faith does not modify in one sense rather than another an already existing power to know God in a supernatural manner. It imparts that very power. Without faith the intellect would not in any degree know God as he is known supernaturally. Charity does not take and give a certain fixed disposition to an already existing faculty of loving God. It gives to the will the aptitude to love God. The will can love the good. It could love God as revealed by reason. It is utterly powerless of itself to give itself the slightest movement toward God as an object of supernatural affection. The will of its own natural resources can love God naturally: it cannot love him supernaturally.

In spite of the fact that the infused virtues confer no faculty of action, they merit the name of virtues. For they perfect man relative to his final end.[26] For virtue is what makes a man good and his action good. Certainly the supernatural infused habits fulfill this definition. They make a man good, and they make his actions meritorious. They adapt him to his final end. They put a man's footsteps on the way that leads to supernatural beatitude. These habits admit of constant increase, but, unlike the natural virtues, their development, like their origin, is from without. It is the action of God that gives them increase. They grow in the soul inasmuch as God, the Author of all grace, gives fresh infusions of them. The soul can but dispose itself for such infusions. By repetition of acts of ethical temperance, one would acquire the natural virtue of temperance. By the repetition of acts of supernatural charity, one simply removes from the will the dispositions that impede the free and agreeable exercise of the virtue of charity. In the natural order of things, the acquisition of the moral and intellectual virtues would mark the crowning and consummation of the moral struggle. This would be the state of acquired perfection of man and would immediately merit the reward of final bliss. The infusion of the

[25] Cf. Terrien, *La Grâce*, vol. I.3.
[26] *S. Th.* I, II, q. 62, a. 1.

supernatural virtues marks the inauguration, not the consummation, of spiritual combat.

With every new "largesse" of sanctifying grace is given an increase in faith, hope and charity. Grace and the infused virtues are intimately connected. The former is related to the latter in much the same way as the essence of the soul to its faculties. Just as the essence is not immediately operative of itself but needs the intellect and the will to produce the operations proper to it, so grace puts forth its characteristic activities through the infused virtues. But the analogy cannot be pushed too far. If the essence of the soul were destroyed, the faculties would share its fate. Grace can disappear, and, though charity suffers dissolution with it, hope and faith do not necessarily do so. They often survive its loss. This can be so because grace resides in the substance of the soul, whereas the virtues do not. They inhere in the faculties—faith in the intellect, and hope and charity in the will. Nevertheless, though faith and hope can remain in the intellect and the will after grace has taken its departure from the essence of the soul, their condition in this state of survival is for them somewhat violent and unnatural. They are struck with sterility. They are, in the expressive theological term, *"informis."* It is not fanciful to trace an affinity between this term and its classical counterpart. The adjective *"informis,"* in classical literature, is used of that which is misshapen: hideous, ugly, lacking what is its own form.[27]

By faith man is given a participation of the divine intellect. Now, just as the power of his intellect has to be supernaturally reinforced in order to be able to contemplate the divine, so too his will must have its native power of loving transformed, elevated and given a more than natural strength in order that it should be emboldened and empowered to conceive a personal, intimate and filial love for God. Those who are born to the Christian inheritance scarcely realize how stupendous a thing it is to be privileged to aspire to a lover's relation with God. It needs courage on the part of a lowly and obscure and unprepossessing person to seek in marriage the hand of a high-born, highly endowed and very beautiful princess. But what is disparity of birth compared with the disparity that reigns between God and the creature! Left to our native resources we should never dare to lift our thoughts so high as to aspire to union with God. From such a dizzy eminence we should turn in awe and shrinking fear. God has to intervene in order to aid us to overcome our timidity or, to be more exact, our utter powerlessness to lift our eyes to him. The will, reinforced and elevated by the divine virtue of hope, dares to tend confidently toward affectionate union with God. Charity gives effect to this tendency and binds the soul to God in the bonds of a mutual love. It is comparatively easy to understand the impossibility for the human intellect, left to its own native resources, to enjoy the intuitive vision of God. Yet how many are there who do not fully realize that it is as radical an impossibility for the human will to love God with

[27] See Froget, *De l'Habitation*, p. 362.

the love of friendship? The infused virtue of charity alone removes this disability.

It is not possible for man, during his earthly pilgrimage, to have God as the unique, direct and exclusive object of his soul's acts. His social life makes multiple calls on his attention. He is in constant contact with his fellow men and with the energies of his own nature. His intelligence and will have to be exercised on a multiplicity of concerns. Frequent are the demands on him for actions which have for their object the regulation of earthly concerns and the provision of the requirements of an earthly existence. But in all these activities he has to bear himself as a man—that is, virtuously. What is more, his whole moral life has to be illuminated by the light of faith. It is not sufficient for him to be *reasonable* in all things; he must be *faith-full* in all things. He must do more than prove himself a man: he must prove himself a Christian. He has to be just in his transactions with others, prudent in his undertakings, temperate in his usage of things, and brave in the face of hardships, difficulties and dangers. If in any of these multiple forms of activity he proves false to the rule of reason and of faith, he becomes, by the fact, a traitor to his God. Such treachery is incompatible with the abiding presence of the Holy Spirit and argues a resistance to his influence. Man cannot have his soul united to God in faith and charity if he violates the rights of his neighbor by injustice or seriously impairs his own dignity as a man and a child of God by intemperance or cowardice. To arrive at the end destined for him, man must deal rightly with God, rightly with his neighbor and rightly with himself. The law that he is to follow, if he is "to press forward toward the mark, to the prize of the upward call of God in Christ Jesus,"[28] comprises two commandments closely interrelated. To the doctor of the law inquiring about the supreme rule of life, Jesus said: "Thou shalt love the Lord thy God with thy whole heart, and with thy whole soul, and with thy whole mind. This is the greatest and the first commandment. And the second is like to this. Thou shalt love thy neighbor as thyself. *On these two commandments dependeth the whole law and the prophets.*"[29]

As has been said, the life of man both in its individual and in its social aspect is for him the path he has to traverse to reach his goal. Life in its multiple human aspects is a means by which man is to make his way to his final end. To achieve himself he has to deal with God and he has to deal with men. By faith, hope and charity, he is set right with regard to God. To love his neighbor and to love himself as befits a man and a Christian and to love both practically he needs further good habits. He cannot regulate his peculiarly human activities as it becomes a child of God to regulate them unless his nature is equipped with the cardinal or moral virtues. God has provided for this need. With the three theological virtues there are infused, with grace, into man's soul the four moral virtues of prudence, justice, fortitude and temperance.

[28] Phil 3: 14.
[29] Mt 22: 37–40.

It is true that one cannot adduce an explicit statement of the teaching authority of the Church asserting the existence of these infused moral virtues, as can be done in the case of faith, hope and charity. Nevertheless, there is little doubt as to what is the mind of the Church in this matter. In the thirteenth century, Pope Innocent III, giving his views on a theological question that divided the doctors of his time, stated that the opinion which held that faith and charity *and the rest of the virtues* were not imparted to infants at their baptism was not that of the greater number of theologians. The phrase "the rest of the virtues" could not be applicable to the single theological virtue of hope and must therefore refer to the infused moral habits. In the year 1312, at the Council of Vienne, Clement V, dealing with the same controversy, pronounced, without making it a dogma of faith, that the opinion, according to which habitual grace *and the virtues* are conferred on all who are baptized, whether adults or children, is the more probable and the one most in harmony with the teachings of saints and theologians.[30] As the controversy turned on what were referred to, a century previous, as faith and charity and the *other virtues*, the obvious implication of this pronouncement is that not only the theological but also the moral habits are the apanage of grace. This doctrine is more than insinuated in Scripture and tradition.

It is to St. Peter—not, strange to say, to St. Paul, who had such an unrivaled theological knowledge of the Christian mystery—that we owe the text that gives us the deepest insight into the nature and the wonders of the divine adoption. The head of the apostolic college pens the following words in his second epistle. As by almighty God through Jesus Christ "all *things of his divine power, which appertain to life and godliness, are given us* . . . by whom [that is, Jesus] he hath given us most great and precious promises, that by these you may be made partakers of the divine nature, flying the corruption of that concupiscence which is in the world. And you, employing all care, minister in your faith, *virtue;* and in virtue, *knowledge;* and in knowledge, *abstinence;* and in abstinence, *patience;* and in patience, *godliness;* and in godliness, *love of brotherhood;* and in love of brotherhood, *charity."*[31] These verses set forth a lengthy enumeration of permanent qualities of soul that, with grace, are bestowed on the Christian.[32] The function of these qualities is pointed out as consisting in the exercise of those acts of virtue which are called forth not only in man's relations with God but in his relations with his fellow men and with himself.

St. Augustine, in a passage stamped by the felicity and grace habitual with him, makes himself an echo of St. Peter's words: "He who gives praise to God by word of mouth, cannot be so engaged always; he who extols him by deeds of virtue can do so unceasingly. *Works of mercy, acts of kindness, holy devotedness, blameless chastity, sober restraint*—these one must practice at all times, whether we are at home or in the public places, whether we are in the company of men or in the privacy of our apartments,

---

[30] Clement V, *Conc. Vien., De Summa Trinit. et Cathol. Fide.*
[31] 2 Pet 1: 3–7.
[32] Cf. Billot, *De virt. infusis,* 5th ed., p. 121.

in speech, and in silence, in activity or in repose, for these virtues dwell in the heart. Who may enumerate all? They are as an army of the Great King that thrones in the center of the soul. The ruler carries out his purposes by means of his troops. So the Lord Jesus, our Savior, once he has taken up, by faith, his dwelling in the inner man, makes use of these virtues as so many servitors to accomplish his designs."[33]

The opinion maintaining the infusion into the soul of the four cardinal virtues and the subordinate virtues which group themselves around these, as around four centers from which they respectively radiate, has in the course of years firmly established itself in the Schools. In present times the vast majority of theologians, following St. Thomas, teach that, in the regeneration even of infants, grace enters the soul at the head of a glittering cortege of virtues, which have as their function to deify at their source all the activities of human life, those that have direct reference to God as well as those that deal with the ordinary concerns of earthly existence.

Indeed, it would be strange were it otherwise. Since man has to tend to God in the totality of his deliberate activity, it would be incongruous that his acts should, in their principle, be "deiform" when they are concerned with the end of life, namely, God himself, and should not be so when they deal with the means to that end, that is, man's everyday existence. This would argue a kind of dislocation in man's supernatural being, a want of balance and proportion—a veritable deformity. The dignity and elevation, what might be appropriately termed "the supernatural culture," which are called for in the soul's direct dealings with God, must be extended to those contacts and interchanges with his fellow men which form the warp and woof of the Christian's daily life.

When man becomes a child of God, all he does, no matter how ordinary, must bear the impress of the nobility of his origin. He must conform to lofty standards in all his ways. The moral virtues in him must have a supernatural tonality. His temperance must be a loftier thing than the philosophic restraint that preserves a man from indulging himself beyond the limits prescribed by reason. The temperance of the adopted child of God must be spiritualized with the ethereal beauty of self-abnegation. The Christian's justice must be transfigured by a generous spirit of sacrifice. The fortitude of the followers of Jesus must know no calculations where the interests of God and divine truth are concerned. Mere natural prudence will enable a man to walk warily and circumspectly so as to secure against possible obstacles that might bring failure on his undertakings. Supernatural prudence shows a man how to make use of the risk of failure and even failure itself as a means to the attainment of the end of human striving. The social and individual virtues of Jesus were not of that cold and calculating nature that belongs to the ethical standards set by the philosophers. So, too, a supra-rational elevation must manifest itself in the good actions of his followers.

[33] St. Augustine, *Tract. 8 in Epist. Joan.*, no. 1, quoted by Billot, *De virt. infusis*, p. 121.

"Different in spirit and inspiration," says St. Thomas, "is the virtue that distinguishes the citizen of the heavenly city from that which is characteristic of the citizen of the earthly city."[34] What is good in the case of the latter is not sufficiently good relative to the former. He points out in another place that the infused virtues and the acquired differ in their regulative principles. They regard from totally different angles the matter with which they deal. "There are two ways," he says, "of distinguishing between good habits. One way is by having regard to the formal aspects of their objects. The object of any virtue is what is good for man in a certain department for things within which the virtue finds its exercise. For instance, the object of temperance is the 'good' to be found in the pleasures of the sense of touch. In the matter of these pleasures, the formal aspect comes from the reason which determines the due human measure to be observed in such things. The material aspect is supplied by these desires themselves. Now it is clear that the due measure in pleasures varies according to how it is determined: by human reason or by a divine ruling. Thus in the matter of the satisfaction derived from food, reason condemns only such excess as would be injurious to health or would interfere with the exercise of reason. But the ruling of the divine law in such matters is that man should chastise his body and reduce it to subjection by a voluntary abstinence in food and drink and things of the kind. Hence it is clear that acquired or natural temperance is specifically different from the infused habit of the same name."[35]

The gratuitous infusion of the cardinal virtues and their subordinate good qualities by which man's life is to be made "deiform" in all its details does not dispense man from moral effort. The infused virtues give to the faculties the power to elicit supernaturally good acts: they do not bestow, of themselves, any facility or promptitude in the exercise of such acts. The hard stone is not more rebellious to the efforts of the artist to shape it to a form of artistic beauty than are the intellect and the will of man to receive the impress and the movement of the divine. This recalcitrancy of will and intellect to act according to the supernatural has to be worn down by the constant and sustained practice of the acts of the different virtues. This is the significance of the exhortations of Scripture and of the masters of the spiritual life, in which they urge the necessity of acquiring virtue. The infused virtues cannot be acquired, but their free and unimpeded play can be procured by the removal of the obstacles that oppose themselves to their exercise. According to how the faithful soul perseveres in doing good, the practice of the infused virtues becomes more prompt and easy. As iron made malleable in the fire readily receives the shape imposed on it by

[34] St. Thomas, *Quaest. disp. de virtute,* in comm. a. 9; cf. Terrien, *La Gloire,* vol. 1.3, chap. 3: "The man on whom God confers the gift of grace is invested with a 'new being'—with a being which makes of him a God by participation. Wherefore his moral life must correspond to the mode of being which is bestowed on him. It is congruous that his moral life should be of a loftier character and should, in consequence, proceed from principles superior to those which preside at the origin of purely natural activity."

[35] *S. Th.* I, II, q. 63, a. 4.

the artificer, so the human faculties, their hard resistance disappearing through their being perseveringly exercised in righteousness, promptly and with docility, receive the direction of the Holy Spirit.[36]

In order that man's will and intellect be quickly and constantly responsive to the direction impressed on them by the supernatural moral virtues, the obstacles in these faculties to that direction must be eliminated. These obstacles are reducible to self-seeking in all its forms. Self-indulgence of every kind establishes in the will evil dispositions which do not disappear with the infusion of the supernatural habits. Willfully entertained prejudices, precipitation, and intellectual sloth make in their turn the intellect rebellious to the impulses of the infused virtue of prudence. These evil dispositions must be undone by acts of self-denial—affecting both the will and the intellect. A man must love truth in all things and labor to attain to it. He must steadily refuse gratification to the passions that stir him to intemperance, cowardice, fear or unlawful pursuit of gain. In a word, he must practice daily self-denial. According to how he does so, the infused virtues become more and more deeply rooted in his soul. They tend to exercise a more undisputed sway over its inner movements and over outward acts. The instigations of the infused virtues are more promptly responded to by the faculties. By this steady self-denial it comes to pass, in process of time, that a man finds an ease and delight in carrying out the hard prescriptions of the Christian moral law—prescriptions which at the outset encountered intense repugnance in a nature prone to self-indulgence. As it is only God who can bestow the supernatural moral virtues, so to him alone it belongs to give them increase. But man can dispose himself for that increase by faithfully obeying the injunction of the Savior: "If any man will come after me, let him deny himself and take up his cross daily, and follow me."[37]

---

[36] St. Thomas, explaining how it comes to pass that a person having, through grace, the infused virtue of justice can yet experience a repugnance to acting justly, writes: "It sometimes happens that a person having a certain good habit finds difficulty, nevertheless, in acting according to it and takes no delight and satisfaction in right action, through some obstacle coming from without. A 'Savant,' at times, finds difficulty in thinking because of sleep or bodily infirmity. In like manner the infused moral virtues can find a difficulty in their exercise, on account of opposing dispositions left in the faculties by previous bad acts. Such a difficulty does not exist in the case of the acquired virtues, because the adverse dispositions are removed by the very acts through which the virtues are acquired" (*S. Th.* I, II, q. 65, a. 3, ad 2).

[37] Lk 9: 23.

13

The Gifts, the Fruits and the Beatitudes

THE conquest of beatitude is an adventure of divine magnitude. Since beatitude is synonymous with life as lived by God, its attainment calls for divine resources, divine energies and divine direction. To so arduous an enterprise God alone is equal. Naturally speaking, men and angels are utterly inadequate to it—inadequate with an infinite inadequacy. Hence the necessity for them, if they are to share God's bliss, of having their native capacities of action reinforced with divine strength. This reinforcement, rendered imperative by the objective to be reached, consists in sanctifying grace and in the virtues, theological and moral. But though divine grace and its attendant virtues do, to a large extent, remove the disabilities under which man labors in his efforts to gain a heavenly kingdom, they do not supply all that he has need of—if his enterprise is to be brought to a successful issue. St. Thomas expressly teaches that the gifts of the Holy Spirit are necessary for the securing of salvation.[1]

The reason for this necessity is to be sought not only in the sublime nature of the goal to be reached but also in the humble quality of him for whom is traced such lofty achievement. The very nature of things demands that there must be a proportion between meritorious action and its reward. It is only action up to a divine standard that can claim as its due recompense a divine reward. It is only in the case of the human life of Christ that this proportion was faultlessly achieved. On the evening of his resurrection, to two of his incredulous disciples, he painstakingly explained the exact balance that existed between his toilsome life on earth and the glory that awaited him in heaven. Jesus did righteous human acts divinely. He walked the earth as God. A divine distinction marked his every act of virtue. His doings and his endurings could be submitted to the exacting tests of divine, not merely human, standards of perfection and emerge with success from the trial. This was because, in all that he did and suffered, he responded with perfect docility to the inner direction of the Holy Spirit. This is the significance of statements in the Gospel such as: "And Jesus, being full of the Holy Spirit, returned from the Jordan and was led by the Spirit into the desert,"[2] and "in that same hour he rejoiced in the Holy Spirit."[3] It was not only in isolated instances that the acts of Jesus were a lightning-like response to the promptings of the Holy Spirit.

In all the details of his deliberate life, in his every decision and act, his soul showed itself as sensitive to the breath of the Spirit of sanctification

[1] *S. Th.* I, II, q. 68, a. 1.
[2] Lk 4: 1.
[3] Lk 10: 21.

as the tremulous aspen leaf to the stirrings of the zephyr. His responsiveness to the divine stimulus was quick, constant and entire. Such responsiveness was the fixed habit of his life. This sustained pliability to divine inspiration was insinuated in the words of Isaiah the prophet when, speaking of the Messiah, he said: "The Spirit of the Lord *shall rest upon him;* the spirit of wisdom and of understanding, the spirit of counsel and of fortitude, the spirit of knowledge and of godliness. And he shall be filled with fear of the Lord."[4] The italicized words mark the abiding influence of the Holy Spirit on the soul of the Redeemer.

Action of a divine stamp and conforming to divine standards flowed effortlessly from Christ: it does not do so in the case of the Christian. Even when the soul has been transformed by grace and its faculties strengthened by the infused virtues, theological and moral, it still experiences an immense difficulty in realizing the exalted program of human life traced for it by the Divine Master. Christ's followers are bidden to be "perfect as their heavenly Father is perfect."[5] A divine bearing, a divine deportment and divine manners in dealing with life and life's circumstances are demanded of man because of his adoption into the family of God. Made participant in the Divine Sonship, made co-heir with Christ and called to share in the communicable prerogatives of the firstborn of God, the soul comes under the obligation of learning the ways of God's household and shaping its behavior in accordance with the high traditions of the divine circle. To do this it needs constant tutelage and guidance. It needs, moreover, to be apt to receive and profit by the divine instructions.

Human reason, even when supernaturalized by the divine virtues, cannot cope with all the difficulties of the tasks that the soul's high station imposes on it. This incapacity of grace and the virtues—if unaided by other divine resources—to conduct man infallibly to his final supernatural end is not due to any inadequacy inherent in grace and the infused virtues. These suffice in themselves to enable man to elicit salutary acts and so merit eternal life. But man's will and his intelligence do not become, at the infusion of grace, flexible to the tendencies of the virtues. Charity imparts to the human will the power to love God. It does not, unfortunately, take from it the fatal power to love what is not God. The virtues give the ability to elicit acts meritorious of beatitude: they do not bestow facility, promptitude, and satisfaction in producing such acts. When a natural virtue has been acquired, the virtue and the faculty which it has modified in the direction of the good habit are perfectly adjusted. They function in perfect unison. They are related to each other as the perfect rider to the perfectly trained steed. Acts of temperance are quasi-instinctive on the part of the man who has won his way to the acquisition of the cardinal virtue of temperance. The case is entirely different where there is question of the supernatural habits. These have but an uneasy, unstable, and precarious hold on the faculties to which, nevertheless, they impart new energies. The

[4] Is 11: 2–3.
[5] Mt 5: 48.

reason, even at its best, cannot be entirely sympathetic with the aims of grace. It is incumbent on man, as adopted child of God, to live a righteous life, not merely humanly but divinely. Reason, even as operating through faith and charity, will tend to dictate salutary acts contracted to the measure of human excellence. Reason, even when supernaturalized, will tend to impose reason's standards of right action. Hence the infused virtues are hampered in their functioning in a twofold manner.

The will and the intellect, when subject to tendencies which are directly contrary to those of the infused habits, always impede and often inhibit the action of these habits. For instance, a man who has, over the years, been given to unfair dealings with his fellowman will find, if he reforms and reenters into grace, that the vicious habits contracted by years of fraud do not immediately disappear. Their force, on the contrary, will appear to have increased rather than diminished. He has, it is true, the infused moral virtue of justice, but the evil dispositions developed by practices of injustice conflict with the action of the virtue. It is only when, through the constant and prolonged exercise of fair dealing in judgment and in act, the vicious dispositions are gradually eliminated that the infused moral virtue will find in the will a ready response to its dictates. But even when the opposition of evil habit has been taken away, there still remains a difficulty which cannot wholly be overcome by the resources of the virtues. This difficulty has been touched upon above. Man, elevated by grace, has to do rightly, not according to the standards of human but divine virtue. As long as reason, even as informed by grace, is the proximate principle of his supernatural acts, a certain stamp of humanness will be found in these acts. They will not be quite worthy of a child of God. Nor will they adapt him perfectly and completely for the heavenly court. The right adjustment of means to end demands that the actions by which man merits a beatitude which is divine should themselves bear a divine impress, both as to the manner in which they are done and as to the standards to which they are to conform.

At best, the infused virtues operate with great difficulty when they are at the service of human reason. They have a work of divine art to achieve, and they find themselves hampered by the constricting limitations of created standards. It is as if an artist's hand were encased in a gauntlet of steel and then applied to the execution of a work of art demanding extreme delicacy of touch, with deftness and ease of movement. Reason is perfectly competent to execute tasks to human measure. The faculties of man, if perfected by the acquired moral and intellectual virtues, will enable him to bring his conduct into line with the canons of rational perfection. This is because, in the case of the acquired virtues, there is a smooth, frictionless adjustment between faculty and habit. The two work as one. Such a frictionless and perfect adjustment between powers of will and intellect and the divine virtues which are infused into them is not possible. St. Thomas explains this matter clearly. He says: "Man's reason receives a twofold perfection from God, one, a natural perfection given by the light of reason, the other, a supernatural perfection conferred by the theological virtues. Though this latter perfection is, in itself, much superior to the former, nevertheless, *it is possessed in a much less perfect manner.* The perfection given by reason may be fully possessed, that given by the infused virtues can be but in imperfect possession. For it must be that through faith and charity it is but in an imperfect manner that we can know and love God. It is evident that once a being possesses perfectly a nature or a form or a virtue, it can of itself (always, of course, with the ordinary concurrence of God) exercise an activity in harmony with that form. But when a being possesses a form or nature or virtue imperfectly, it cannot of its own resources produce an act corresponding to that form, unless it receives external assistance." He illustrates this doctrine by a very apt and homely example taken from surgery: "A medical student," he says, "who has but an imperfect hold on the art of surgery cannot successfully carry through a delicate operation, unless he is aided by his master." Wherefore, we must conclude that reason suffices man in the acquittal of those things that are to reason's measure and correspond with what would be the natural end of man. But in respect of the final supernatural end of man, to which he has to guide himself by his reason, informed only to a certain measure and incompletely by the theological virtues, reason proves inadequate and requires to be supplemented by the direct influence (movement and instinct) of the Holy Spirit.

The gifts of the Holy Spirit are God's divine inventions to remedy the native incapacity of the virtues to elevate man to the perfection to which he is called. The gifts are necessary to man if he is to walk worthily of his vocation. That is to say, they are necessary for salvation.[6] Their function is to enable man to do righteously in a superhuman way and to bring his actions into line with God's own standards of conduct. The gifts enable man to live his human life as God would live a human life. The gifts are of absolute necessity for the Christian, if the Christian is to walk this earth after the manner of Jesus Christ. Without them the complete imitation of, and mystical union with, the Son of man is impossible.

When man has been reborn of water and of the Holy Spirit, he is in the difficult position of one who comes under the obligation of setting out toward a distant goal, handicapped with insufficient knowledge of the road and insufficient strength in himself to overcome the obstacles that strew his path. The vision of God—that is, the intuitive knowledge of God—is the goal. To know God as he is—that is a knowledge that belongs to God himself. It is only God who knows God. "No one knoweth the Son, but the Father; neither doth any one know the Father, but the Son." [7] This intimate knowledge is, with the divine nature, communicated in its entirety to the Third Divine Person. "For the Spirit searchest all things, yea, the deep things of God." [8] It is only he who knows who can reveal. Hence it is that on the Holy Spirit devolves the function of revealing God. If man is to set his course straight for his objective, he needs enlightenment from

[6] See *S. Th.* I, II, q. 68, a. 2.
[7] Mt 11: 27.
[8] 1 Cor 2: 10.

the Holy Spirit. It is true that a certain knowledge of the intimate life of God is given to man by faith, but this grasp of divine things is very weak and nerveless. The instruction on the constitutive elements of the beatitude of God has to be conveyed in words borrowed from human experience. These terms, while conveying what is true, necessarily deform and, to a certain extent, distort the truth they present. The soul, strongly under the influence of grace—that is the experience of all God's servants—chafes against the imperfect knowledge of God imposed on it by its natural way of knowing divine things. God's friends yearn to discern the object of their desire more perfectly. Here, the gift of understanding comes to reinforce faith. The gift takes away some of the limitations of the virtue. It does not give sight. That belongs to the realm whither the regenerated soul is journeying. But it gives a perception of what to faith is but a matter of assent.

St. Thomas says: "Faith implies but an assent to those things which are proposed to the reason for acceptance, but Understanding imparts a kind of perception of the truth." [9] And again, in another context, he writes: "The Gift of Understanding, after the saying of St. Gregory, enlightens the mind with regard to the things that come by hearing, in such ways that a man, even here below, enjoys a foretaste of the clear manifestation that is to be." [10] This luminosity projected through the obscurity of the divine objects of thought is something that can never glow on the intelligence as long as it is confined to functioning in its natural manner, using the concepts through which it comprehends the things of faith. In things which are beyond reason, the human mind receives from faith that perfection which empowers it to attain to them—faith being like gazing on divine things in a mirror and in concepts which express the divine enigmatically. But that spiritual things be seized, as it were, in their unveiled truth, this is entirely above the normal human mode of apprehension and is due to the operation of the gift of understanding. [11] The contrast between the working of the virtue and that of the gift is being continually obtruded on one's notice in the lives of the followers of Christ. The faith of the saint is the same as the faith of the ordinary Christian, and yet how different! The difference is entirely due to this, that in the case of one, faith is reinforced by the activity of the gift, whereas in the case of the other, it does not come under its influence.

Man, therefore, though equipped with grace, cannot effectively fare toward his beatitude unless he is directed and helped by the Holy Spirit. He cannot have a knowledge of God which will act as a beacon light to direct his steps unerringly and undeviatingly toward God unless he receives interior illuminations from the Holy Spirit. He cannot have

[9] *S. Th.* II, II, q. 8, a. 5, ad 3.
[10] *S. Th.* III., sent., d. 34, q. 1, a. 1; *"Intellectus—intus legere,"* i.e., to read in the depths of a thing, to explore the heart of it, is the Latin equivalent for that "gift" of the Holy Spirit which in English is termed "understanding." The Latin form is the more expressive of the two.
[11] See *S. Th.* III, sent., d. 34, q. 1, a. 2.

strength to surmount all the difficulties of the journey unless he is upheld by the same Divine Spirit. The path to God through the judgments, decisions and actions of life is difficult to discern. It often seems to lose itself in a maze of tracks beaten out by narrow worldly wisdom, misleading passion and perplexing circumstance. There is need of vision, divinely keen, to trace in all this confusion the way approved by God. The human reason is incapable of unravelling the complexity presented by the different courses of action which offer themselves. " 'For the thoughts of mortal men are fearful, and our counsels uncertain.' [12] Therefore man has need, in his quest of the right counsel to adopt, to be instructed by God, who sees and knows all. By the Gift of Counsel man is guided as though he received his direction from God himself." [13] In these cases of exceptional difficulty it is not the exercise of man's own reasoning, working in the light of faith, that hits upon the right course to follow. The Christian's judgment is formed in consequence of a direct intimation of the Holy Spirit, operating through the gift of counsel. This is a mode of coming to a decision which is above the ordinary human way of long inquiries, laborious investigation and hesitant decision. That a man should know what is to be done here and now, as though instructed on the matter by the Holy Spirit himself, in a manner admitting of neither doubt nor hesitation, this is not in accordance with the nominal process of the human mind. It is due to the gift of counsel. [14]

The virtue of prudence is competent by itself to deal with affairs which do not overtax the powers of reason. In a similar way, the cardinal virtue of courage enables a man to confront the ordinary dangers and difficulties of life, with which he has sufficient strength of character and purpose to deal. But adherence to God, occasionally, as in times of exceptional temptations or of great trials and persecutions, calls for a courage which is beyond the resources of man to furnish. Martyrdom and betrayal of God are alternatives which frequently face God's servants. Involving one's friends in material ruin, forfeiting the means of existence for one's dependents, committing oneself to death with torture—from this, mere human courage could not but shrink. The martyrs did not calculate their endurance by the measure of human fortitude but by the measure of divine strength, and it was for this reason that they did not falter in the trial and prove incorrect in their calculations. Their native courage was, in their trials, reinforced by the gift of fortitude.

In a similar way the virtue of justice inclines the Christian to give to each man his due and to act in all conjunctures sincerely and with affability. The man who shapes his conduct according to the rules of justice measures all his actions by what is due to himself and to his neighbor. The gift of piety inspires a man to conform to much loftier standards in his dealings with his fellows. It is regard for God and a power

[12] Wis 9: 14.
[13] S. Th. II, II, q. 52, a. 1.
[14] S. Th. III, sent., d. 34, q. 1, a. 2.

to discern something of God in those with whom they are brought in contact that move the true children of God in their acts of kindness. Inspired in all their actions by a childlike love for God, they find it easy to look upon others as members of the vast family of God, to which they themselves have the privilege to belong.

Temperance commands a reasonable use of things that contribute to a man's pleasure. Under the influence of the gift of fear, a man will, out of a reverential love for God, shrink from such delights even as are permissible and will repute them as dross in comparison with the satisfactions that flow from attachment to the Lord and from the graces he bestows on his friends. The human intelligence already enlightened by faith is further perfected by those gifts of knowledge and wisdom. Under the influence of the former, man forms a quick, unerring, and yet unreasoning[15] judgment on the value of all human things in their relation to God and in their bearing on the supernatural destiny of the soul. Wisdom, by creating a close affinity between the human soul and God as the ultimate source of all things, imparts the power of judging of everything by means of a certain divine taste. The soul's evaluations are unerring because it shares the tastes of God himself.

It is clear from all this that the function of the gifts is to strengthen and perfect the operations of the virtues. Wisdom, understanding and knowledge come to the aid of faith; counsel takes away the hesitations of prudence; piety gives a loftier aim to justice; fear replaces the cautious dictates of human reason by the exigencies of the good pleasure of our heavenly Father; and fortitude reinforces the virtue of the same designation. It is worthy of note that there is no gift to complete and crown the operations of the theological virtues of hope and charity. The reason is that these virtues reside in the will. This faculty in dealing with God does not suffer from the disabilities and limitations that press upon the intellect. Our knowing of God is necessarily through the distorting concepts of created things. But in exercising the act of love toward God the will does not impose any created forms on the divine in its approach to the divine. By charity man loves God as he is in himself. There is no more perfect mode of loving God than this. Hence, as regards the will, there is no inherent imperfection in its manner of operation for the overcoming of which a gift would be needed.[16]

What is true in the case of charity is true also where there is question of hope. Any imperfection that attaches to the acts of this virtue does not

---

[15] Unreasoning but not irrational. By the gift man forms an unerring judgment but has not to arrive at it through the slow processes of reasoning.

[16] St. Thomas writes: "The will in us does not suffer, by reason of itself, any imperfection in the mode of its functioning, as does the intellect. This latter faculty is necessitated, in the act of knowing, to dependence on the images of the imagination. Hence here below, we love God in his essence. We do not contemplate that essence. Wherefore over and above that virtue which is in the will, there is no need to look for any gift to impart to it a more perfect mode of operation than belongs to the virtue" (*S. Th.* III, sent., d. 24, q. 1, a. 1, sol. 5, and a. 2, sol. 1).

arise from a want of perfection in the mode of operation of the will, but solely from the remoteness and arduousness of the object toward which the will strives.

Although the operation of the gifts is revealed most commonly in those superhuman achievements and heroic deeds of virtue which illustrate the lives of the great servants of God, it would be a mistake to conclude that works on this grand scale form the proper and exclusive field of activity for the gifts of the Holy Spirit. Acts of heroic virtue are not necessary, in the ordinary course of events, for salvation. And St. Thomas expressly states that it is not possible for the soul to reach heaven unless it is equipped with those supernatural habits which have appropriated for themselves the name of gifts.[17] It follows from this that these reinforcements of the supernatural virtues must, at times, enter into play, even in the common circumstances of the Christian life. The reason has been indirectly intimated in a preceding page. As long as we live on this earth, we are, as far as regards the living of our divine life of grace, in the condition of children—with the powers but also with the weaknesses of childhood. The humanity on which our divine sonship is ingrafted fetters and renders awkward the movements of the child of God. Regenerated, we can, using grace and the virtues, direct ourselves toward the divine objective that has become ours by reason of our divine adoption. But our steps are the tottering, feeble, uncertain steps of childhood. Because of the fatigue of the journey or the difficult nature of the obstacles to be met with or the obscurity of the road, we, like children, need at times to be carried in the arms of our Divine Guide and to have our course through the perplexing maze of circumstance traced for us by him.

At the Last Supper, the apostle Thomas uttered a profound truth, unconsciously, when he said: "Lord, we know not whither thou goest, *and how can we know the way?* " [18] The Master's reply to the apostle showed that the latter was in error when he thought that he was in ignorance of the road which led to the house of God. Thomas did know, but knew so imperfectly that his knowledge was almost ignorance. There is One to whom is clear with a divine clarity every stage of the divine life and its blissful consummation. Him, Christ would send to be man's constant support and guide throughout the whole length of his earthly pilgrimage. "And I will ask the Father," he said, "and he shall give you another Paraclete, that he may abide with you for ever." [19]

Unless that Divine Companion of our way intervenes, from time to time, to sustain our weakness and to enlighten our darkness, inevitably we shall fail to reach our goal.[20] Acting directly on our intelligence by special illuminations and invigorating our will by direct infusions of energy and

[17] *S. Th.* I, II, q. 68, a. 2.

[18] Jn 14: 5.

[19] Jn 14: 16.

[20] St. Thomas says explicitly: "Effectively no one arrives at that heritage, which is the country of the blessed, unless he is led thither and sustained on the way by the Holy Spirit" (*S. Th.* I, II, q. 68, a. 2).

strength, he enables us to triumph over our dullness of perception and over our natural weakness. In these instances men go forward, in virtue of a strength that is not their own. They participate in the divine perspicacity and in the divine force. The initiative in their determinations and the vigor in the execution of their decisions is traceable not to their reason fortified by the virtues but to the Holy Spirit himself. *They are borne onward rather than make their way ahead.* Such is the characteristic privilege of the sons of God. "For whosoever are led by the Spirit of God, they are the sons of God." [21] In regard to our final supernatural end, said St. Thomas, "Since our rational faculties direct us to it, as being but in a certain measure and imperfectly energized by the theological virtues, they cannot do so effectively; their action needs to be reinforced by the prompting and impulse of the Holy Spirit." [22]

It is normal for the Christian to direct the course of his supernatural life, leaving the initiative in his decisions and acts to his intellect and will operating through the infused virtues. This he does in the very ordinary and simple circumstances of his existence. But at times he is liable to fail if he is left, with these resources only, to grapple with events. An external factor has to be invoked. That the light and strength he requires for action should come from without and not from within is something that is utterly beyond the human mode of acting. *It is this superhuman mode in the way of doing and suffering, not the greatness of the things to be done and suffered, that marks the activities of the gifts.* The name by which these most necessary habits of the soul's faculties are designated in Scripture indicates this markedly. The inspired writer speaks of them as "spirits." The prophet Isaiah writes: "The Spirit of the Lord shall rest upon him, the spirit of wisdom and of understanding, the spirit of counsel and of fortitude, the spirit of knowledge and of godliness." [23] Spirit and inspiration and breath are akin in signification. To inspire a person means to communicate from oneself to that person one's own enthusiasm or one's own ideal. The application of the word "spirit" to the Seven Gifts implies that the power, energy and movement they impart come from an external source. The quality which is manifested in the act has its origin not in the human spirit, even as transformed by grace, but in the Divine Spirit himself. [24]

A question arises here naturally. Why cannot the Holy Spirit act on the will and intellect directly? Wherein lies the necessity of these permanent dispositions to mediate between his action and the soul? The answer to these questions serves to complete the analysis of the nature of the

[21] Rom 8: 14.

[22] *S. Th.* I, II, q. 68, a. 2.

[23] Is 11: 2.

[24] St. Thomas, quoting the text of the prophet Isaiah where the Seven Gifts are enumerated, reasons thus: "From the application of the term 'spirit' to this *'Sacrum Septenarium'* we are clearly given to understand that they are in us in virtue of a divine inspiration—that is, a breathing on us by God. For inspiration signifies a movement that has its source from without that which is moved. Now in man there is a dual principle of his deliberate acts: one is interior, namely, his own reason, the other external, that is, God."

"*Sacrum Septenarium.*" There is a great disproportion between the mind and the will of the Creator and the mind and will of the creature. The distance is infinite. Hence, naturally speaking, there is a lack of adaptation between man's reason and the wisdom of God. It is difficult—extremely difficult—for the creature to catch the accents of the Creator. The divine whisperings are so subtle, spiritual and ethereal that they cannot affect the gross and dull hearing of the creature. God's own language and his direct teachings based on divine omniscience are unintelligible for us—unless we receive a special preparation for the apprehension of that teaching and of the accents through which it is transmitted. Here the human will suffers from a disability similar to that which affects the intellect. It finds an immense difficulty in allowing itself to be caught up in and carried onward by the movement of the divine will.

A teacher may be endowed with great knowledge and exceptional powers of exposition and yet may fail to produce any effect on his pupils if these are too backward to grasp his teaching. Metaphysics, no matter how beautifully and exactly expounded, runs the risk of being wasted on dull and untrained pupils. A great professor used to say that students took from a class proportionately to what they brought to the class. It is useless for God to enlighten us unless we are made capable of receiving such enlightenment. The intellect must be "co-apted" to God's instruction. It would be idle for God to impress a movement on man's will unless that will were adapted to receive that impress. The specific function of the gifts is to adapt the soul to receive effectively the illuminations and the impulses of the Holy Spirit dwelling within it. Just as the moral virtues are certain good habits developed in the will and in the appetitive tendencies of the sense nature in man, by which these, in their movements, are made amenable to the control and direction of reason, so, by the gifts are man's intellect and will made tractable to the direction of the Holy Spirit.[25]

The gifts raise the soul to that standard in which it becomes capable of receiving profitably the divine instructions and guidance. They serve to take away the dullness from our hearing, the dimness from our vision, and the sluggishness from our will so that all the spiritual powers may become sensitive and responsive to the action of God on them.[26] The gifts render

[25] *S. Th.* I, II, q. 68, a. 3.

[26] St. Thomas thus explains: "It is evident that if anything is to be influenced by another, it must be adapted to receive such influence. The more lofty the source of the influence, the more perfect the disposition required in order to be affected by it. For instance, we remarked that the mental equipment and training of a pupil must be all the greater, according to how the teaching he receives is the more abstruse. Clearly, the ordinary virtues give man that perfection which enables him to follow the dictates of reason and shape his conduct accordingly. But he needs a higher perfection than that imparted by the virtues, if the Divinity itself is to be the inspiration of his thought and conduct. Such perfection is imparted by the gifts—so called, not merely because they are infused by God, but because by them man is so disposed that he becomes promptly responsive to the divine impulse" (*S. Th.* I, II, q. 68, a. 1). A little further on, in article 8 of the same question, he writes: "The gifts of the Holy Spirit are [dispositions] whereby all the faculties of the soul are established in a condition of submission to the divine movement when imparted to them."

the soul flexible to the action of the Holy Spirit upon it and pliable under his hand so that the impress of the Divine Spirit can be left upon its human acts. This impress is needed in those special circumstances in life where the weak motive force of human reason as elevated by faith must be replaced by the direct promptings and impulses of the Holy Spirit. In such circumstances, the Holy Spirit must be the originating principle of the acts man has to elicit in view of his salvation. It is as when a loving father, watching his child's laborious and ineffectual efforts to trace intelligible signs on paper, takes the infant's hand in his own and firmly and surely guides it to the formation of the required words. In some such manner the Holy Spirit, by whom we are made capable of murmuring "Abba, Father," in the ear of God, at certain times takes us in hand and with our free cooperation aids us to the accomplishment of acts meritorious of eternal life.[27]

It has been said that in the economy of the supernatural order the gifts come to the help of, and reinforce, the infused virtues. According to how the action of the former becomes more constant and regular in the life of the Christian, a very pronounced change takes place. The infused virtues become more and more thoroughly "imbibed" into the will and the intellect. An adjustment ever more perfect steadily develops. The virtue and the faculty begin to move in unison and with little or no friction. There grows a unity of action that resembles that which exists where there is question of the acquired virtues. The imperfect hold that the supernatural habit has on the will or on the intellect tends to disappear and to be replaced by a more perfect hold. The result is that supernatural acts of virtue come to be accomplished no longer with difficulty but with facility, promptitude and satisfaction. The fruit is the product of a plant, when this has reached its maturity. It is pleasant to the taste and is that in view of which the plant is tended and cared. Virtue is possessed and cultivated in view of the good actions which fructify therefrom. Acts are, by metaphor, called the fruits of virtue when they carry with them, like the products of the garden trees, a certain delectation.[28] When, owing to the soul's sustained docility to the Holy Spirit dwelling within it, the supernatural infused virtues fructify in virtuous acts having savor and pleasantness in the doing of them, rightly are such good acts termed the

---

[27] In theological language the function of the gifts is expressed by saying that, by them, man is disposed to follow with docility the *instinct* of the Holy Spirit. *"Dona sunt perfectiones quibus homo disponitur ad hoc quod bene sequatur instinctum Spiritus Sancti."* The term "instinct" means a prompting, a spurring on, a stimulus to thought or action. The Latin word *"instinctus"* is derived from the verb *"instinguere,"* which means to incite, to impel, to stimulate. The word suggests, moreover, that the acts, originating in this divine enlightenment given to the intellect and impulse imparted to the will, have somewhat of the character of those actions in us which spring spontaneously from nature without study and without reflection. Men acting in this way are said, in ordinary language, to act on instinct. Irrational animals have this characteristic in a more pronounced manner than beings endowed with reason (see *S. Th.* I, II, q. 68, a. 3, and Terrien, *La Grâce*, vol. 1.3, chap. 5, p. 206).

[28] Cf. *S. Th.* I, II, q. 70, a. 1.

fruits of the Holy Spirit. St. Paul enumerates twelve classes of them.[29] This number is not meant to be exhaustive, for every good supernatural act that is accomplished with ease and delight merits the name of "fruit." [30]

The prompt and joyous execution of acts of virtue does not, to the full, exhaust either the possibilities or the energies of divine grace. There are still greater heights which it is open to the human spirit to scale, aided by the ever-growing strength of the divine life within it. When through the sustained practice of the theological and moral virtues the soul has learned throughout all its extent to sway obediently to the breath of the Holy Spirit, it eventually reaches a state where the characteristics of the life of reason, even when transformed by grace, are gradually left behind. It is the state of consummate virtue and has been enjoyed here on earth by very many of God's saints. Acts springing directly from the energies of the gifts are invested with a superhuman grandeur and perfection. Virtue enables a man to use rightly and wisely worldly advantages, such as wealth and honors. Man is lifted above himself when he despises them and practically, not merely theoretically, treats them as naught. Attaining to this in practice induces that blissful condition of life which is promised in the first beatitude. "Blessed are the poor in spirit, for theirs is the kingdom of heaven." [31]

It is already much to observe due measure in the satisfactions accorded to the senses. To reject them utterly and, going farther still, to embrace pain and affliction by deliberate choice—this is to retrace in one's own life that unearthly disposition to which expression was given in the words "I have a baptism wherewith I am to be baptized. And how am I straitened until it be accomplished?" [32] Those who arrive at this attitude toward suffering are elevated above the normal condition of humanity, for to bear suffering with patience and with fortitude is already, in itself, a mark of high virtue. Hence it is that those who voluntarily make sufferings their portion merit to be filled with divine consolation. "Blessed are they that mourn, for they shall be comforted." [33]

In a world where injustice is rife, it demands heroism to be constant in fair dealing, to be perfectly sincere in action and in word, and to accord to each one his due. Not to be satisfied with this, but passing beyond the limits traced by the highest human virtue, to spend oneself with the recklessness of the God-man in the service of one's fellows, that is divine. Those who, in dealing with others, allow themselves to be moved by no other considerations than the necessities of these others, reproduce in their acts of benevolence the inexhaustible compassion and mercy of God.[34]

---

[29] "But the fruit of the Spirit is charity, joy, peace, patience, kindness, goodness, long-suffering, mildness, faith, modesty, continency, chastity" (Gal 5: 22, 23).

[30] *S. Th.* I, II, q. 70, a. 2.

[31] Mt 5: 3.

[32] Lk 12: 50.

[33] Mt 5: 4.

[34] "Blessed are the merciful, for they shall obtain mercy" (Mt 5: 7).

Faith reaches an extraordinary degree of intensity in souls that are thus far removed from the emotions and passions that fret and disturb mankind. Purified of all earthly tastes and desires, their contemplation of God is not blurred or dimmed by the mists that form in the valley of tears. "Blessed are the pure of heart, for they shall see God."[35] "Even here below," writes St. Thomas, "when the sight of the intellect is purified by the gift of understanding, God can, in a certain sense, be seen."[36] The Beatitudes in St. Matthew are eight in number, but in their multiplicity they but ring the changes on the same theme.[37] In them the Savior points to the immense possibilities opened to the human soul, even in this life, by the divine life of grace, which he came to give mankind.

In the opening words of the Sermon on the Mount, the Savior invites his hearers to give free play to the energies of the grace within them and thereby rise to those achievements of consummate virtue which, by the aid of the Holy Spirit, they can accomplish. By such acts the soul is made ripe for heaven and, as it advances with assured step toward it, becomes flushed with the rays of the glory that is to be. The firm hope of that beatitude which consists in the vision of God can be ours in a twofold sense. It can exist in the presence of a certain state of preparedness or adaptation to the bliss that is to be. This is the hope based on merit. But the firm assurance may be ours in another sense. It can consist in a certain foretaste or imperfect beginning of the glory of heaven, such as has been enjoyed by holy men in the life here below. Hence, in the list of the Beatitudes those statements that are concerned with merit refer to preparations or adaptations to beatitude. "Whereas the parts of the sentences that speak of reward imply either perfect beatitude and have reference to the perfect beatitude of heaven; or they imply that beginning of beatitude such as is enjoyed by the perfect and, in this case, have application to the present life."[38]

The acts of superhuman virtue which effect this blissful condition of soul that so perfectly adapts man for the life of heaven are the direct outcome of the unimpeded activities of the gifts of the Holy Spirit. As to the Holy Spirit it belongs to initiate the soul into the divine life of God by grace, so on him too it devolves to bring this life to its full maturity. It is he who, having set the soul's steps on the road to heaven, conducts it to the very gate and, finally, according to the words of the Psalmist, ushers it into the abode of the blessed. "Thy good spirit shall lead me into the land where is my destiny."[39] "In this happy land, everlasting bliss shall consist in justice, and peace and joy in the Holy Spirit."[40] For in that realm of happiness "the glorified soul embraces God, through God, that is to say, through the Holy Spirit. God has given us the Holy Spirit in order that

[35] Mt 5: 8.
[36] S. Th. I, II, q. 69, a. 2, ad 3.
[37] S. Th. I, II, q. 69, a. 4, ad 1.
[38] S. Th. I, II, q. 69, a. 2.
[39] Ps 142: 10.
[40] Rom 14: 17.

the beatified soul might give back to God love for love, and thus in him find its repose."[41]

The Holy Spirit, the Eternal Gift and the Uncreated Love, is, therefore, the alpha and the omega, the beginning and the end of our spiritual life.[42]

[41] *De Beatitudine* 2.
[42] Cf. S. Kolipiniki, C.S.Sp., *Le Don de l'Esprit Saint.*

EPILOGUE

"It is written that eye hath not seen nor ear heard, neither hath it entered into the heart of man what things God hath prepared for them that love him."[1] How exact an application these words find in the marvelous grandeur that becomes the lot of him who is "born of water and the Holy Spirit"! Men instinctively hunger for greatness, and yet it must be confessed that when this wondrous greatness which infinitely surpasses anything that earth can show is proffered them, they, a few exceptions apart, manifest little or no enthusiasm in its regard. It may be that the distinction conferred on them by baptism makes little appeal to them in comparison with that which they crave from the world. The Savior once said to those who held the chief place in the religion of Jewry: "How can you believe who receive glory one from another and the glory which is from God alone you do not seek?"[2] This attitude is comprehensible in the unspiritual—in those earthly souls for whom spiritual realities mean little. But the same reproach could, with justice, be addressed to a great number of Christians. Is the explanation in this, that there is in them an instinctive and subconscious shrinking from the obligations that a clear view of the grandeur that is theirs would render it impossible to evade? *"Noblesse oblige."* A too keen realization of their nobility would impose on Christians a sustained elevation of conduct which the multitude might find a strain. Hence it is, perhaps, that many prefer not to study too closely their titles of nobility. This is true to some extent, but it is not the whole explanation, nor does it cover all the cases. Christians, perhaps more generally, fail to rise to the greatness that is their prerogative and consequently do not feel it an imperative duty to shape their conduct habitually in a manner consonant with their real station, because of a certain kind of a practical disbelief.

It is hard for the average person to reconcile the wonders of which his soul, his faith tells him, is the theater with the very ordinary and commonplace individual which he is conscious to himself of being. One may assent notionally, and in a manner of indefinite and universal application, to the teachings of faith and yet fail to bring them home to oneself as an individual. It is difficult for the average person to have the practical conviction that God, in very truth, thinks so much of him as to be willing to establish with him those intimate relations made possible by grace.

Mary of Nazareth is the condemnation of this practical unbelief. She makes all the wonders of grace credible. When the infinite and eternal God can achieve such a bewildering reversal of roles as to become, while remaining God, a child nestling in a mother's arms and depending on a woman's care and affection, nothing that God deigns to do in our own

[1] I Cor 2: 9; and Is 64: 4.
[2] Jn 5: 44.

regard should seem unthinkable. The immense God contracted himself, so to speak, to the narrow circle of a woman's arms and addressed that woman as mother, and there was no fiction in this address. When God was prepared to assume the condition of a child born of a woman—a woman whose bare feet, very likely, trod an earthen floor under a humble roof—it ought not to surprise us that he should be prepared to stoop to intimacy with beings so commonplace as ourselves. Mary was declared blessed by one of her countrywomen because she had borne Jesus.[3] The Savior did not question the truth of this observation but pointed out that the basis of Mary's blessedness was other than the woman thought. It lay, he insinuated, in the wealth of divine grace with which her soul was enriched and which constituted her suitability to be chosen as his Mother.[4] Jesus seized the occasion offered by the woman's enthusiastic exclamation to teach that, while Mary's privilege as Mother of God was unique, the divine quality of soul, which won for her the regard of God and occasioned his choice of her, can be shared by others.

If God condescended to stand in such a relation to Mary, we may hold without hesitation that he is ready to stand toward us in that relation which is established by grace.[5] Mary is the rock on which all heresies have been dashed to pieces. Each and every heresy, when analyzed to its ultimate implication, is but an elaboration of man's theory of the mode in which man is to become God. It is man's way, or rather Satan's way, of man becoming as God, knowing good and evil. Mary is the highest exemplification of God's way for man to become as God, knowing good and rejecting evil. She is the pattern of divinization for all the children of Adam. It was a wonderful thing that she, born of parents sharing the ordinary lot of humanity, should believe herself really called to the sublime dignity of being Mother to God. The Holy Spirit himself, through the lips of St. Elizabeth, congratulated her on the wonderful strength of her faith. "Blessed art thou that hast believed, because these things shall be accomplished that were spoken to thee by the Lord."[6]

Would that every Christian in grace shared to some extent in that magnificent faith of Mary and held with firm and practical conviction that God the Holy Spirit dwells in his soul in a close and intimate manner—in a manner that bears an analogy with the indwelling of the yet unborn, Incarnate God in Mary's womb! What a transformation such a conviction would effect in the lives of many who content themselves with the practice of an uninspiring, routine and mediocre Christianity! The mystery of the indwelling of the Holy Spirit in souls is that one among the mysteries of our faith which is the most potent to give an elevated tone to a human life and make it a worthy expression of Christianity. The

---

[3] Cf. Lk 11: 27.

[4] It is on this account that the Fathers and ecclesiastical writers were wont to say of Mary that she conceived God in her soul before she conceived him in her womb (St. Augustine, *Sermon* 215, 4, and St. Leo, *Sermon on the Nativity*, 1).

[5] Cf. Terrien, *La Mère*, vol. 1, p. 50.

[6] Lk 1: 45.

special need of our days is a more thorough and explicit knowledge of the Holy Spirit and of the marvels of the divine grace which he pours forth in the souls of men. An uncompromising assertion of all the wonders and of all the actuality of the supernatural is the best response to the cynical assertiveness of the gross naturalism of the age.

APPENDIX

STUDY GUIDE

REV. ROBERT P. BUCCIARELLI

INTRODUCTION

When Fr. Edward Leen's *The Holy Ghost* (Sheed & Ward, 1939) appeared in print, the Russian Revolution was slightly more than twenty years old. A shudder of apprehension was traversing the world. That apprehension had not as its sole cause the sight of the horrors that the world witnessed in those years. Many Christians had begun to feel that perhaps all may not be right with themselves.

There were yet more horrors to come with the global conflicts of the Second World War. Yet these also would have the effect envisioned by the author in his day, namely, the awakening of the averagely good Christian to the danger he ran in allowing himself to drift with the current of the social life about him.

As part of this reaction, Fr. Leen saw a renewed interest in the spiritual life, "an eagerness to have a deeper and more accurate knowledge of the Holy Spirit" (p. 12). As the year 2000 approached , Pope John Paul II called for "a renewed appreciation of the presence and activity of the Spirit" (Apostolic Letter, *Tertio anno adveniente*, 1994, no. 45).

It is the purpose of this study guide to serve not only the purpose that Fr. Leen had in writing this book, namely, to promote devotion to the Holy Spirit, but also the objective that the Holy Father had set for the faithful as the millennium approached.

In the summary that follows, an attempt has been made to extract from each chapter a single theme along with examples to illustrate the point. Some contemporary references have been added, principally from Pope John Paul II and Blessed Josemaría Escrivá.

The first three chapters study the love of God manifest in creation (chapter 1), then in God himself (chapter 2) and in the Incarnation (chapter 3). Chapter 4 considers humanity's participation in the divinity, seen as the purpose of the Incarnation. Then, the Holy Spirit is viewed as the fountain of the life that comes through this supernatural elevation (chapter 5). Chapter 6 studies the Holy Spirit as the first of God's gifts.

Chapter 7 initiates the considerations on God's love of friendship for the soul in grace with a study of the mission of the Holy Spirit. Chapter 8 takes up this mission as indwelling. Chapter 9 shows the effects of the activity appropriated to the Third Person. Chapter 10 examines divine filiation that comes with being born of water and of the Holy Spirit. The last three chapters, 11, 12 and 13, deal with the principles of supernatural growth.

I. THE FIRST MODE OF GOD'S LOVE—HIS LOVING KINDNESS TO HIS CREATURES

Scripture teaches both in the Old Testament and the New that God alone is good. This divine goodness is both ontological and moral. God is good in his being (*ontos* in Greek) and in his activity.

In his being, that is, as he is in himself, God is supremely lovable. He is like a magnet that attracts love. In his activity, he is the source of all good. He bestows good on things, first of all, by giving them their existence. "His absolute goodness makes him eminently unselfish and therefore well disposed in the highest manner toward his creatures" (p. 18). His being good and his doing good inspire trust and confidence.

It is to our own best interests that we approach God and allow ourselves to be changed for the better by our contact with him. If in our experience "men of noble, kind and generous dispositions can so uplift others, how much more potent might be the effect of God on his creatures. This effect would be secured if the creatures would but allow themselves to come to God as to one whose sole object in his relations with them is to influence them for good. 'If you then, who are evil, know how to give good gifts to your children, how much more will your Father who is in heaven give good things to those who ask him!' (Mt 7: 11)" (p. 20).

The sense of our unworthiness, the awareness of our lukewarmness and sinfulness should never persuade us that God does not love us or that he does not want our love. His love is not repelled by our lack of love. He continues to love us even when we are not as we should be. Contrary to the way we love, God does not require that something first be good before his will goes out to it. We love things because they are good. God makes them good in loving them.

God is always kind and benevolent toward us; this is what benevolence means, to wish someone well. "All things have been the recipients of the effect of his benevolence. If inanimate things, plants and animals can be the objects of ceaseless attention on the part of the Almighty, is it to be wondered at that rational creatures, even if they are sinners, should draw on themselves a far greater measure of the same kind of regard?" (p. 22).

Toward sinners, the Lord has a certain kind of love even as they are, and he aims at loving them more perfectly if they accept the actual graces

he sends for them to repent. "Can a woman forget her sucking chil[d]
she should have no compassion on the son of her womb? Even these
forget, yet I will not forget you" (Is 49: 15).

We should never become discouraged or hopeless. God loves us with
his benevolent love even when we have offended him. "The more weak
and the more sinful we find ourselves, the more we ought to dwell on the
thought that God is our Creator and our Benefactor and that in spite of
our waywardness we are still objects of his regard" (p. 25).

For sinners and for the lukewarm, the consideration of God's loving
kindness is not only a motive to expect his forgiveness but also a strong
incentive to virtue.

2. THE HOLY SPIRIT—DIVINE LOVE SUBSISTENT

Having seen God's love of benevolence for his creatures, we now consider
this love in himself.

All divine life is comprised in the activity of the divine intellect and the
activity of the divine will. God in comprehending himself conceives an
idea of himself which fully and perfectly signifies God. There is a similitude of this in our own process of understanding. We grasp or understand
something in a concept or idea or mental word. In that word our mind
understands the nature of a thing. God conceives an idea of himself that is
so perfect an image that it is himself, with the only distinction that it
proceeds from himself.

Through the other divine operation, God's will, there emerges a divine
reality to which Scripture and Catholic theology give the name "Holy
Spirit." There is good reason why this name "Spirit" should be given to
what proceeds from the Father and the Son through divine love.

Here too there is a similitude to our way of loving things. When our will
is captivated by the appeal of an object, there follows a strong impulse
toward it. "So, in God, when the infinite charm of the Divinity stands fully
revealed in the Word, there arises a mighty onrush of impetuous movement toward the object of wondrous appeal. That movement arising from
the depths of the Godhead, sweeping toward its object with impetuous
force, is naturally likened to a rushing wind—a strong sigh of affection—a
mighty breath proceeding from within under the pressure of love" (p. 31).
St. Thomas teaches: "In God that which proceeds by way of love does not
proceed as begotten but rather as a breath (*spiritus*), i.e., a breathing or
sigh arising from love. By this term is meant a vital movement or impulse,
inasmuch as one is said to be moved or impelled by love to do something"
(p. 32 and n. 13). In the Acts of the Apostles, the descent of the Holy Spirit
is described in terms of a rushing wind: "And suddenly a sound came from
heaven like the rush of a mighty wind" (Acts 2: 2).

The Spirit is called "holy." Creatures are holy in the exact measure in
which they submit to the attraction of the divine goodness. "The Father
and Son are carried toward it with an impetuous movement of infinite

e it is that Scripture and theology, aiming at characterizing
ame the mode in which the Third Divine Person proceeds
d the Second, have designated the Third Person 'the *Holy*
also called 'Love,' and this name belongs to him as the term
proper to the Son" (p. 32).

ve personified, the Holy Spirit may be described as being "all
"Everyone understands what is meant when a person is described
being 'all heart.' One who is so described is a person endowed with a
loving and generous nature, and impelled by that nature to pour forth all
its resources in the service and in the interest of others" (p. 33). He is, as it
were, the uncreated heart of the living God.

In Jesus, perfect God and perfect man, the Sacred Heart gives us the
outstanding feature of his human character—his love. "Now, what the
sacred heart is in the God Incarnate, *that* the Holy Spirit is in the God that
dwells in light inaccessible—it is that unseen God contemplated as 'Love
personified'—in the literal sense of this phrase" (p. 33).

With this love, God the Father and God the Son love us. When we
begin to realize the truth that this love is a divine person, we see that we
may know and love him in the same distinctive way in which we have
learned to know and love God the Father and God the Son.

> Get to know the Holy Spirit, the Great Unknown, the one who has
> to sanctify you.
>
> Don't forget that you are a temple of God. The Paraclete is in the
> center of your soul: listen to him and follow his inspirations with
> docility (J. Escrivá, *The Way*, no. 57).

3. GOD WITH US—THE WORK OF THE HOLY SPIRIT.
THE SECOND MODE OF GOD'S LOVE

God's benevolent love extends to all his creatures. He loves man particu-
larly and shows this with the rich nature he has given him. To those in the
state of grace, he bestows a gift that the slightest amount is greater than the
whole natural order. Yet sinners also have every motive to trust in his
merciful kindness. For all human beings, whatever their condition, God
becomes a friend of man in the strict sense when he takes on our human
nature in the Incarnation. The Word becomes flesh and dwells among us.
This is another deeper mode of the divine love for us.

The Incarnation is the great work of the Holy Spirit. Jesus has a human
voice and all else that pertains to true humanity because he was conceived
in the womb of the Blessed Virgin Mary "by the power of the Holy Spirit."
The archangel Gabriel said to Mary: "The Holy Spirit will come upon
you, and the power of the Most High will overshadow you. And therefore
also the child to be born will be called holy, the Son of God" (Lk 1: 35).
The Holy Spirit "has smoothed away the difficulties that attend the efforts
of frail, sinful man to enter into relations of intimacy with his Creator.

There is an encouragement for souls in the thought that the God to whom they are striving to return is human like themselves, with a human understanding and a human power of sympathy" (pp. 40–41).

Jesus Christ is the bridge that spans the space between Creator and creature. In the common humanity shared by God and man is found the bond of union between the two. "Friendship," says St. Thomas, "is based on some fellowship in life: since nothing is so proper to friendship as to live together. Now, irrational creatures can have no fellowship in human life, because this life is regulated by reason. Hence friendship with irrational creatures is impossible except metaphorically speaking" (p. 37 and n. 6). We cannot, in a true sense, be friends with a horse, with wine or with a team. Friendship, and the love that goes with it, requires a certain equality and a community of life.

If the relation of friendship between us and the irrational creature is impossible due to the lack of equality, it is even more impossible that we be friends with God due to the infinite distance between ourselves and our Creator. Aristotle said that "one can lay down no accurate definition as to how great must be that discrepancy between two men which makes friendship between them impossible. Though they may be widely separated from the point of view of personal advantages, friendship may still continue. But when the gap is very wide, as, for instance, between men and God, friendship is no longer possible" (pp. 37–38 and n. 7).

Even sin does not exclude the sinner from the friendship of the God-man. St. Thomas, quoting Aristotle, says that men are not to withhold friendship from their friends who have taken to evil ways. If it is praiseworthy to help a friend recover a lost fortune, how much more praiseworthy is it, by devoted affection, to help him recover his virtue (see p. 38 and n. 8). "Jesus in his lifetime was called the friend of sinners. He did not disclaim the title. Rather, he gloried in it and, in his most touching parables, amply justified it" (p. 39). In the Old Testament, God is spoken of as merciful and forgiving toward sinners. But only in the New Testament is he said to be the "friend of sinners" (Mt 11: 19; see Lk 15: 2).

The Holy Spirit is the bond of union between the Father and the Son. He fulfills the same role between God and God's rational creatures. It is the Holy Spirit who has fashioned the sacred humanity of Christ. Jesus is the gift made to us by the goodness of God. The act of giving is especially appropriate to the Third Person, who himself is the gift of God and through whom every gift comes from God. All the endearing qualities of Jesus are the expression of the Spirit of Jesus. "The gracious character of the Savior is, at one and the same time, the creation and earthly reflection of the character of the Third Person of the Blessed Trinity" (p. 46).

"As we become friends with Jesus fresh horizons open up before us. The desires of our heart are enlarged and he is able to satisfy these new desires as he did those that prepared the way for them. The Holy Spirit has given us the sacred humanity of Jesus, by which, in spite of our sinfulness . . . we can feel God as a friend to us. The work of the Holy Spirit does not end there. This but prepares the way for more intimate relations with the Divinity. It is his self-appointed task to establish those relations between God and men" (p. 46).

> Jesus is your Friend—*the* friend—with a human heart, like yours, with most loving eyes that wept for Lazarus.
>
> And as much as he loved Lazarus, he loves you (J. Escrivá, *The Way,* no. 422).

> Our Lord Jesus wants it: we have to follow him closely. There is no other way.
>
> This is the task of the Holy Spirit in each soul, in yours too. You have to be docile, so as not to put obstacles in the way of your God (J. Escrivá, *The Forge,* no. 860).

4. JESUS WAS BORN OF THE FLESH THAT WE MIGHT BE BORN OF THE HOLY SPIRIT

God did not become man simply in order that we should pass from human imperfection to human perfection. The Second Person of the Blessed Trinity became man to make us like to God and not just perfect men. The sacred humanity of Jesus is not an end in itself but a way to the Divinity. If the Incarnation is to fulfill its purpose, we have to make the divine life of Jesus our own. "The human charm of Christ is meant to *attract,* not to *arrest,* the gaze of the soul. Its function is to draw us to the Divinity, which reveals itself to us through the human features of the Savior in a manner calculated to win our confidence and affection" (p. 51).

The holy humanity of our Lord was formed by the Holy Spirit. To him we also owe the record in Scripture of Christ's attitude of friendship toward all men, including sinners. When he walked the earth, his sanctity did not repel them. On the contrary, "the tax collectors and sinners drew near unto him to hear him" (Lk 15: 1). St. Matthew tells us that on another occasion that it came to pass that "as he sat at table in the house, behold, many tax collectors and sinners came and sat down with Jesus and his disciples" (Mt 9: 10). They would not have done this unless they were sure he truly loved them. They felt free to approach him. He did not discourage them. Jesus has not changed his character or dispositions since then. All this is the effect of the Incarnation, which is due to the Holy Spirit and verifies the Third Person's title of "Paraclete" or "Comforter."

Yet "God stooped to our condition for the express purpose of raising us to his condition" (p. 55). We need to cooperate in this task. Jesus' human life must be lived in us—lived in its spirit. "To live our life in the spirit of Jesus means that the attitude of soul, the ideals and principles that characterized, governed and directed the conduct of Jesus, must be made to govern and direct our conduct. . . . He lived in docile subjection to God. 'I always do the things that please him' (Jn 8: 29), he said. It is in this fundamental attitude of soul that we are to be *one* with him" (p. 52).

Before Pentecost, the apostles did not realize that our Lord wanted his life to be in them. They admired and loved him as their teacher, their rabbi, their leader. Before the descent of the Holy Spirit, they recognized him as Savior but didn't really know what salvation meant. Only after the Third Person came did they grasp that they were supposed to share Christ's life. At Pentecost they understood that "the lives of Christ and of his members were not to be as two distinct circles having merely external contact, but rather as two circles tending to become concentric. The Paraclete showed that the way of salvation (or sanctification—for it is one and the same thing) for man was that he should . . . merge his life in that of Christ" (p. 53).

When this happens, we are able to love the God-man not only with a human friendship, we are able to love the God in him with a friendship that is divine. It is the Paraclete himself who makes this possible, "because God's love has been poured into our hearts through the Holy Spirit who has been given to us" (Rom 5: 5). With our mind and will we can know and love the same object on which the intellect and will of God converge—God himself, infinite truth and infinite good. He gives us his own love with which to love himself and others. We can participate in the divine energy of God loving himself.

In effect, we can love God as his daughters and sons. St. John says: "But to all who received him, who believed in his name, he gave power to become children of God" (1: 12). These words are not a metaphor. "One has a totally inadequate conception of the effect of sanctifying or habitual grace, as it is called, if it is regarded as producing a condition of soul characterized by merely negative properties—such as freedom from sin and from the punishment due to sin. The infusion of habitual grace into our souls is the genesis of a life, the vital activities of which far transcend the energies of the highest form of moral life. . . . *By grace we are empowered to love not only the man in the man-God, but even the God in him, and that, too, with the love of friendship*" (p. 56).

By pouring God's own love, charity, into our soul, the Holy Spirit *divinizes* the soul. He raises us so we are in the condition of God, as much as we can be, which "permits the creature and the Creator to embrace in an affection which is in its mode divine and truly bears the name of friendship" (p. 57). God made friendship with man possible by taking on a human nature in the Incarnation. Now, to bring about a community of nature on the divine plane, God divinizes man. He has made it possible that God should love us with the love of friendship, both humanly and divinely, and we can love him likewise, with a friendship both human and divine. Christ has merited the supernature that divinizes us. It is the Holy Spirit, the giver of all gifts, who forms it in us. We are born spiritually in the Holy Spirit, becoming, as Scripture says, "partakers of the divine nature" (2 Pet 1: 4; see pp. 57–58).

A basic truth emerges from examination of the Gospel texts: what Christ was, and what he is for us, cannot be understood apart from the Holy Spirit. That means that not only is the Holy Spirit's light necessary for penetrating Christ's mystery, but the influence of the

Holy Spirit in the Incarnation of the Word and in the entire life of Christ must be taken into account to explain the Jesus of the Gospel. The Holy Spirit left the mark of his own divine personality on the face of Christ (John Paul II, General audience, March 28, 1990).

This is the great boldness of the Christian faith: to proclaim the value and dignity of human nature and to affirm that we have been created to achieve the dignity of children of God, through the grace that raises us up to a supernatural level. An incredible boldness it would be, were it not founded on the promise of salvation given us by God the Father, confirmed by the blood of Christ, and reaffirmed and made possible by the constant action of the Holy Spirit (J. Escrivá, *Christ Is Passing By*, no. 133).

5. THE HOLY SPIRIT—THE FOUNT OF LIFE

The Holy Spirit enables us to mold our thoughts, desires and actions to the form of the human doings of Christ. Yet this is not the final end of the Spirit's activity. Having formed us, by his graces, to the form of Christ, the Holy Spirit communicates to us the life of God which is in Christ. St. Paul concludes his second letter to the Corinthians: "The grace of the Lord Jesus Christ and the love of God and the fellowship of the Holy Spirit be with you all" (2 Cor 13: 14).

Now we will see what is meant by divine life and how appropriate it is that the Holy Spirit be called "the fount of life" (from the hymn *"Veni Creator Spiritus"*).

Life manifests itself in self-movement which is never aimless. A living being sets itself in motion to reach a definite end, a point of repose where the movement stops. God is intensely active because he is intensely alive. "But his activity is an infinite repose, because he is in full possession and the active enjoyment of all that can be the term of endeavor, namely, life. God has not only fullness of life, he is life itself. . . . His repose is not a repose of inactivity but the repose of a fully satisfied and satisfying activity, free from pain and effort" (p. 65). When speaking of analogy, Ronald Knox refers to an ancient hymn in the Liturgy of the Hours that tells us that God is "motionless." It is not that God is like a rock that cannot move. God is motionless because he has no need to move; "he can be everywhere without moving. In him, it is not the absence of a perfection, but the absence of a defect" (see *The Hidden Stream*, chap. 4, "Our Knowledge of God by Analogy"). Similarly, when we say God is alive, we add that there is no movement in him, not as ascribing a defect to him but attributing to him a perfection, indeed, the highest, most absolute and infinitely perfect possession of the fullness of life, as expressed in the divine operations of perfect knowledge and perfect love.

God has the highest *quality of life.* "The value of life . . . is in exact proportion to the nobility of what constitutes the object of thought and the term of endeavor" (p. 66). God's object of thought is himself, which is also the object of his love. There is nothing better that can be known and loved. If we humans are to rise to God's life, we must share in the nobility of his thoughts and affections. This participation is made possible when the Holy Spirit is given to us, "for the Spirit searches everything, even the depths of God" (1 Cor 2: 10).

"The Holy Spirit is in us by grace. In him we see God. . . . To enable us to enter into his own life, God gives us his own Spirit—the Holy Spirit—to be in us the source of the vision of the divine, and of the love of the divine. . . . We have . . . through the Holy Spirit, the same object of thought and the same object of affection as God himself has—that is, we have God's own life. The Holy Spirit is the source of this life in us: he is *Fons Vivus*," a living fount (pp. 68–69).

Our life turns divine to the extent that the intellect permits the Holy Spirit to enlighten it, becoming open to what he reveals about the divine truths. When these are accepted with faith, they can be loved. If the highest life consists in knowing and loving what is best, life resolves itself for us here on earth into the love of God. When we are devoted to the Holy Spirit, who makes this possible, our conviction of its reality will be great, as will be our appreciation of its value and our desire for its growth.

> We do not exist in order to pursue just any happiness. We have been called to penetrate the intimacy of God's own life, to know and love God the Father, God the Son, and God the Holy Spirit, and to love also—in that same love of the one God in three divine Persons—the angels and all men (J. Escrivá, *Christ Is Passing By*, no. 133).

6. THE HOLY SPIRIT—GIFT OF GOD MOST HIGH

Theologians teach that "Gift" is a more appropriate name for the Holy Spirit, even more than "Love." We now see why.

Self-centeredness is a virus that works against God's plan for mankind to form one mystical body, united together by the bond of divine charity. John Paul II distinguishes between individualism and personalism. "Individualism presupposes a use of freedom in which the subject does what he wants, in which he himself is the one to 'establish the truth' of whatever he finds pleasing or useful. He does not tolerate the fact that someone else 'wants' or demands something from him in the name of an objective truth. He does not want to 'give' to another on the basis of truth; he does not want to become a 'sincere gift.' Individualism thus remains egocentric and selfish. . . . Personalism is altruistic: It moves the person to become a gift for others and to discover joy in giving himself. This is the joy about which Christ speaks (cf. Jn 15: 11; 16: 20, 22)" (*Letter to Families*, 1994, no. 14).

"Generosity in giving is an excellent antidote against the virus that has been introduced into our 'spiritual system' by original sin" (p. 72). It has a unifying effect by establishing a bond between the one who gives and the recipient. There are several conditions that must be met for a gift to be truly such: the giving must proceed from love; its object must be to the advantage of the recipient and not of the donor; it must be something in the moral power of the donor to transfer; it must be apt for giving.

God is the great giver. In him all the conditions for a gift are perfectly met. God does everything out of sheer love. He gives with perfect disinterestedness; he has nothing to gain spiritually or materially from his creatures. It is in his power to communicate himself. In fact, through faith we learn that our purpose is to serve God in order that he may be able to give himself to us, to fill our spirit with his life and so bring us to that fullness of existence we long for. "We are bidden to serve God and to keep our wills in harmony with his uniquely because that is the condition to be realized on the part of the creature in order that the Creator may be given—may become for the creature a gift actually received" (p. 77).

"If a man loves me, he will keep my word, and my Father will love him, and we will come to him and make our home with him" (Jn 14: 23). "I will pray the Father, and he will give you another Counselor, even the Spirit of truth, whom the world cannot receive, because it neither sees him nor knows him; you know him, for he dwells with you, and will be in you" (Jn 14: 16–17). "These texts show conclusively that when we are in such dispositions that our will is conformed to that of Jesus, then God, Father, Son and Holy Spirit, communicates himself to us. . . . In his human life our Lord showed us how to serve God and remain united with him, union being a consequence of service. Disservice spells disunion" (pp. 78–79). When we strive to imitate Jesus in doing the will of the Father, when we live according to the principles which governed his actions, then God bestows himself on us as a gift.

Sin made the communication of God impossible. The entrance of the gift into the soul was blocked by the deliberate action of man's will. "Sin not only emptied the soul of the Divinity but left in it, as well, an aversion from the divine. But sin did not change God. He always remained communicable, always remained *a gift*, ready and apt to be given to his rational creatures. In order that from being communicable he should be actually communicated nothing was needed but that the aptitude to receive him should reappear once more in man. The Word became flesh to restore this receptivity in fallen humanity and actually revived it in those who consented to enroll themselves in his following: 'But to all who received him, who believed in his name, he gave power to become children of God' (Jn 1: 12)" (p. 79).

After the Redemption, all that is needed for man to receive the gift is that he should desire God above all things, with all other things in subordination to the love of God. Man is not the cause of the gift, but he is the cause of its absence. This is similar to a sunlit room. Man does not cause the light that streams in from outside, but he can cause the darkness by drawing the curtains. In the *Ascent of Mt. Carmel*, St. John of the Cross compares God's gift to "a ray of sunlight striking a window. If the window is in any way stained or misty, the sun's ray will be unable to illuminate it and transform it into its own light, totally, as it would if it were clean of all these things, and pure; but it will illumine it to a lesser degree, in proportion as it is less free from those mists and stains; and will do so to a greater degree, in proportion as it is cleaner from them, and this will not be because of the sun's ray, but because of itself; so much so that, if it be wholly pure and clean, the ray of sunlight will transform it and illumine it in such wise that it will itself seem to be a ray and will give the same light as the ray. . . . God communicates to it his supernatural being, in such wise that it appears to be God himself, and has all that God himself has" (bk. II, chap. 5, 8).

"In the communion of the Blessed Eucharist, the presence of the Incarnate God endures only as long as the Sacred Species remains unassimilated to our substance—at most a comparatively short space of time. But in the communion in which God gives himself to the soul, *the presence of God is not transient. God is given as a gift and therefore to be our permanent possession.* God remains in the possession of the soul as long as the soul wills to hold him as its own" (p. 78). It is only when we rebel against God's will that we break with Jesus and so lose the infinite gift that has been given us—God himself.

God's providence extends to all his creatures, but his love is given to those who choose him in preference to all creatures. The first gift he gives is his love itself. "Is it not because we love a person that we gratuitously confer a benefit on him? The first thing that we give him is the love by which we wish that what is good should be his. Consequently love is the first gift, since from it flow all other gifts" (p. 80 and n. 18). God gives us not merely signs of love, which he certainly does in many ways. He gives us his Love itself, the Holy Spirit. Thus, in the hymn "*Veni Creator Spiritus,*" the Church assigns him the title "Gift of God Most High" (*Altissimi Donum Dei*). "Created love can reach its object only by representation. Love itself must remain imprisoned in the human heart. It is part of the creature's being and not detachable from it. But if the love which is felt for us could take substantial form and come to us not merely in representative signs, but in its own reality, as a living entity, how inexpressibly dear to us would this living love be!" (p. 102).

Of the two proper names for the Holy Spirit, "Love" and "Gift," the second is in fact more proper. "Love" as a term designates an activity, something accidental. "Gift" refers to an entity, a substance. Yet the terms are related. "Since a gift means something that passes from the benefactor to the beneficiary because of the love of the former for the latter, it can be appropriately applied to the Holy Spirit, who proceeds from the love of the Father and the Son and is bestowed on us because of the love of God for us" (p. 82).

7. THE MISSION OF THE HOLY SPIRIT—THE THIRD MODE OF GOD'S LOVE

The apostles did not understand at first how anyone could take our Lord's place. Yet, at the Last Supper, Jesus tells them that he will be replaced by another. "And I will pray the Father, and he will give you another Counselor"—the Paraclete—"to be with you forever, even the Spirit of truth, whom the world cannot receive, because it neither sees him nor knows him; you know him, for he dwells with you, and will be in you" (Jn 14: 16–17). Jesus deliberately states that he must depart in order for the Paraclete to come. "If I do not go away, the Counselor will not come to you; but if I go, I will send him to you" (Jn 16: 7).

Jesus was not thinking only of the Twelve. He has in mind the entire body of Christians throughout all time. "It is clear, too, that he envisaged the 'mission' or the sending of the Holy Spirit by his Father and by himself ... as the grand event to which his whole life was directed" (p. 84). We cannot understand the supernatural adequately without a good grasp of the mission of the Holy Spirit and all that flows from that mission.

St. Thomas says that "a Divine Person is capable of being sent insofar as he exists in someone in a new way; and of being given insofar as he is had (i.e., held or possessed) by someone; and it is sanctifying grace that accounts for both these effects" (p. 85 and n. 10). The sending or mission of the Holy Spirit is connected with the conferral of sanctifying grace.

From the perspective of the Creator, infusing grace into a soul is infinitely superior to anything he causes in nature. God is present in everything he creates. The Holy Spirit has been in the soul by virtue of the fact that God is everywhere. But when the soul has been justified by the blood of Christ, the Third Person begins to take up new functions there. He is invested by God the Father with the role of ambassador to the court of man's soul. "A mere cessation of hostilities between states is an unsatisfactory condition of things. When enmity has ceased, the warring powers have to be drawn close together in the bonds of friendship. The parallel holds in this great drama of redemption. The Son of man had established the terms of peace, and in that his work as mortal man was ended. It devolved on the Holy Spirit to strengthen, consolidate and perfect that peace so dearly purchased. Jesus had swept away *misunderstanding*; it remained for the Holy Spirit to create a *perfect understanding*. It is for that he is sent. When a treaty has been struck between two powers, a representative from each is sent to reside close to the seat of government of the other. Christ our chief has ascended to the court of our heavenly Father, where he lives, always living to make intercession" for us [see Heb 7: 25]. ... The Creator ... at the request of Jesus, sends his ambassador to represent his interests in the world of souls. That divine envoy is none other than the Holy Spirit" (p. 98). An ambassador is said to be sent to a government even though he has been there already in a different capacity; once he is appointed, he takes up his ambassadorial functions.

St. Teresa of Avila writes: "It seems to me that the function of mediator between God and the soul devolves on the Holy Spirit" (p. 98, n. 42). The divine ambassador is always faithful to the interests of the one from whom he has been sent. "He devotes all his efforts to developing in the soul a perfect sympathy with divine things. He strives to make it one with God in aspirations, tastes, ideals. He leaves no means untried to create a perfect understanding between the creature and the Creator. He pours actual grace upon actual grace into the soul in order to impart to it what may be aptly termed 'the heavenly mind.' He initiates it into the knowledge of divine things" (p. 99).

The ambition of the Holy Spirit is to make us more and more conformable to what is divine. Christ won for us the power to be born of God. "But to all who received him, who believed in his name, he gave power to become children of God" (Jn 1: 12). It is the mission of the Holy Spirit to bring us to this birth and stamp on our souls the image of God. "Unless one is born of water and the Spirit, he cannot enter the kingdom of God" (Jn 3: 5). The Holy Spirit forms us as God's children and develops in us the love that springs from our filiation. He imparts to us a divine manner.

> The Holy Spirit enables the soul to share in Jesus' filial love for the Father, so that, as St. Paul says: "Those who are led by the Spirit of God are children of God" (Rom 8: 14). He enables the Father to be loved as the Son has loved him, i.e., with the filial love which is shown in the cry "Abba" (see Gal 4: 6; Rom 8: 15), but it pervades the entire activity of those who, in the Spirit, are children of God. Under the Spirit's influence their whole life becomes an offering to the Father, filled with reverence and filial love (John Paul II, General audience, May 22, 1991).

> Alone! You are not alone. We are keeping you close company from afar. Besides, living in your soul in grace is the Holy Spirit—God with you—giving a supernatural tone to all your thoughts, desires and works (J. Escrivá, *The Way*, no. 273).

8. THE HOLY SPIRIT—THE SOUL'S DELIGHTFUL GUEST

In the previous chapter, we have seen the action of the Creator in sending the Holy Spirit to the soul. We now consider the effect of that activity in the creature.

St. Thomas Aquinas says that "in the very gift of sanctifying grace, the Holy Spirit is possessed by and dwells in a man" (p. 102 and n. 2). "Habitual grace gives to the soul a power of reaction which makes it capable of holding God vitally—of possessing him—of having him as its own. It is not in virtue of the action of God but of the consequent reaction of the soul that the latter is made the temple of God" (p. 105). "If, for instance, the marble on which Michelangelo worked developed life as well as form under the strokes of his chisel; and if, instead of a lifeless statue, a living thing of radiant beauty emerged from the shapeless block on which his genius wrought; and if that living thing of beauty, the perfect reflex of the artist's mind, recognizing in the artist the author of the life and beauty that it possessed, were to enfold him in its embrace in an act of loving recognition and gratitude, we would have an image of what is meant by saying that it is in virtue of the soul's power of reaction given by grace that God is said to dwell in the soul" (pp. 105–106).

God is in everything, because wherever anything is, God must be there. God is present in the rational creature that has no faith. He is present in a more intimate way in the soul that has faith but no charity because of mortal sin. In this case, the person with faith, but with unforgiven mortal sin, can continue to know God as he is in himself, one nature in three persons. "God, as the God not of philosophy but of revelation, remains under the gaze of the soul, but that gaze is dull, unheeding, cold and uninterested when faith is divorced from charity. God is present *with* the soul, but not present *to* the soul. It is just as when in a crowded apartment our eyes rest on individuals there present who mean nothing to us; we see, in a certain sense, without seeing. On such occasions the act of vision is merely physical: there is no soul contact or interest accompanying it. It is only when, among the crowd, our glance lights on one in whom we are interested or to whom we are bound by the bonds of affection, that we can be said, in the full sense of the term, to see the person on whom we fix our eyes. We see not only with the organ of sight but, in a sense, with our heart and soul as well" (p. 116).

Thus it is that the soul in the state of grace envelops God by the operations of knowledge and love. St. Thomas teaches that "above and beyond the common or ordinary manner in which God is in all things, there is a singular and special manner which belongs exclusively to the rational creature, in which God is said to be present as what is known is present in the knower and what is loved is present in the lover. Because a rational creature by knowing and loving attains to God himself, it comes to pass that God according to that special manner of presence is said not only to be present in the rational creature but to dwell in it as in his temple" (p. 117 and n. 40).

The mission of the Second Person of the Blessed Trinity gives to our intellect a participation in his own personal character, one in whom understanding excites interest. "He who is the living knowledge of God impresses on the soul that mode of knowing God which generates the desire of drawing closer to that infinite good which is being revealed. The Word of God gives to the soul's glance that animation and that penetration which makes God, from being present *to* us, become present *in* us." The mission of the Third Person "impresses on the soul the stamp of his personal character, which is love" (p. 116)

God begins to dwell, as it were, under our roof as one to whom the soul cleaves in the bonds of intimate knowledge and affection, no longer as a stranger.

Charity does not make God present, since he is present everywhere, "but it completely transforms the nature of the universal presence which the soul shares with all creatures. . . . Charity transmutes merely spatial presence into a vital presence" (p. 118).

On Mt. Tabor, St. Peter was ecstatic about building three tabernacles (see Mt 17: 4). His desires are fulfilled not materially but spiritually in the indwelling that results from the mission of the Holy Spirit. By acts of faith, hope and charity, the soul constructs a tabernacle in which God, the Holy

Spirit, dwells. "God dwells with much contentment in this new and immaterial tabernacle because it not only houses him, it also enfolds him in knowledge and love. It shelters him and worships him" (p. 119).

God is at home more or less perfectly in the soul according to the degree of its charity. "According to the extent we lend ourselves more perfectly to his operations in us, more flexibly to the movements that he impresses on our spirit, more ardently in love of God, the more we begin to realize the great fact that God is within us, not merely as creator, ruler and judge, but as guest, friend and lover" (p. 119).

Blessed Josemaría Escrivá urges us to pray to the Paraclete:

> Divine Guest, Master, Light, Guide, Love, may I make you truly welcome inside me and listen to the lessons you teach me. Make me burn with eagerness for you, make me follow you and love you (*The Forge*, no. 430).

> We are all equally called to sanctity. There are no second-class Christians, obliged to practice only a "simplified version" of the Gospel. We have all received the same baptism, and although there is a great variety of spiritual gifts and human situations, there is only one Spirit who distributes God's gifts, only one faith, only one hope, only one love (cf. 1 Cor 12: 4–6; 13: 1–13). And so we can apply to ourselves the question asked by the Apostle: "Do you know that you are the temple of God, and that the Spirit of God dwells in you?" (1 Cor 3: 16). And we can understand it as an invitation to deal with God in a more personal and direct manner. For some, unfortunately, the Paraclete is the Great Stranger, the Great Unknown. He is merely a name that is mentioned, but not Someone, not one of the three persons in the one God, with whom we can talk and with whose life we can live (*Christ Is Passing By*, no. 134).

9. FINGER OF GOD'S RIGHT HAND

We need to become more aware of the purpose and effect of the indwelling of the Holy Spirit in our souls. "Marvellous and happiness-giving consequences flow from the divine indwelling in the measure in which the Christian cooperates with the action of the Blessed Trinity in the interior of the soul" (p. 121). We now see how he makes us friends of God.

God longs to dwell in the soul. Once he is there, the Holy Spirit is preoccupied with one project: in actively molding the soul to an ever closer resemblance with God. The Holy Spirit's special function is to make man and God friends after having been enemies. "He does this by taking away all the obstacles to that friendship which exist in man's soul and establishing in their place the dispositions themselves of friendship" (p. 124).

When Jesus was about to leave his disciples, he promised them that he would send them another Paraclete, "another Counselor" who would abide with us forever (see Jn 14: 16). This promise was fulfilled on the morning of Pentecost. The Holy Spirit is prepared to fulfill perpetually the requirements of friendship by truly being a comfort to us at all times.

The Holy Spirit comforts us in times of loneliness and isolation, when we have to face the opposition of the world as our Lord foretold. But hostility does not come only from those who are "officially" against Christianity. "Even in the bosom of Christian circles, those who show an unflinching and whole-hearted loyalty to the teaching of the Savior meet with an opposition which hurts more than does the opposition of the enemies of the Christian name" (p. 126). The experience of loneliness is offset by the presence of the indwelling Spirit, a person who by the Word of God has been declared to be a Consoler, a person who is love personified. He is a "tremendous lover" who is ever faithful, in contrast with human affection, which is always subject to change.

Furthermore, the Holy Spirit endows us with the capacity to bear up under trials. St. Thomas says that as the Holy Spirit makes us friends of God and makes God abide in us and us in God, "it follows that it is through him, the Third Person of the Blessed Trinity, that we find joy in God and comfort in all the trials and adversities of life. Because of this the Savior names the Holy Spirit, Paraclete, that is, Comforter" (p. 128 and n. 17).

As a friend, the Holy Spirit not only consoles hearts, he enlightens minds as well. The Holy Spirit knows the deepest truths about God. "For the Spirit searches everything, even the depths of God. . . . No one comprehends the thoughts of God except the Spirit of God" (1 Cor 2: 10–11). Thus the Holy Spirit illuminates the words of Scripture and lights up the mysteries of religion, disclosing their inner harmonies and correspondence with all the needs and aspirations of the human heart. A great love for revealed truth then follows, and with it its moral obligations are easier to observe.

This was the case of the apostles. "During three years Jesus shared divine secrets with the inner circle of those he drew about him. 'No longer do I call you servants, for the servant does not know what his master is doing; but I have called you friends, for all that I have heard from the Father I have made known to you' (Jn 15: 15). But because their knowledge of what he so painstakingly communicated to them remained largely superficial, that knowledge did not render them strong when the hour of trial came. On the other hand, the intoxication of soul caused by the revelation of Pentecost rendered them indifferent to persecution and death. It was not that new truths were given them but that new light was shed on the old truths taught them by Jesus, as, at the Last Supper, he said would be: 'But the Counselor, the Holy Spirit, whom the Father will send in my name, he will teach you all things and bring to your remembrance all that I have said to you' (Jn 14: 26). For the mysteries illuminated for them by the Holy Spirit, the apostles conceived an attachment proof against the menace of death" (pp. 128–129).

Finally, the Holy Spirit makes us more lovable in God's sight and hence the object of ever-increasing divine gifts. "God's love for the soul grows in accordance with the soul's growth in attractiveness for him. It is the Holy Spirit who imparts this attractiveness which wins the favoring regard of the Almighty. He does it by giving ever more and more grace" (p. 131).

Justification takes place in an instant. Sanctification is a process that endures a lifetime. "To the Holy Spirit is appropriately attributed the beginning, the continuance and the crowning of this mysterious process. . . . He is the subsistent sanctity of God" (p. 130). Unfortunately, we can prevent the Holy Spirit from doing his work by placing an impenetrable obstacle between ourselves and the source of all holiness. "The barrier removed, the Holy Spirit at once exercises his function as the 'Spirit of Sanctification.' In us he is truly the source of charity by which we, in imitation of God, love the Divine Good" (p. 130).

In the hymn "*Veni Creator Spiritus*," the Holy Spirit is called "Finger of God's Right Hand." He is compared to an artist who delineates on the soul the features of God. St. Cyril of Alexandria speaks of God imprinting his image on souls which receive him, "as a seal on wax, and thus communicating his own likeness to our nature, retraces therein the beauty of the divine archetype, and restores in men the image of God" (p. 131 and n. 29).

The created sanctity of our Savior's holy humanity was the perfect human expression of the holiness of the invisible God. "He reflects the glory of God and bears the very stamp of his nature" (Heb 1: 3). The Holy Spirit has made his humanity perfect, flawless, even in the eyes of God. "It devolves on the Holy Spirit, having formed the head of the regenerated human race, to proceed to the formation of the members" (p. 132).

"Under the action of the Divine Artisan, the features of Jesus show ever more and more distinctly in those who make progress in sanctity. They become continually more Christlike. It is, to use another comparison employed by the Fathers, as when, under the patient chiseling of the sculptor, the human features and the human shape of the model emerge from the formless block of marble. So from the human soul, that has been shapeless and formless by sin, is hewn, by the Divine Sculptor, a living image of Christ. Each fresh infusion of sanctifying grace brings its own touch of perfection to the work, helping to make the resemblance more striking. Each time that the creature, responding to the impulse of its Divine Guest, performs an action into which it casts all the fervor of charity . . . it makes a step forward in the process of sanctification—it grows in resemblance to Jesus" (p. 133 and n. 38).

> Don't hinder the work of the Paraclete: seek union with Christ so as to be purified, and feel with him the insults, the spit, the blows, and the thorns, and the weight of the cross . . . , and the nails tearing through your flesh, and the agony of a forsaken death.
>
> And enter through our Lord's open side until you find sure refuge there in his wounded heart (J. Escrivá, *The Way*, no. 58).
>
> Our Lord Jesus Christ wants it: we have to follow him closely. There is no other way.

This is the task of the Holy Spirit in each soul, in yours too. You have to be docile, so as not to put obstacles in the way of your God (J. Escrivá, *The Forge*, no. 860).

10. BORN OF WATER AND THE HOLY SPIRIT

The effects of grace can be studied from several points of view. The one that we are now going to explain is the effect of the soul's *deification,* whereby the soul and its faculties are endowed with a certain divine quality.

From the start, we must bear in mind what St. John Damascene says about deification. It does not involve an "inconceivable metamorphosis of our nature into that of God" (p. 135 and n. 2). This must be accepted if we are to understand St. Augustine correctly when he states that "God became man that man might become God" (p. 135 and n. 4). St. Thomas follows this expression closely: "If the Son of God became man and underwent circumcision in the flesh, it was not for his own sake, but in order to make us 'gods' by grace and to merit for us circumcision of the spirit" (p. 135 and n. 3). In describing the transformation that grace brings about, Scripture speaks of regeneration, renewal in the Holy Spirit (Tit 3: 5), born of God (1 Jn 3: 9), begotten of God by the word of truth (Jas 1: 18), created after the likeness of God (Eph 4: 24), created anew in Christ (2 Cor 5: 17). Our contact with God does not consist in the mingling of human nature with the divine nature. Yet grace produces a change that makes our soul become like God.

Sanctifying grace forges in man a likeness to the Son of God. "For those whom he [God] foreknew he also predestined to be conformed to the image of his Son, in order that he might be the first-born among many brethren" (Rom 8: 29). The only-begotten is the first-begotten of many. By grace, according to words of St. Peter, we are made "partakers of the divine nature" (2 Pet 1: 4).

The word "nature" is key to what sanctifying grace is and what it does. Nature is the essence of a thing considered as a source of activities proper to anything. It has its powers but it also differentiates it from other natures. A man can think since he has a rational nature, but it is not in his nature to fly like a bird. When we say that through grace we participate in the divine nature, we mean that we share in God's operations in some way. St. Thomas speaking of habitual grace says: "That which exists substantially in God, that same perfection exists in the manner of an accident in the soul that participates in the divine goodness" (p. 139 and n. 20). That which is in God is in the soul, but differently. In God, it is substantially, whereas in the soul, it is found like a quality, "in the manner of an accident." If it were our substance we would no longer be men but would be changed into God's own substance, something which St. John Damascene, as we have seen, says is inconceivable.

Grace is what enables us to achieve the supernatural end which God has set for our nature. We do not have a merely human goal. Ours is a supernatural destiny. "Just as creatures move, in virtue of the nature in them, to the conquest of their final end determined for them by their Creator, so, too, in the supernatural order, God infuses a 'form' or 'nature' into the soul by which it is able to exercise those operations which put it in possession of its final supernatural end which is divine" (pp. 140–141 and n. 22).

The participation does not mean that a part of the divine nature is given us. God is simplicity itself and cannot be divided. "What the phrase 'participate in the divine nature' does mean is that there is wrought in the creature, by the action of God, a perfection which bears a resemblance to, is modeled on, and has its source and principle in the divine nature itself" (p. 141).

In God, his nature is possessed equally though distinctly by three persons. In transforming the soul through grace, he undertakes to form an image, a finite reproduction, of the inner processions of knowing and willing that are the source of the divine persons.

Sanctifying grace prepares the soul for an even greater good. "It is a preparation for the communication of the Holy Spirit coming in person into the soul of the just, accompanied by the Father and the Son, and uniting himself to that soul, in an ineffable manner, as object of its knowledge and love" (p. 145).

There is, then, a twofold element in the process of deification, "one created, the other uncreated. The created element serves as a sort of connecting link between God and the soul, adapting the latter for the indwelling of the Divine Persons. Such is the function of grace. The uncreated element . . . constitutes the term of our aspirations and the summit of our perfection; it is that supreme good, the enjoyment of which, even in its initial stage is a foretaste of heaven. It is the Holy Spirit himself giving himself to us, coming to dwell in our hearts" (p. 145-146).

Nature is the principle of operation. By sharing in the divine nature, we are given an aptitude for divine operations. Grace enables us to share in that intimacy which exists among the Divine Persons themselves. "It is by and through its faculties that the soul is able to lay hold of and possess God. It is united to him through the activities of the divine infused virtues of faith, hope and charity residing in the intellect and will. Grace modifies the substance of the soul; the divine virtues that issue from it have their place in the soul's faculties" (p. 146).

Our souls reproduce an image of the divine processions. When we put on the divine form, we necessarily reproduce the character of the divine life. Blessed Josemaría Escrivá says, "Faith teaches that man, in the state of grace, is . . . filled with God" (*Christ Is Passing By,* no. 103).

F. Ocariz writes: "The participation possesses the eternal dynamism of the intra-Trinitarian divine processions, accomplishing the supernatural marvel of 'the action of the one Spirit himself, who by making us Christ's brethren leads us toward God the Father' (J. Escrivá, *Conversations with Msgr. Escrivá,* no. 67). . . . This is the substance of the supernatural order:

the Trinitarian mystery projected onto us or, better still, our adoption, or introduction, to live in God through filiation, through the Son" (*God as Father*, pp. 14–15).

> Our heart now needs to distinguish and adore each one of the divine Persons. The soul is, as it were, making a discovery in the supernatural life, like a little child opening his eyes to the world about him. The soul spends time lovingly with the Father and the Son and the Holy Spirit, and readily submits to the work of the lifegiving Paraclete, who gives himself to us with no merit on our part, bestowing his gifts and the supernatural virtues! (J. Escrivá, *Friends of God*, no. 306).

II. THE SPIRIT OF ADOPTION

Through grace man can have an ideal in common with God. The ideal toward which all of God's energies are directed is the intellectual vision and total possession of his own being. That is, his aim is beatitude, the highest good for an intelligent nature (p. 149 and n. 5). The vision of the divine essence is also the final end toward which man is directed by God's grace. God wills that man desire the same objective that is proper to himself. This is possible only through charity, the created image of divine love. "It is in the Holy Spirit that God loves the divine beauty. The Holy Spirit is sent by the Father and the Son so that we, in our turn, might through him be enamored of the same divine beauty. According to how the loving attraction develops, the creature becomes . . . inflamed with God's enthusiasm and, united with God and sustained by his friendly, ever ready help, bends all its energies toward the conquest of that beatitude to which its Divine Friend beckons it. This conquest becomes the absorbing passion of the life of the creature that is responsive to the interior action of the Holy Spirit" (p. 150).

This common goal, beatitude, is the tie that binds creature and Creator in friendship. "Life has no meaning except as spent in tending toward that goal. To live for such a one is to know and to love God" (p. 150). The saints have shown this in their life of prayer. They thirst after the life of God. Knowing that God desires beatitude for them, they eagerly search for the means to attain that goal. They speak with him about how to surmount the obstacles that present themselves. "This friendly communing with God on a topic of common interest is what mental prayer should be, at least in its initial stages. . . . The spirit of friendship—and real friendship is established by the Holy Spirit between God and man—demands that the soul should have a clear consciousness of this consoling truth, namely, that in the mutual contact of Creator and creature, God is solely preoccupied with the friendly object of enlightening the soul as to the steps it is to take in order to make its way to the position in which its divine lover stands, and of giving it the strength it needs to make that arduous journey, in spite of the repugnances of fallen nature" (pp. 150–151).

God loves the one who presses forward ardently to the divine union. "The human does not disappear before the onrush of the divine; it is simply sublimated and endowed with a more than human potency. Through the operation of the Holy Spirit in the justified soul, there is produced a physical reality endowed with the properties of the intimate nature of God" (p. 151). St. Basil the Great provides a classical description of the soul's transformation and the benefits that accrue to others through its union with God. "Just as crystalline objects, when touched by a ray of sunlight, themselves become resplendent and shine forth, so also the souls in whom the Spirit dwells are illuminated by the Holy Spirit and themselves become spiritual and send grace to others" (*Liber de Spiritu Sancto,* 9, 23).

Grace gives a right and title to the inheritance of God. This is ours because we are born of God. The great "preoccupation" of God remains as always that the inheritance of heaven should be for his children. "And if children, then heirs, heirs of God, and fellow heirs with Christ, provided we suffer with him in order that we may also be glorified with him" (Rom 8: 17).

If the exercise of the infused virtues of faith, hope and charity becomes so habitual "that a sustained and permanent disposition is created in the soul . . . the way is prepared for that experience of God within us which is a real foretaste of the bliss of Paradise" (p. 154). "On earth God can be seized only in and through faith and, therefore, he is held very incompletely and imperfectly. The soul enjoys him in hope, not in complete attainment. . . . This hope in which the Christian lives is not wavering or timid. . . . While awaiting the revelation, he is admitted to close friendship with almighty God. He can embrace the Lord in charity—even if, always, what he loves is obscure for him" (p. 155).The full realization of the experience of God takes place in heaven.

Grace is a creature and an accident that modifies the soul in its essence and its faculties. It does not have an independent existence in itself. But this by no means makes it insignificant. Only God can create grace. Scripture speaks of it as a new creation: "For neither circumcision counts for anything, nor uncircumcision, but *a new creation*" (Gal 6: 15). "Therefore, if any one is in Christ, he is *a new creation*" (2 Cor 5: 17).

God pours into the soul a stream of actual graces so that it can effectively advance toward the attainment of the beatific vision. "The creature becomes dear to God when it flings itself generously into the conquest of that which God himself prizes as the supreme good. God delights in seeing man, spurred on by the forces of graces liberally given, pressing forward ardently . . . to the divine union" (p. 151).

The beginning of the new life is acquired through the grace of divine adoption. This is obtained for all by Christ through the redemption and extended to all by the Holy Spirit. By grace, the Spirit remakes and, as it were, recreates man in the likeness of the only-begotten Son of the Father. In this way the incarnate Word renews and reinforces God's "gift of self," by offering man through the redemption that "participation in the divine nature" mentioned in the Second Letter of Peter (1: 4). St. Paul also, in the Letter to the Romans, speaks of Jesus Christ as "designated Son of God in power according to the Spirit of holiness by his resurrection from the dead" (1: 4).

The fruit of the resurrection, which realizes the fullness of the power of Christ, Son of God, is therefore shared with those who are open to the action of the Spirit as a new gift of divine adoption (John Paul II, General audience, July 26, 1989).

Ure igne Sancti Spiritus! Burn me with the fire of your Spirit, you cried. You then added: "My poor soul needs to fly again as soon as possible, and not stop flying until it rests in God!"

I think your desires are admirable. I will pray for you often to the Paraclete. I will invoke him continually, so that he may nestle in the center of your being, presiding and giving a supernatural tone to all your actions and words, thoughts and desires (J. Escrivá, *The Forge*, no. 516).

12. THE PRINCIPLES OF SUPERNATURAL GROWTH

In granting man the supernatural life of grace, God preserves an analogy with the natural life it raises and transforms. The gift of habitual grace is a birth to supernatural life. Furthermore, it is a pure gift of God. The creature has no right to it. All it has is a mere aptitude to be raised to a life on a higher plane, what theologians call an obediential potentiality.

This bestowal of grace is the beginning of a process of growth. The Christian who would be content with being in grace and without any ambition to bring about its growth would be like a person "content to contract his mind and limbs to the measure of the cradle during his entire existence" (p. 160).

Along with habitual grace, God gives his creature principles of activity that are essentially superior to the faculties he naturally possesses, his intellect and will. Appointing a divine goal as the final end, he furnishes man with the means to carry him to that goal. These principles of action are the virtues of faith, hope and charity. With the passing of years, there should be an advance in the practice of these virtues.

Along with the virtues of faith, hope and charity, called theological because they have God (*theos*, in Greek) as their object, there are the infused moral virtues corresponding to the cardinal virtues of prudence, justice, fortitude and temperance. "It is true that one cannot adduce an explicit statement of the teaching authority of the Church asserting the existence of these infused moral virtues, as can be done in the case of faith, hope and charity . . . [yet] in present times, the vast majority of theologians, following St. Thomas, teach that, in the regeneration even of infants, grace enters the soul at the head of a glittering cortege of virtues, which have as their function to deify . . . those [activities] that have direct reference to God as well as those that deal with the ordinary concerns of earthly existence" (p. 170). The latter are the infused moral virtues.

Not only man's acts that are concerned with the end of life, namely, God himself, should be "divinized" but also whatever else he does, no matter how ordinary, should have a supernatural tonality. The temperance of a son of God has to be characterized by self-denial and not just by a golden mean that condemns only that excess which would harm health or interfere with the use of reason. Divine law holds that man should chastise his body and reduce it to subjection by voluntary abstinence in food and drink. Likewise, "the Christian's justice must be transfigured by a generous spirit of sacrifice. The fortitude of the followers of Jesus must know no calculations where the interests of God and divine truth are concerned. Mere natural prudence will enable a man to walk warily and circumspectly so as to secure against possible obstacles that might bring failure on his undertakings. . . . The social and individual virtues of Jesus were not of that cold and calculating nature that belongs to the ethical standards set by the philosophers. So, too, a supra-rational elevation must manifest itself in the good actions of his followers" (p. 170).

St. Thomas says: "The rule of action for the justified is the divinity itself as participated in by man, in a certain fashion. He is therefore bound to act, no longer as becomes a mere man, but as becomes one who is, as it were, made God by participation in the divinity" (p. 165 and n. 24).

If a man is to act as a son of God, it is not sufficient that he simply be ethical. "It is not sufficient for him to be reasonable in all things: he must be faith-full in all things. He must do more than prove himself a man: he must prove himself a Christian. He has to be just in his transactions with others, prudent in his undertakings, temperate in his usage of things, and brave in the face of hardships, difficulties and dangers. If in any of these . . . he proves false to the rule of reason and of faith, he becomes, by the fact, a traitor to his God. Such treachery is incompatible with the abiding presence of the Holy Spirit" and implies resistance to his influence (p. 168).

We need to try constantly to remove obstacles to the supernatural moral virtues. These obstacles are "reducible to self-seeking in all its forms. Self-indulgence of every kind establishes in the will evil dispositions which do not disappear with the infusion of the supernatural virtues. . . . These evil dispositions must be undone by acts of self-denial—affecting both the will and the intellect. A man must love truth in all things and labor to attain to it. He must steadily refuse gratification to the passions that stir him to intemperance, cowardice, fear or unlawful pursuit of gain. In a word, he must practice daily self-denial" (p. 172). By doing so, the Christian responds more promptly to the Holy Spirit, who inspires him to perform the acts of the infused virtues. Only God can infuse these virtues and increase them; but man can dispose himself for that increase by heeding our Lord's calls to take up our cross daily to follow him (see Lk 9: 23).

The whole Christian life is lived in faith and charity and in the practice of all the virtues, according to the interior action of the renewing Spirit, who imparts the grace which justifies, vivifies and sanctifies. With this grace comes all the new virtues which constitute the fabric of the supernatural life. This new life is developed not only by the natural faculties of man—intellect, will and senses—but also by the new capacities that are added on along with grace, as St. Thomas Aquinas explains (*S. Th.* I–II, q. 62, a. 1 and a. 3). They give to the intellect the ability to adhere to God-Truth in faith; to the heart the ability to love in charity, which in man is like "a participation in the divine Love itself, the Holy Spirit" (II–II, q. 23, a. 3, ad 3). They also give to all the powers of the soul and in some way to the body, too, a participation in the new life with acts worthy of men elevated to participating in the nature and life of God in grace: *consortes divinae naturae,* as St. Peter says (2 Pet 1: 4) (John Paul II, General audience, April 3, 1991).

A director. You need one so that you can give yourself to God, and give yourself fully . . . by obedience. A director who understands your apostolate, who knows what God wants, who can effectively second the work of the Holy Spirit in your soul without taking you from your place, filling you with peace, and teaching you how to make your work fruitful (J. Escrivá, *The Way,* no. 62).

13. THE GIFTS, THE FRUITS AND THE BEATITUDES

Even with the virtues that are infused in the soul with sanctifying grace, we cannot perform acts that are proportionate to our destiny, the vision of God in heaven. The divine reward is given as due recompense only to actions that measure up to a divine standard. There must be a proportion between actions and reward. Only in the case of the human life of Christ is this proportion perfectly achieved. This was due to his response to the promptings of the Holy Spirit. "Jesus did righteous human acts divinely. He walked the earth as God. A divine distinction marked his every act of virtue. His doings and his endurings could be submitted to the exacting tests of divine, not merely human, standards of perfection and emerge with success from the trial. This was because, in all that he did and suffered, he responded with perfect docility to the inner direction of the Holy Spirit" (p. 173).

Our case is different. The infused virtues by themselves suffice to produce acts meritorious of eternal life, but we possess them in an imperfect manner. For example, faith gives us some knowledge of the intimate life of God; we believe that he is three persons in one nature, a truth that we would not know unless we accept divine revelation. But this knowledge is very weak. It is conveyed in human terms which are true as far as they go, but they express the sublime reality imperfectly. "It is evident that once a being possesses perfectly a nature or a form or a virtue, it can of itself (always, of course, with the ordinary concurrence of God) exercise an activity in harmony with that form. But when a being possesses a form or nature or virtue imperfectly, it cannot of its own resources produce an act corresponding to that form, unless it receives external assistance" (p. 176 and n. 6). St. Thomas gives examples: "Thus the sun, which possesses light perfectly, can shine by itself; whereas the moon, which has the nature of light imperfectly, sheds only a borrowed light. Again, a physician, who knows the medical art perfectly, can work by himself; but his pupil, who is not yet fully instructed, cannot work by himself, but needs to receive instructions from him." Hence, we have to be moved from outside if we are to act in a perfect, divine manner. That is, to attain our eternal destiny, we need, in addition to the infused virtues, to be moved and led there by the Holy Spirit. "The gifts enable man to live his human life as God would live a human life. The gifts are of absolute necessity for the Christian, if the Christian is to walk this earth after the manner of Jesus Christ. Without them the complete imitation of, and mystical union with, the Son of man is impossible" (p. 176).

Likewise St. Thomas continues: "The gifts of the Holy Spirit are habits whereby man is perfected to obey readily the Holy Spirit" (see p. 182 and n. 25). That is, there must be permanent dispositions that prepare to be acted on by the Third Person. "A teacher may be endowed with great knowledge and exceptional powers of exposition and yet may fail to produce any effect on his pupils if these are too backward to grasp his teaching. Metaphysics, no matter how beautifully and exactly expounded, runs the risk of being wasted on dull and untrained pupils" (p. 182). The gifts of the Holy Spirit adapt the intellect and will to receive effectively the inspirations of the Holy Spirit.

The *gift of understanding* gives a kind of perception of the truth, reading into the depths of the articles of faith. The *gift of counsel* guides man as though he received his direction from God himself, enabling him to know what is to be done here and now, without doubt or hesitation. The *gift of fortitude* reinforces natural fortitude, above all in the face of great trials. The *gift of piety* inspires a man to conform to much loftier standards in dealing with God and also with his fellow human beings, whom he sees as members of the vast family of God. "Under the *gift of fear,* a man will, out of a reverential love for God, shrink from such delights even as are permissible and will repute them as dross in comparison with the satisfactions that flow from attachment to the Lord and from the graces he bestows on his friends" (p. 179). Under the influence of the *gift of knowledge,* man forms a quick, unerring judgment "on the value of all human things in their relation to God and in their bearing on the supernatural destiny of the soul" (p. 179). The *gift of wisdom* "imparts the power of judging of everything by means of a certain divine taste. The soul's evaluations are unerring because it shares the tastes of God himself" (p. 179).

These reinforcements of the supernatural virtues enter into play in the common circumstances of the Christian life. It is the superhuman mode in the way of acting and reacting, "not the greatness of the things to be done and suffered, that marks the activities of the gifts" (p. 181). In the normal course of events, we think and make decisions with the help of God's grace and the virtues. But with these resources only, we may fail. We need additional light and strength from above and beyond ourselves. St. Thomas explains: "Whether we consider human reason as perfected in its natural perfection or as perfected by the theological virtues, it does not know all things, nor all possible things. Consequently it is unable to avoid folly and other like things. . . . God, however, to whose knowledge and power all things are subject, by his motion safeguards us from all folly, ignorance, dullness of mind and hardness of heart, and the rest" (*S. Th.* I–II, q. 68, a. 2, ad 3). "It is as when a loving father, watching his child's laborious and ineffectual efforts to trace intelligible signs on paper, takes the infant's hand in his own and firmly and surely guides it to the formation of the required words" (p. 183).

When the action of the gifts becomes more constant in the life of the Christian, the infused virtues take more perfect hold of the intellect and will. "The result is that supernatural acts of virtue come to be accomplished no longer with difficulty but with facility, promptitude and satisfaction. . . . When, owing to the soul's sustained docility to the Holy Spirit dwelling within it, the supernatural infused virtues fructify in virtuous acts having savor and pleasantness in the doing of them, rightly are such good acts termed the fruits of the Holy Spirit" (pp. 183–184). St. Paul gives twelve classes of them: charity, joy, peace, patience, kindness, goodness, long-suffering, mildness, faith, modesty, continency, chastity (Gal 5: 22–23). But this number is not meant to be exhaustive, "for every good supernatural act that is accomplished with ease and delight merits the name of 'fruit'" (p. 184).

Through the sustained practice of the theological and moral virtues and docility to the gifts of the Holy Spirit, the soul reaches a state where his acts of virtue not only merit a reward in heaven, but also enable him to find happiness in the very things that the worldly try to avoid at all cost. "Blessed are the poor in spirit, for theirs is the kingdom of heaven. Blessed are those who mourn, for they shall be comforted . . . " (Mt 5: 3–11). St. Matthew gives eight "beatitudes." By the acts of the beatitudes, the soul is prepared for heaven and, at the same time, has a foretaste of that bliss. "Because when a man begins to make progress in the acts of the virtues and gifts, it is to be hoped that he will arrive at perfection, both as a wayfarer and as a citizen of the heavenly kingdom" (*S. Th.* I–II, q. 69, a. 2).

> Only when a man is faithful to grace and decides to place the cross in the center of his soul, denying himself for the love of God, detaching himself in a real way from all selfishness and false human security, only then—when a man lives by faith in a real way—will he receive the fullness of the great fire, the great light, the great comfort of the Holy Spirit.

It is then, too, that the soul begins to experience the peace and freedom which Christ has won for us (see Gal 4: 31), and which are given to us with the grace of the Holy Spirit. "But the fruit of the Spirit is: charity, joy, peace, patience, kindness, goodness, long-suffering, mildness, faith, modesty, continency, chastity" (Gal 5: 22–23), and "where the Spirit of the Lord is, there is freedom" (2 Cor 3: 17) (J. Escrivá, *Christ Is Passing By*, no. 137).

Come, O Holy Spirit: Enlighten my understanding in order that I may know your commands; strengthen my heart against the snares of the enemy; enkindle my will. I have heard your voice, and I do not want to harden my heart and resist, saying, "Later . . . tomorrow." *Nunc coepi!* Right now! Lest there be no tomorrow for me.

O Spirit of truth and of wisdom, Spirit of understanding and of counsel, Spirit of joy and of peace! I want what you want, because you want it, as you want it, when you want it (Prayer composed by Blessed Josemaría Escrivá in April 1934).

EPILOGUE

Mary is a model for the workings of God's grace in the soul and of what a person who corresponds to grace can achieve for self and for others. She is the greatest example of God's way for man to become as God, knowing good and rejecting evil. She is the pattern of divinization for all mankind.

Elizabeth congratulated Mary on her wonderful faith. "Blessed is she who believed that there would be a fulfillment of what was spoken to her from the Lord" (Lk 1: 45). "Would that every Christian in grace shared to some extent in that magnificent faith of Mary and held with firm and practical conviction that God the Holy Spirit dwells in his soul in a close and intimate manner—in a manner that bears an analogy with the indwelling of the yet unborn, Incarnate God in Mary's womb! What a transformation such a conviction would effect in the lives of many who content themselves with the practice of an uninspiring, routine and mediocre Christianity! The mystery of the indwelling of the Holy Spirit in souls is that one among the mysteries of our faith which is the most potent to give an elevated tone to a human life and make it a worthy expression of Christianity" (p. 188).

The "Nazareth event" described by Luke in the Gospel of the Annunciation is therefore a perfect image—and we can call it the model—of the God–man relationship. God wills that this relationship be founded in every person on the gift of the Holy Spirit, but also on personal maturity. At the threshold of the new covenant the Holy Spirit gave Mary a gift of immense spiritual greatness. He obtained from her an action of dedication and living obedience, which is an example for all those who are called to faith and to the following of Christ, how "the Word was made flesh and dwelt among us" (Jn 1: 14). After the earthly mission of Jesus and Pentecost, the call, God's "self-gift," the action of the Holy Spirit which continues the Nazareth event will be repeated throughout the whole future of the Church. And it will always have to be that man's answer to the call and to God's gift be given with the same personal maturity which radiated throughout the *fiat* of the Virgin of Nazareth during the annunciation (John Paul II, General audience, April 18, 1990).

How men like to be reminded of their relationship with distinguished figures in literature, in politics, in the armed forces, in the Church!

Sing to Mary Immaculate, reminding her:

Hail Mary, daughter of God the Father! Hail Mary, Mother of God the Son! Hail Mary, Spouse of God the Holy Spirit! Greater than you—no one but God! (J. Escrivá, *The Way,* no. 496).